Understanding Latino Families

Understanding Families

Series Editors: *David M. Klein, Notre Dame University*
Bert M. Adams, University of Wisconsin

This book series examines a wide range of subjects relevant to studying families. Topics include parenthood, mate selection, marriage, divorce and remarriage, custody issues, culturally and ethnically based family norms, theory and conceptual design, family power dynamics, families and the law, research methods on the family, and family violence.

The series is aimed primarily at scholars working in family studies, sociology, psychology, social work, ethnic studies, gender studies, cultural studies, and related fields as they focus on the family. Volumes will also be useful for graduate and undergraduate courses in sociology of the family, family relations, family and consumer sciences, social work and the family, family psychology, family history, cultural perspectives on the family, and others.

Books appearing in **Understanding Families** are either single- or multiple-authored volumes or concisely edited books of original chapters on focused topics within the broad interdisciplinary field of marriage and family.

The books are reports of significant research, innovations in methodology, treatises on family theory, syntheses of current knowledge in a family subfield, or advanced textbooks. Each volume meets the highest academic standards and makes a substantial contribution to our understanding of marriages and families.

The National Council on Family Relations cosponsors with Sage a book award for students and new professionals. Award-winning manuscripts are published as part of the **Understanding Families** series.

Ruth E. Zambrana, Editor

Understanding Latino Families

Scholarship, Policy, and Practice

UNDERSTANDING
FAMILIES

SAGE Publications
International Educational and Professional Publisher
Thousand Oaks   London   New Delhi

For information address:

SAGE Publications, Inc.
2455 Teller Road
Thousand Oaks, California 91320

SAGE Publications Ltd.
6 Bonhill Street
London EC2A 4PU
United Kingdom

SAGE Publications India Pvt. Ltd.
M-32 Market
Greater Kailash I
New Delhi 110048 India

Printed in the United States of America

Library of Congress Cataloging-in-Publication Data

Main entry under title:

Understanding Latino families: scholarship, policy and practice/
    edited by Ruth E. Zambrana.
        p. cm.—(Understanding families; 2)
        Includes bibliographical references and index.
        ISBN 0-8039-5609-6 (alk. paper).—ISBN 0-8039-5610-X (pbk.   :
    alk. paper)
        1. Hispanic American families.   I. Zambrana, Ruth E.   II. Series.
    E184.S75U4   1995
    306.8'08968—dc20   95-8202

The cover photograph shows the mural *VIVA LA VIDA* by artist Gregory Mejia. The mural was commissioned by the Midwest Latino Health Research, Training, and Policy Center for Medical Treatment Effectiveness Program (MEDTEP) at the University of Illinois at Chicago, 1640 W. Roosevelt Rd., Chicago, Illinois, where it is on display. Used with permission.

This book is printed on acid-free paper.

95 96 97 98 99   10 9 8 7 6 5 4 3 2 1

Sage Production Editor: Diana E. Axelsen

Dedication

This book is dedicated to my mother and father and to my children. By words and example, Mami instilled in me the strength to persist, in the face of maltreatment, toward higher goals, so that I could contribute to the forward movement of our community. This book has also been inspired and pushed forward by the lives of my children, Amad and Jahan. In particular, my son confronted, without warning, the insidious and demeaning force of racism in a public school system. Those same forces contribute to the persistent lack of achievement of many Latinos in the U.S. educational system. Thus, this book is also written to recognize and honor all Latino children and youth and their parents, who have struggled against the contradictions in this society that espouses equality and delivers inequity.

CONTENTS

Preface

The uniqueness of this book is its integrated focus on the Latino family, with attention to various Latino subgroups, and its inclusion of applied knowledge about ways to work with Latino families. This book aims to establish a Latino/Hispanic perspective on families by reviewing relevant statistical and empirical research, as well as "think pieces," in three areas: social and demographic profiles of Hispanic/ Latino groups in the United States; empirical and conceptual reviews of Latino/Hispanic family approaches; and practice and policy implications for Central American immigrants, Latino youth, and families and parenting programs, with a special focus on Latino fathers. The last section discusses health and human services reform and new themes and directions for scholarship and practice.

The book does not include all past and current work conducted on Latino/Hispanic groups. The authors derived their material from existing studies, which have tended to focus on the deviant aspects of the Hispanic culture, have not examined intragroup differences, and have often used frameworks that have failed to adequately capture change and strength in family processes and normal developmental milestones. Thus, the book represents a modest effort to advance social science scholarship on Hispanic/Latino families. Its intent is to serve as a catalyst to encourage a more dynamic and relevant conceptual departure for the study of Latino families. Equally important, the underlying hope is that this book will serve to inspire a new generation of scholarship that focuses on the strengths of the Latino/Hispanic groups, those structural processes that impede their progress, and those cultural and familial processes that enhance their intergenerational adaptation and resiliency.

An important contribution of the book is its emphasis on distinguishing characteristics of Latino subgroups across socioeconomic status, place of birth, and generational status. All the contributors recognize that the Hispanic/Latino population represents a heterogeneous group in terms of language, race, and cultural customs and practices. Yet an abundance of evidence shows that the Hispanic/Latino population in the United States shares a distinct set of experiences, demonstrated by their low educational attainment, high levels of poverty, and high levels of fertility, all of which shape the quality of their lives. Thus, the book's focus is on the significant portion of the Hispanic population that has been the subject of most studies and is underserved and underrepresented. A second major contribution is its focus on proposing a clear theoretical direction for the study of Latino families and a research agenda for future work. The authors represent a group of scholars who are knowledgeable about Latino families and their respective topic areas.

The organization of the book is designed to provide the reader with an understanding of the changing characteristics of Hispanic/Latino families and a statistical profile of social and demographic trends. The emphasis in Chapter 2 is on the economic well-being of Latino families, including income, size of family, fertility patterns, labor market participation, structural patterns, and family characteristics. Chapter 3 reviews major past and current research in the social sciences on relevant family issues, such as gender roles, familism, generational patterns, identity, kinship, child-care patterns, and aging. Chapter 4 highlights the central contemporary focal concerns of Latino children and adolescents. Its emphasis is on life chances of Latino youth, including education, employment, health, upward mobility, opportunities for children, acquisition of human capital, peer culture, and developmental pattern.

The next three chapters describe "real world" data collection experiences and how these data are used to create relevant and sensitive programs for the Hispanic/Latino community. Scientific knowledge is usually derived or generated from experiences in specific contexts. The transfer and application of knowledge to community settings represents a critical phase of the research process. In other words, there is a continuous need to assess the utility of science in real-life situations. Chapter 8 discusses the health and human service needs of Latino children and families, identifying current policies and legislative issues that may benefit Latino families. Chapter 9 proposes an expanded theoretical paradigm that would enable a more meaningful and culturally sensitive set of investigations to advance knowledge in the study of Latino families. The last chapter summarizes the major themes that have been derived from the study of Latino scholarship to date and proposes areas of future research, policy, and practice.

I intended this book to be used in undergraduate and graduate courses in sociology of the family, racial and ethnic studies, counseling and clinical psychology, anthropology, public health, and social welfare. Further, this collection can serve to assist investigators, practitioners, and policymakers to have a broader perspective on Latino families, women, and children, to assure a more responsive set of future activities.

I and several of the authors gratefully acknowledge the foresight of the Interuniversity Program and Social Science Research Council in appointing the Latino Family Working Group and providing a grant to convene the group, commission four papers, and develop an annotated bibliography. I am also deeply grateful to all the authors, who contributed their chapters in spite of exceedingly busy schedules and innumerable commitments. Equally important, this book could not have been completed without the commitment, editing, proofreading, and unending energy of Claudia Dorrington. Her own interest in the subject area and unparalleled perseverance and attention to detail have contributed immensely to the quality of this book. I also want to thank Maxine Baca Zinn, who is in spirit my coeditor. She provided sound advice and encouragement as the book unfolded over the last 5 years.

The staff at Sage Publications also deserves special mention. Marquita Flemming and Diana Axelsen provided encouragement and excellent follow-up. Jim Nageotte assumed his role with enthusiasm, understanding, and a delightful sense of humor. I thank them all.

Finally, Catherine Dorosewicz, Administrative Assistant at the Center for Child Welfare at George Mason University, provided unending support in the final stages of book production. I am deeply grateful for her assistance and commitment in this effort.

RUTH E. ZAMBRANA

PART I

LATINO FAMILIES

Conceptual Approaches and Overview

1

The Study of Latino Families

A Point of Departure

WILLIAM A. VEGA

This chapter presents a theoretical overview of important themes in the Latino family literature and a discussion of how recent social and economic trends may be affecting the Latino family. Many powerful ideas framing research on Latino families are a synthesis of old and new concepts. From various academic sources and traditions, an orienting conceptual framework is emerging, one that reflects the most important social issues and intellectual movements of the past few decades (Vega, 1990).

The theoretical substrate of current Latino family research is informed by diverse anthropological, sociological, and social psychological studies that focus on immigrant and intergenerational patterns of family structure, social support, gender-role behaviors, socialization, communication, and dysfunction. Most of these studies take as their point of departure the notion that Latino families are highly familistic and routinely confronted by hardships stemming from immigration, poverty, and minority status (Ramirez & Arce, 1981). Latino family research is increasingly influenced by the growing body of American and European cultural theory and, in turn, is contributing to it as well (Nelson, Treichler, & Grossberg, 1992). Culture theory assumes continuous cultural interchange, syncretisms, and adjustments as human groups respond to new environmental circumstances and structural inequalities. Human experience is held to be innately subjective and creative and must be studied with this perspective in mind. Therefore, culture theory is antithetical to notions of static culture or cultural hegemony. The influence of cultural theory is contextual and offers a philosophical basis for reconceptualizing familism in a non-pejorative way. This creates intellectual space for critical thinking and research about the complexity of Latino families, their functions, and forms.

Conceptual thinking about immigrant settlement, culture change, and socioeconomic incorporation has existed for many decades in American social science, especially sociology (Burgess, 1926; Glazer & Moynihan, 1975; Gordon, 1964; Park, 1936; Thomas & Znaniecki, 1918-1920; Wirth, 1928). However, this earlier work was focused primarily on European immigration into New York and Chicago. Latin American immigration brought with it new conceptual possibilities and requirements to explicate race and social class issues (de la Garza, Bean, Bonjean, Romo, & Alvarez, 1985). The multiregional and multigroup reality of Latino immigration also invokes the need for theoretically driven comparative studies in order to grasp how differing Latino ethnic groups with similar family values are accommodating to local opportunity structures and social conditions (Portes & Bach, 1985).

Latino family research has coalesced around two broad general interest areas. One is research about the role and internal dynamics of families and social networks for communication, socialization, distribution of resources, preservation of cultural forms, family reformation, and immigrant resettlement. The second area covers feminist perspectives on changing family life and gender-role patterns—simply put, how Latinas experience and perceive their family situations and how they are managing domestic role obligations and associated strains and conflicts in the context of outside employment. The customary depiction of the Latino family as committed to traditional family values, behaviors, and extended family structures has not diminished in contemporary research (Staples & Mirandé, 1980). This remains an important intellectual resource for theory building and empirical studies. The contemporary literature critically evaluates oversimplifications and inaccuracies inherent in broad generalizations about Latino families and extends the level of analyses to include new information and conceptual approaches. It also reflects the use of increasingly sophisticated and varied research designs and methods.

The current emphasis is away from traditional family models, which carry the assumptions implicit in the "culture of poverty" and "underclass" theories of the past. These are seen as intellectually weak and inconsistent with the empirical evidence, or worse still, stigmatizing and disempowering. Cultures and families are dynamic, adjustable, and poised to solve problems in living. Current family theory and research are more concerned with understanding the accommodations, vulnerability, and resilience of the Latino family, as well as the mutability and continuity of cultural forms within it. Reflecting the importance of the social adaptation perspectives in Latino family research, the next sections identify some of these important studies and their underlying premises.

Family Morphology and Socioeconomic Circumstances

Griswold del Castillo (1984) provides a powerful historical example of family arrangements among Mexican Americans in southwestern cities during the latter half of the 19th century, concluding that a large proportion of households (38%) were female-headed, even though extended, two-parent families remained the "ideal type." Men were frequently away from home for extended periods; therefore, men's and women's roles were not highly differentiated. These families were "flexible, pluralistic, and adaptive to survive" (p. 132) the rigors of economic marginality and frontier life. Disruptions and reformulations in family structure were commonplace, but family networks were durable.

Research about contemporary Latino life comes to similar conclusions. Studies of immigration and social network reformation attest to the structural flexibility of families and their instrumental role. Family networks are used to solve logistical problems associated with immigration, to garner information about employment, and to sustain and offer shelter to immigrants or migrants until they have established an economic foothold (Portes & Bach, 1985). Some studies have pointed out that intercommunity and transnational linkages of Mexican-origin families provide an important new way for understanding how families remain viable over time, irrespective of national borders, thereby creating a more enduring binational family system than was heretofore possible (Alvarez, 1987; Massey, Alarcón, Durand, & Gonzalez, 1987).

Chávez (1985, 1988) investigated the relationship between family structure and legal residence. He found that undocumented immigrants were more likely to be in family households that were laterally extended, indicating a predominance of households where "the additional relative is of the same kinship generation, for example, a brother, sister, cousin" (1985, p. 323). Legal immigrants were more likely to be both laterally and up-extended, with households also including mother, father, aunt, or uncle. A second study (1988) showed how immigrants who intend to settle in the United States, even if they are undocumented, are more likely to reshape family units. Undocumented migrants—even recent arrivals—living in households composed of family units were much more likely to consider their employment to be permanent. Therefore, despite the obvious fluidity and transience associated with undocumented status and fluctuating labor market conditions, these families have a rapid rate of family reconstitution (Browning & de la Garza, 1986).

Disrupted families and cohabitation have increased dramatically among second-generation Puerto Rican migrants on the mainland (Muschkin & Myers, 1989). This trend contrasts both with family patterns in other Latino ethnic groups and with families in Puerto Rico, emphasizing the importance of understanding impacts of environmental and associated economic factors on Latino families to better assess their current and future viability (Pelto, Roman, & Liriano, 1982). Puerto Rican migrants have diversified their social networks into "household structures, extra-household ties, and general patterns of helpful exchange" (Pelto et al., 1982, p. 54). Similar developments may already be occurring among other Latino ethnic groups, although past research has not adequately focused on this important and potentially controversial issue. The relationship between disrupted families, economically stressed environments where unemployment is common, and the increase in female-headed families should be studied in several regions where Latino ethnic groups reside. Changing family structures, including marital disruption and cohabitation, could represent the most important issue for Latino family theory and research in the decade ahead. These changes will have far-reaching effects in redefining Latino familism and the effectiveness of family-based socialization.

Familism and Continuity of Family Values

Latino family literature is framed by discussions of familism, the behavioral manifestations of Latinos that reflect strong emotional and value commitments to family life. Although other ethnic groups are also family oriented, the style of Latino familism presumably makes it qualitatively distinct from the behavior of non-Hispanic Whites. However, the empirical evidence is sparse and inconsistent, and the traditional family archetype is controversial because the social science literature has attributed negative social outcomes to it (Baca Zinn, 1982-1983). Although theoretical approaches in Latino family research have expanded well beyond an exclusive preoccupation with this issue, familism remains a frame of reference for research and policy development despite, or perhaps because of, the absence of conceptual precision and empirical evidence in previous research (Alvirez, Bean, & Williams, 1981).

Interaction and social support patterns have been most extensively studied among Mexican American families. These behaviors include participation in relatively large kin networks, where high levels of visitation and exchange behaviors are practiced (Keefe, 1984). In contrast, non-Hispanic Whites have fewer family contacts and are satisfied to maintain these at long distance. Although both ethnic groups value kin relationships, they also report disadvantages to close family ties. Nevertheless, Mexican Americans are reported to be more likely to use family as a resource for solving problems and are more likely to reside in a cluster of extended kin households, thereby facilitating familistic reciprocity behavior. Non-Hispanic Whites are more likely to live in nuclear family units that are some distance from other family members. Mindel (1980) found that non-Hispanic Whites actually migrated away from kin networks, whereas Latinos migrate toward them. He believed that maintaining family ties among Latinos was a coveted obligation that provided satisfaction to family members.

Several studies have reported that Mexican American immigrants have smaller social networks than nonimmigrants, because immigrants rely primarily on family members for emotional support and instrumental assistance (Golding & Burnam, 1990; Griffith & Villavicencio, 1985; Vega & Kolody, 1985). Native-born Mexican Americans interacted in multigenerational social networks of both friends and family. Griffith and Villavicencio (1985) reported that education and income were the best predictors of availability of support and more contact with network members. In a study involving Mexican American women, social support was highest among women who were employed and could drive a car (Vega, Kolody, Valle, & Weir, 1991). Furthermore, the same study found that immigrant women were most likely to receive their social support from the family of origin, such as brothers, sisters, and parents, but were not likely to report receiving support from adult children living in separate households. Perhaps some family reciprocity behaviors are asymmetrical because of the economic marginality that characterizes these newly established households of adult children.

Valle and Bensussen (1985) have provided a conceptual scheme for understanding the multiplex character of social support and exchange behavior in Latino families and extended support systems. This work is useful for understanding that not all supportive behavior is effective for solving problems. In addition, social support for problem solving frequently emerges from nonfamily sources. In their three-generation study, Markides, Hoppe, Martin, and Timbers (1983) found that older Mexican Americans and non-Hispanic Whites reported similarly high levels of satisfaction with family relationships. Mexican American elderly were likely to expect more support from children and not receive it, which may indicate intergenerational differences in expectations occasioned by acculturation. However, in a later article, Markides, Boldt, and Ray (1986) reiterated the familistic orientation by stating that the family is the dominant source of advice and assistance in all generations. Weeks and Cuellar (1981) found that Hispanic elderly believe they should be able to count on support from their children if they request it, but the elderly were reluctant to seek such assistance because to do so would reflect negatively on their sense of self-reliance.

Assessing the profundity and meaning of affiliational patterns is elusive. Too often, family behaviors and attitudes are abstracted from their contexts in daily living, which has a tendency to bias self-report research in the direction of moral idealism rather than the textured subjective emotions and conflicts that actually accompany real human relationships in families. This is a difficult pitfall to avoid, given the limitations of survey research. Family histories are rich with meaning for individual family members, and perhaps the emotional enigmas of family relationships are more adequately captured in qualitative studies and diary approaches.

The current literature is characterized by a redundancy in accounts of Latino familism. Yet it must be frankly stated that many studies are limited in theoretical scope, generalize findings from limited or nonrepresentative samples, and have inadequate controls for demographic factors such as family composition. The following section discusses recent studies on traditional gender roles, another primary area of interest in Latino family research.

Traditional Values and Gender Roles

Even in contemporary studies the traditional gender-role ascriptions remain dominant, but with important modifications (Ortiz & Cooney, 1985). There is a movement away from simplistic descriptive explanations predicated on *machismo* and toward understanding gender roles as flexible and responsive to environmental conditions (Baca Zinn, 1982a). For example, Kutsche (1983) studied Latino families in rural New Mexico and found strong allegiance to traditional gender roles but no strict division of labor, because men often worked away from home for extended periods. These prolonged absences required women to fulfill the role obligations that were normative for males who resided at home. Childrearing was also seen as a joint parental obligation. Bird and Canino (1982) report that in Puerto Rico, family decision making is either a joint parental process or the function of the mother. The fact that increasing numbers of Latino families are headed by females may increase egalitarian gender participation in families, posing a direct challenge to male dominance as a culturally preferred mode. Given the work of Griswold del Castillo (1984), cited above, it is clear that Latinas have always been capable and prepared to step forward and assume role obligations usually associated with male gender roles. However, women have often been put into the position of symbolically reaffirming male role prerogatives, rather than directly challenging male dominance in household or family affairs.

Therefore, although continuity with traditional cultural role expectations is a feature of contemporary Latino families, recent studies show that role transformations are occurring among women, facilitated by acculturation as well as socioeconomic and labor market conditions (Baca Zinn, 1982a; Gonzalez, 1982). For example, Baca Zinn (1980) found that availability of employment was the most important determinant of whether Mexican American women worked outside of the home. Ortiz and Cooney (1985) reported educational attainment was the most important determinant of labor force participation by Mexican American women. Similar findings have been reported for Puerto Rican women in New York (Moore & Pachón, 1985). Therefore, when gender-role research is refocused from professed values about gender roles to actual contexts of social behaviors and functional relationships, quite a different perspective on Latino families emerges. Gender-role expectations are fluid, responsive to changing family structure and economic demands. Ybarra (1982) found a wide variety of gender-role arrangements in families, from the most traditional, patriarchal, role-segregated structures to purely egalitarian, joint-role structures.

Increasing employment among Latinas who would otherwise be involved in domestic role obligations has multiple implications for these women. Working women have higher levels of social support, in part because they have higher income and they are more likely to drive. However, employment for Latinas, as for all women in American society, creates certain conflicts and role strains. Kelly and Garcia (1989) compared employed Mexican women in Los Angeles and Cuban women in Miami who were immigrants, reporting that working was a culturally anomalous behavior that required continuing negotiation, conflict, and justification. Unlike Cuban women, who left the workforce after achieving short-term financial goals, Mexican women were more likely to continue employment, as required by family economic marginality. Under these circumstances, employment could be considered an indicator of family structural weakness and vulnerability. Canino and associates (1987) found that working women have more depressive symptoms than married men, and these authors interpreted their findings as meaning that employment outside the home represents a different social status for the two genders.

Family Process and Acculturation

Conceptualizing Latino family process is intertwined with considering how families change in values and communication patterns during the intergenerational process of acculturation. This is a profound process, rooted in cultural changes of both immigrants and their children. Szapocznik and Hernandez (1988) showed that the pace of acculturation is more rapid for children than for their parents. Further, culture change may also be more chaotic and disorganizing for youth, because they are attempting to develop a coherent sense of identity by learning and integrating differing cultural expectations, which at times may be in conflict or become the source for intergenerational conflicts (Szapocznik & Kurtines, 1988). The acculturation process may also involve adjusting to minority status, low life chances, and dangerous environments where risky behaviors and lifestyles are commonplace (Vega & Amaro, 1994; Vega, Hough, & Romero, 1983).

Although acculturation is apparently not a destabilizing factor for most Latino immigrant families, the long-term consequences of acculturation on the viability of Latino families have not been carefully studied. An expanding body of studies indicates that acculturation is associated with family dysfunction and higher levels of personal disorganization, especially adolescent pregnancy, deviant behavior, and drug use (Amaro, Whitaker, Coffman, & Heeren, 1990; Gil, Vega, & Dimas, 1994; Vega & Amaro, 1994). Gil, Vega, et al. (1994) have shown that, because of changing family composition and deteriorating family functioning, Latino adolescents are more vulnerable to illicit drug use than non-Hispanic White or African American peers.

There is a dearth of theory about how acculturation affects Latino family adjustment, especially models that are focused on adaptation rather than dysfunction. Martinez (1986) has presented a model of family socialization based on the premise that individual family members participate in multiple social groups, which makes them adaptable and opportunistic. Furthermore, socialization through multiple group membership is progressive, embedding the family in a more complex array of community-based networks over time. In turn, this forms "interconnective relationships of the individual, the family, and society" (Martinez, 1986, p. 266). This means the entire family is changing, due to these synergistic processes of communication.

A few comparative studies have been conducted to determine whether family socialization varies between Latino families and other cultural/ethnic groups. Jaramillo and Zapata (1987) studied perceptions about siblings' and parents' roles among Mexican American and non-Hispanic White children, controlling for socioeconomic status.

They found that birth-order dynamics were similar for both ethnic groups, indicating that socialization of children differed very little, except for last-born children. This is an interesting finding, pointing out the essential point that sound research should control for socioeconomic status. Furthermore, acculturation level and generation in the country of birth of the parents should also be ascertained for more accurate comparisons and interpretations of family research.

Two other studies have looked at family processes, and both report that low-acculturation families have somewhat different dynamics. One study (Vega et al., 1986) looked at levels of family cohesiveness and adaptability, using a well-known assessment instrument (the Faces) and the circumplex model of Olsen, Russell, and Sprenkle (1980). Low-acculturation Mexican American families were more likely than high-acculturation peers or non-Hispanic White families to be low in stress and to be satisfied with family life and spouse personality during the stage of childrearing. A second study (Vega, Kolody, & Valle, 1988), involving immigrant Mexican women, reported that low-income and low-acculturation women reported more nonreciprocity of spouse: for example, marital strain based on the spouse insisting on having his own way. Nonetheless, women who were low in acculturation were less likely to be frustrated by their spouse's inability to provide adequately for them.

Strengths and Sources of Challenge:
Looking Ahead

In recent years, the theoretical and empirical bases for thinking about the Latino family have moved toward a nascent "social adaptation" paradigm. However, there is little uniformity, depth of conceptualization, or confirmatory work evident in this research (Rothman, Gant, & Hnat, 1985). In addition, the knowledge base about Latino families is primarily based on theory, findings, and anecdotal accounts about Mexican Americans. Currently, there is a rapid increase of research about other Latino ethnic groups, including Central Americans and Dominicans. More research is needed about other Latino ethnic groups and, preferably, coordinated studies or replications of carefully conducted studies, as well. Furthermore, there is a need for studies focused on four interrelated areas:

1. The social stratification and trends of Latino families
2. The effects of fertility and social class on each other, and their mutual effects on Latino family structure and familism
3. Changing gender-role statuses and functional transformations in household types by social class
4. Intermarriage trends, social correlates, and cultural diffusion (Jiobu, 1988)

Poverty, immigrant adjustment, acculturation stresses, and minority status have been endemic in the social history of Latinos and their settlement in this country. In response, Latino families and their extended networks have remained flexible and adaptive. So what has changed? Specifically, declining American affluence, a shrinking labor market for unskilled and semiskilled workers, deterioration of public education, a climate of violence, and a citizenry embittered about immigration. The unprecedented growth of the Latino population is causing concern among segments of U.S. society. This demographic change was predicted by scholars (Hayes-Bautista, Schink, & Chapa, 1988), who urged the rapid expansion of educational opportunity for Latinos in order to keep pace with population growth. However, popular opinion is crystallizing around a very different perspective: cutting public services and limiting immigration.

The current structural changes in the U.S. economy—including the movement of jobs away from states where large Latino populations reside, the serious decline of public education, and neighborhood social disorganization—are potent challenges to the survival of thousands of Latino families. The inevitable impacts are being felt in the destabilization of low-income Latino families in several ways: unstable or unpredictable income levels due to unemployment and underemployment, prolonged absence of family members due to job seeking in other areas, demoralization resulting from employment conditions, preoccupation with the well-being of children in unsafe environments lacking child care or adequate recreational facilities, and a growing feeling of lack of opportunity, as well as isolation and racial animosity from non-Latinos.

Despite the provocative and dismaying array of hardships confronting Latino families, we have already seen that they are not defenseless. The existing academic and popular literatures agree that the cultural behaviors of Latinos are strongly familistic. Furthermore, from the empirical evidence thus far available, the quality of social support provided by Latino family networks suggests powerful protective effects on health and emotional well-being. Therefore, it is important to explore issues and conditions affecting Latino families in order to gain some insights about how these families are enduring and transforming in the context of these volatile socioenvironmental circumstances.

Historical accounts point to the plasticity of Latino family forms. Structures are variable, especially among immigrant families. Household composition ranges from female-headed with children to complex, two-parent, extended-nuclear types. Children of immigrant families are often placed temporarily with adult relatives who are not their parents. Gender-role expectations and behaviors are also fluid and responsive to changing circumstances. The "breadwinner" in immigrant households may become an increasingly abstract concept. Labor market conditions in specific locales will dictate whether men or women, or both, will be viable wage earners contributing to household maintenance in Latino families. Given the anticipation of acculturation and structural changes in families, it will be an important empirical question to determine if constancy of family-centered values can be maintained among U.S. Latinos.

Despite having similar familistic orientations, Latinos are a heterogeneous population. They have diverse national and cultural origins, live in different regions of the nation, and differ greatly in their lifestyles. The environments in which Latinos reside offer dissimilar opportunities for positive identity development of children and for family economic success. For example, in Miami, Latinos are both a majority and minority group, combining large business, professional, and blue-collar classes with more recently arrived destitute immigrants from Central America. The Northeast offers a very different experience of widespread urban poverty, compounded by large-scale Latino immigration from the Caribbean basin. Los Angeles embraces an old, established, Latino working class, a very large middle class, and a torrent of new arrivals from Mexico and Central America. These differences in the "contexts of reception" for immigrants, affecting the socialization and development of subsequent generations, are of primary importance in assessing the future of Latino families in the United States (Portes & Rumbaut, 1990). Complex demographic trends are under way, as both low-income and middle-income Latino families rapidly increase in number, the former as a result of immigration and high fertility rates, and the latter as a consequence of intergenerational socioeconomic mobility.

These differences also signify very different types and intensities of challenges being confronted by Latino families. As shown in recent studies, Latino youth are very sensitive to the importance of family life; when the family is weakened, often the children are also jeopardized. Latino adolescent delinquency and drug use have been linked to changes in household structures, low family pride, and deteriorating family functioning (Gil, Vega, et al., 1994; Gil, Warheit, et al., 1994). By logical extension, if increasing numbers of Latino families are overwhelmed by demands beyond their range of coping ability, we can anticipate a destructive cycle to begin that could seriously increase the number of dysfunctional youth and families. Therefore, we must either hope the problem is self-correcting or improve our understanding of Latino families and endeavor to use this knowledge to develop public policy and improve programs aimed at strengthening Latino families.

From a societal perspective, it is important to preserve Latino familism. It attenuates delinquency and drug use. The low use of health and mental health services by Latinos has been attributed, at least in part, to family supports. Social support has been demonstrated to keep people healthier and help them recover from illness more quickly. Mexican American families are more tolerant than non-Hispanic Whites of members who suffer serious mental or developmental disabilities, and they are more likely to keep such relatives in home care (Karno et al., 1987). To the extent that Latino families function well on their own cultural terms, potentially costly use of remedial and custodial health and human services can be offset.

Effects of Labor Market
Conditions on Family Life

The proportion of Latino families below the poverty line has increased to over one quarter of all families (Beán & Tienda, 1987). School dropout rates among native-born Latinos, the generally low level of educational attainment of most Latino immigrants, and the deterioration of labor market conditions in the face of large-scale immigration have created an unprecedented threat to the economic incorporation of Latinos. In the past, an intergenerational economic "catch-up" was noted for Latino immigrants. Will this occur for the most recent generation of immigrants?

Angel and Tienda (1982a) reported a decade ago that non-nuclear family members are more likely to contribute to household income in Mexican American and Puerto Rican families than in non-Hispanic White families. Logically, this situation can be expected to have increased since this research was conducted. Therefore, although norms of reciprocity underlie these instrumental behaviors, desperation may also be a primary reason for transitions in family structure and for aggregating income. Economic stressors could have important ramifications for a possible decline of the Latino two-parent nuclear family and the increasing feminization of poverty in some sectors of the Latino population, with serious implications for the well-being of Latino children.

A historical precursor to this trend may be the Puerto Rican experience in the northeastern United States, where marital disruption and cohabitation increased dramatically between 1940 and 1970. Using this as an urban environmental case study, it is possible to see how acculturation, low education, unemployment, poverty, and racism combined to assail traditional family structures, leading to numerous alternative adaptations for family life (Muschkin & Myers, 1989) and social network arrangements (Pelto et al., 1982), especially among second-generation migrants. A similar process may occur in California, currently the home of 9 million Latinos. Data gathered by the state showed that about 50% of the U.S.-born Latinas who gave birth in 1992 were not married at the time. Although immigrant Latinas have lower rates of unwed motherhood, their rates are rapidly accelerating.

Under adverse circumstances, families will not disappear; they will be transformed. Latino family theory and research should anticipate the possibilities and attempt to assess these changes, if indeed they occur. Current trends suggest that rates of family transition from nuclear to non-nuclear, from married to cohabiting partners, and to female-headed households with children may all increase sharply in the years to come. Does this signal an irreversible end to the traditional Latino family? Not necessarily, and not in all family cultural forms or functions. High rates of transition away from nuclear extended families may attenuate with improved socioeconomic circumstances. We should recall that female-headed households were widespread in 19th century California during the social and economic reorganization of the state after the U.S.-Mexico War, but the proportion of two-parent families increased again in the 20th century. This shifting toward and away from female-headed households may be cyclical, depending on both temporary and long-term environmental conditions. Latinas perform, often out of necessity, a multiplicity of domestic and nondomestic roles, without reliance on male partners. Moreover, social agility is required because the two-parent nuclear-family model remains a culturally sanctioned norm.

Conclusion

Careful thinking is needed about the policy implications of existing theory and about increasing the rate of knowledge acquisition about Latino families. This volume is a good starting place for these considerations. Theoretical models of the past relied on depictions of Latino families as enmeshed, inert, maladaptive family structures and gender roles, which presumably contributed to replicating lifestyles of poverty. This derogatory and unrealistic view has given way to an exciting new era of possibilities. This new era is premised on powerful intellectual currents, including demography, cultural and feminist theory, and sociological models of immigrant socioeconomic incorporation. These intellectual developments have been accompanied by a growing sophistication in the use of research designs and methods. The next decade of research and policy development will reflect these changes, and policy development will grow in intricacy with a finer appreciation of the primary role of Latino families in optimizing educational attainment, social mobility, health, and community development. Important new challenges, and unforeseen alterations in immigration policies, will undoubtedly impinge on the issues identified in this chapter and invoke future transformations in the Latino family. By gaining an improved understanding of these processes, we can hope to develop rational policies to promote the best interests of Latino families.

2

The Diversity of Latino Families

VILMA ORTIZ

This chapter focuses on Latino families, describing changes over the last 30 years and making comparisons to non-Hispanic White, African American, Asian, and American Indian families. Also, comparisons among Latinos of various national origins— namely Mexican Americans, Puerto Ricans, and Cubans—are made.[1] In the section that follows, an overview of families, and of Latino families, followed by a brief historical overview of different Latino groups is presented. Demographic characteristics (age, place of residence, and migration background), socioeconomic characteristics (education and employment), and family characteristics (marital status, fertility, and family income) of Latinos and other groups are presented in the data section of this chapter.

The data used are from published U.S. census figures (see Appendix for list of data sources).[2] To explore the historical changes that have occurred for these groups, 1960 and 1970 census data were used whenever possible, but these earlier data were not available for all groups. For instance, whereas information on the Mexican-origin and Puerto Rican population was included in the 1960 and 1970 censuses, data for the Cuban population became available only in 1970, and Asian Americans were not identified until 1980. (People of these origins were counted in earlier censuses, but published reports on the data did not isolate them as a separate category.)

More recent figures were obtained from 1990 census publications and Current Population Surveys (CPS), also collected by the Census

Bureau, with the most recent figures available for non-Hispanic Whites, African Americans, and Latinos. As the CPS data gathering is a smaller effort than the decennial censuses, figures are not available for Asians and American Indians. Also, CPS reports do not provide all the characteristics included in census reports.

A comparative perspective is used to examine the status of Latino families. By doing so, we can obtain a better sense of what processes and factors are unique to Latino families and what issues are shared by all families or by all families of color. As demonstrated, Latinos share many commonalities with African American and American Indian families, whereas they differ considerably from non-Hispanic White and Asian families. Moreover, the data show considerable diversity among Latino families.

Overview of Families

That American families have undergone dramatic changes in the last 30 years is well known and documented (Sweet & Bumpass, 1987). There has been a shift from traditional, nuclear families to families consisting of single people, single older people, and unmarried couples. Minority families, including Latino families, have also experienced dramatic changes, although with different end results (Bean & Tienda, 1987; Farley & Allen, 1988). For instance, there has been an increase in the number of single people, especially women, heading families with children. These changes have implications for the economic status and security of minority families. Coupled with overall deteriorating economic conditions, we have seen a deterioration in the well-being of minority families. Latino families have experienced many of these changes, although the extent varies considerably by national origin, regional concentration, and other factors.

Early social science writings on Latino families presented a singular view of families as governed by traditional, patriarchal values and behaviors (Clark, 1959; Madsen, 1973; Rubel, 1966). This characterization was thought to be based on male dominance and age-based authority. Moreover, it hypothesized complete segregation of gender roles, with husbands being the breadwinners and authority figures and submissive, passive wives being full-time homemakers. The function of this family configuration was to insulate families from hostile American institutions, to socialize children, and to inculcate children with traditional Mexican (or Latino) values. Change within families was to occur through an acculturation or assimilation process whereby families moved from traditional forms to the more egalitarian modes of American families (Gordon, 1964).

These traditional portrayals have been heavily criticized from a revisionist viewpoint (Baca Zinn, 1980; N. Williams, 1990; Zavella, 1987). For instance, traditional perspectives on Latino families assumed that American families were models of egalitarianism, ignoring the reality that Western families were themselves patriarchal. The ideology of traditional families was presented, rather than the diverse reality of Latino families. These traditional views also ignored the considerable change that has occurred among Latinos. For instance, Mexican Americans and other Latinos have become primarily urban over the last 30 years. Moreover, class has emerged as a key concept in understanding the relation of Latino families to the larger society.

To gain a full understanding of Latino families, one must examine the role of work for women. Latinas have always been at the bottom of the working-class distribution because of their concentration in women's work: as machine operators, clerical and service workers, and employees in the food processing, electronic, and garment industries (Segura, 1984). The factors influencing the position of Latinas in the labor force include discrimination and lower levels of education.

Women's participation in the labor force is closely linked to their family roles. However, the research evidence does not support the notion that traditional gender-role values have kept women from entering the labor force (Ortiz & Cooney, 1984). Instead, women work out of economic necessity, because their husbands also hold disadvantaged positions in the labor market. The reality deviates sharply from the traditional ideology that relegates wives to full-time housewife status. Instead, wives justify their decisions to work by stressing their roles as providers for their children and sometimes negotiate the decision to work with their families by taking part-time or seasonal work (Zavella, 1987).

Historical and Demographic Overview

While the size of the non-Hispanic White, African American, and American Indian populations has only grown modestly over the last 30 years, the Latino population has increased considerably during this

TABLE 2.1 Population Size (in 1,000s) by Race/Ethnicity, 1960-1990

	1960	1970	1980	1985	1990
Non-Hispanic White	158,838	177,749	189,035	199,117	199,686
African American	18,849	22,550	26,482	28,151	29,986
Asian	—	—	3,726	—	7,274
American Indian	546	764	1,479	—	1,878
Latino	6,900	9,073	14,604	16,940	22,354
Mexican	3,465	4,532	8,679	10,262	13,496
Puerto Rican	893	1,429	2,005	1,036	2,728
Cuban	124	545	806	1,003	1,044

NOTE: Dashes indicate that information was not available.

period—to over 22 million in 1990 (Table 2.1). Moreover, the Latino population is expected to grow by 33% during the next decade (Hayes-Bautista, Schink, & Chapa, 1988). The number of Latinos in California has increased fivefold over the past five decades; they now constitute 25% of the state's population (Hayes-Bautista, 1990). It is estimated that by the year 2030 this figure may easily increase to 45% (Hayes-Bautista et al., 1988). Los Angeles alone has experienced a 97% increase in the Latino population, in contrast to a 24% increase in the African American population.

The sharp increase in population is due primarily to high rates of immigration among Latinos (Table 2.2). Immigration to the United States has been greatest among Mexicans and among Central Americans fleeing political and economic events in their countries of origin. The Immigration and Naturalization Service (INS) recorded just over 3 million immigrants from Spanish-speaking Latin American countries between 1981 and 1991 (Puerto Ricans, who are U.S. citizens, are not included in this count) (Immigration and Naturalization Service, 1991; U.S. Bureau of the Census, 1993d). In the past decade, in California alone, the immigration of Latinos has been at its highest level since 1920.

According to 1992 data, the total Hispanic-origin population was nearly 64% Mexican, 11% Puerto Rican, 4.7% Cuban, and 14% from various Spanish-speaking Central and South American nations. The remaining 6.3% are categorized as other Hispanics (Garcia, 1993). As these populations vary considerably in their socioeconomic and family characteristics, a brief separate discussion follows for each of the three largest groups.

MEXICAN AMERICANS

Latinos of Mexican origin are the largest and most diverse of all Latino groups. Some are indigenous to the southwestern United States and were already residing there when the territory was taken over by the United States in 1848. Since the early 1900s, immigration from Mexico has occurred at a high rate, although the extent of immigration and the level of acceptance of Mexican Americans by non-Hispanic White society have varied with economic conditions: restrictive immigration policies during periods of economic downturns and welcoming policies during periods of labor shortages (Pachón & Moore, 1981). Compared to other Latino groups, the foreign born make up a smaller proportion of the Mexican-origin population, but a larger percentage of the foreign born arrived recently (Table 2.2). Mexican immigrants have typically been poor and from rural areas. Although historically many came to the United States to work in agriculture, more recently most have settled in urban areas. Mexican immigration during the last 20 years has been at its highest level since the 1920s, with a particularly large number migrating as a result of changes in 1965 immigration law allowing for family reunification. Mexican immigrants make up a significant portion of the Latino immigrants in the Southwest. For instance, over 60% of Latino immigrants in California are of Mexican origin (Hayes-Bautista, Hurtado, & Valdez, 1990).

PUERTO RICANS

Although a small community of Puerto Ricans has resided in New York City since the 1920s, large-scale migration did not begin until the late 1940s, with the largest migration occurring during the 1950s and early 1960s. About 50% of the Puerto Ricans living in the continental United States were born in Puerto Rico (Table 2.2).[3] Puerto Rican migrants have typically been young, with little education and low occupational skills. They left the limited employment opportunities in Puerto Rico for the lure of plentiful, low-skilled manufacturing jobs in New York City. Puerto Ricans continue to reside primarily in cities of the Northeast, particularly in New York, Pennsylvania, Connecticut, and Massachusetts. Puerto Ricans have not done well economically in the United States and are very disadvantaged in contrast to other Latino groups (Ortiz, 1986).

TABLE 2.2 Median Age and Migration History by Race/Ethnicity, 1980

	Median Age	Percent Foreign Born	Percent Recent Immigrant[a]
Non-Hispanic White	32.9	4.9	—
African American	26.1	3.1	—
Asian	29.4	58.6	44.7
American Indian	23.4	2.5	—
Latino	23.8	35.2	25.0
Mexican	22.1	26.0	28.5
Puerto Rican	23.3	51.0	20.0
Cuban	39.1	77.9	7.2

NOTE: Dashes indicate that the percentages were too small to be significant.
a. Percent recent immigrant refers to the percent of those foreign born who immigrated in the last 5 years.

CUBANS

Cubans who immigrated to the United States during the late 1950s and early 1960s were predominantly professionals and entrepreneurs who fled Cuba when Castro came to power. Their background, coupled with their being granted refugee status and subsequently resettlement assistance by the U.S. government, has meant that Cubans have done relatively well economically. As their migration occurred during an earlier period, Cuban immigrants are not as young as other Latinos (Table 2.2). This predominantly urban population settled primarily in Florida. In the early 1980s, another influx of Cubans entered the United States. Commonly referred to as the "Marielitos," because they left from the Cuban port of Mariel, this group has not fared as well economically because they were of lower socioeconomic status than the previous Cuban immigrants and also did not receive such extensive resettlement assistance (Portes & Bach, 1985).

Socioeconomic Characteristics

Historically, Latinos have been a disadvantaged community in U.S. society. This is evident in domains such as education, labor force status, occupational status, and earnings, although there has been improvement over time. The status of women is also important to examine, to better understand the economic status of families. Prior

TABLE 2.3 Educational Attainment by Gender and Race/Ethnicity, 1960-1990[a]

	Total Population				1980	
	1960	1970	1980	1990	Men	Women
Percent high school graduates:						
Non-Hispanic						
White	43.2	54.5	68.8	79.1	69.6	68.1
African American	20.6	31.4	51.2	66.2	50.8	51.5
Asian	—	—	74.8	80.4	78.8	71.4
American Indian	17.6	33.3	55.8	—	57.3	54.3
Latina/o	—	32.1	44.0	50.8	45.4	42.7
Mexican	18.4	24.2	37.6	44.1	38.9	36.3
Puerto Rican	16.0	23.4	40.1	55.5	41.3	39.1
Cuban	—	43.9	55.3	63.5	57.7	53.3
Percent college graduates:						
Non-Hispanic						
White	8.1	11.3	17.1	22.0	21.3	13.3
African American	2.5	4.5	8.4	11.3	8.4	8.3
Asian	—	—	32.9	39.9	39.8	27.0
American Indian	1.5	3.8	7.7	—	9.2	6.4
Latina/o	—	4.5	7.6	9.2	9.4	6.0
Mexican	1.8	2.5	4.9	5.4	6.1	3.7
Puerto Rican	1.5	2.2	5.6	9.7	6.5	4.8
Cuban	—	11.1	16.2	20.2	19.7	13.2

NOTE: Dashes indicate that information was not available.
a. In 1960, based on those 14 years old and over; in 1970, 1980, and 1990 based on those 25 years old and over.

research has documented that women in general are in worse economic positions than men, although gender comparisons have not been satisfactorily conducted among Latinos and other people of color. This section compares educational levels, labor force participation, and employment characteristics of Latinos and Latinas with other racial/ethnic groups.

EDUCATIONAL ATTAINMENT

Most Latinos have an especially low educational level, although it has improved over time (Table 2.3). Except for Cubans, Latinos have lower educational levels than other racial/ethnic groups, including

TABLE 2.4 Labor Force Participation of Women by Race/Ethnicity, 1960-1990 (16 years old and older)

	All Women				Women With Children (1980)		
	1960	1970	1980	1990	Unmarried	Married	Difference
Non-Hispanic White	33.6	40.6	49.4	57.5	71.9	51.4	+20.5
African American	42.2	47.5	53.3	57.8	60.0	67.8	−7.8
Asian	—	—	57.7	—	69.3	58.8	+10.5
American Indian	25.5	35.3	48.3	—	56.3	50.7	+5.6
Latina	—	39.3	49.3	53.5	50.6	48.2	+2.4
Mexican	28.8	36.4	49.0	52.9	58.6	46.7	+11.9
Puerto Rican	36.3	32.3	40.1	41.4	27.4	42.9	−15.5
Cuban	—	51.0	55.4	57.8	67.5	60.3	+7.2

NOTE: Dashes indicate that information was not available.

American Indians and African Americans. Mexicans and Puerto Ricans had similar levels of high school completion in 1960—less than 20%. By 1980, about 40% had completed high school. By 1990, a smaller proportion of Mexicans (44%) had completed high school than Puerto Ricans (55%). Cubans have a higher educational level than other Latinos. Although the rate of high school completion among Cubans is lower than among non-Hispanic Whites, their rate of college completion is similar.

Among Mexicans and Puerto Ricans, men and women are similar in their educational attainment, whereas among Cubans, men have a slightly higher educational level than women. African American and American Indian men and women had similar educational levels in 1980. On the other hand, Asian men have significantly higher rates of high school and college completion than Asian women. Among non-Hispanic Whites, there is no gender difference in high school completion, but men are more likely to complete college.

LABOR FORCE PARTICIPATION

Table 2.4 presents labor force participation of women (meaning the percentage who are employed or looking for work). As has been well documented in the literature, labor force participation among all women has increased dramatically over the last 20 to 30 years. Although African American women have historically had the highest rate of labor force participation, their participation has not increased to the same extent as other groups since 1960. In 1990, their level of participation was similar to that of non-Hispanic Whites.

The labor force participation of Mexican women also increased sharply between 1960 and 1990. Puerto Rican women have an unusual pattern: Their participation rate actually declined between 1960 and 1970 and then increased after that. This may be linked to the decline of manufacturing jobs in New York City, jobs that Puerto Rican women tended to hold (Cooney, 1979). Cuban women have had a higher rate of participation than other Latinas.

Table 2.4 also presents the labor force participation rates by marital status for women with children in 1980. Generally speaking, labor force participation varies by the presence of children and marital status. Unmarried women with children are more likely to be in the labor force than married women with children.[4] This is not surprising, given that unmarried women with children face the economic necessity of working to support their families. Married women have spouses who help support the family, although many married women, even those with young children, work outside the home. This pattern was clearly evident among Mexican, Cuban, and non-Hispanic White women; however, among Puerto Ricans and African Americans in 1980, married mothers were more likely to work than unmarried mothers.

This pattern may reflect several factors operating at once. Unmarried Puerto Rican and African American mothers may work less because they have fewer opportunities to find employment that would adequately support their families. One reason for this is that both groups are more likely to reside in the Northeast and Midwest, where lower-skilled jobs are declining in number and higher-skilled jobs are increasing (Karsada, 1985). These reduced employment opportunities may discourage unmarried mothers from working. On the other hand, married women may find that their husbands cannot support the family entirely on their own, given the employment difficulties that Puerto Rican and African American men face (Bean & Tienda, 1987; Farley & Allen, 1988). Consequently, married Puerto Rican and African American women work to help support their families.

EMPLOYMENT AND INCOME

Table 2.5 presents characteristics of employed women and men in 1979. The first column shows the percentage of women participating

TABLE 2.5 Employment Characteristics Among Employed Persons by Race/Ethnicity and Gender, 1979 (16 years old and older)

	Women				Men			
	Percent Employed Full-Time Year-Round	Percent Professional Occupations	Percent Self-Employed	Income, Full-Time Year-Round Workers	Percent Employed Full-Time Year-Round	Percent Professional Occupations	Percent Self-Employed	Income, Full-Time Year-Round Workers
Non-Hispanic White	40.2	22.4	4.0	$10,512	63.1	25.0	9.9	$17,986
African American	40.3	16.5	1.2	9,583	51.3	11.7	3.5	12,657
Asian	42.4	23.8	4.0	11,502	57.4	33.2	7.9	17,403
American Indian	34.9	17.7	3.0	9,286	48.8	14.7	6.2	13,876
Latina/o	37.4	12.5	2.1	8,923	54.0	12.0	4.9	12,970
Mexican	35.0	10.8	2.0	8,616	52.7	9.0	4.4	12,623
Puerto Rican	38.1	13.4	1.2	9,390	55.1	11.4	2.9	12,108
Cuban	47.1	15.7	2.6	8,982	61.4	22.3	8.3	14,168

in the labor force who worked full-time year-round. Asian women were most likely to work full-time year-round, followed by similar percentages (40%) of non-Hispanic White and African American women. Latina and American Indian women were the least likely to work full-time year-round. Interestingly, Puerto Rican women were slightly more likely to work full-time year-round than were Mexican women, even though Mexican women were more likely to be in the labor force. Consistent with their higher labor force participation, Cuban women were much more likely to work full-time year-round.

Overall, women were less likely than men to work full-time, year-round in 1979. Furthermore, non-Hispanic White and Asian men were the most likely to do so, followed by Latino, African American, and American Indian men. Consequently, the gender difference was greater among Latinos and non-Hispanic Whites, because the men in these groups were more likely to work full-time, year-round than men in other groups.

The second column of Table 2.5 shows the percentage of employed women in professional occupations in 1979. Among non-Hispanic White and Asian women, a higher percentage of those employed were professionals; Latinas had the lowest percentage of professional jobs, with African American and American Indian women falling in between. Among Latinas, Cuban women included the highest percentage of professional workers, and Mexican women had the lowest percentage, followed by Puerto Rican women. This higher percentage among Cubans is not surprising, given that immigrants from Cuba consisted of many professionals and entrepreneurs.

Among non-Hispanic Whites and Asians, a higher percentage of men than of women were professionals. In contrast, among African Americans and American Indians, a lower percentage of men were professionals. Among Latinos, a higher percentage of Mexican and Puerto Rican women were professionals than of men in the same groups, whereas a smaller percentage of Cuban women were professionals. However, women professionals among all groups tended to be in female-dominated and lower-paying occupations, such as nursing and teaching.

The third column in Table 2.5 shows the percentage who were self-employed (or who owned a business) in 1979. Overall, men had higher levels of self-employment than women. Non-Hispanic Whites and Asians had the highest rates of self-employment (4%), and African Americans and Puerto Ricans had the lowest rates (1.2%). Among non-Whites, higher rates of self-employment tended to be among groups with high numbers of immigrants—in particular Asians and Cubans, but also among Mexicans. It is reasonable to suspect that many self-employment arrangements are small, family-owned businesses and that women provide unpaid labor in these businesses.

The last column of Table 2.5 shows the income of full-time year-round workers.[5] In 1980, non-Hispanic White women earned about $10,500, whereas Asian women earned about $1,000 more, and African American and American Indian women earned about $1,000 less. Latinas, especially Mexican and Cuban women, earned the lowest amounts. Interestingly, Puerto Rican women earned more than either Mexican or Cuban women, in sharp contrast to Puerto Rican women's more disadvantaged status on other indicators. The reasons for this may be that they are residentially concentrated in the Northeast region with relatively higher wages and better employment conditions, so that they do better once in the labor force, even though they are less likely to work. Paired with these higher wages are higher requirements for skills in this geographic area; thus, fewer Puerto Rican women and men work, and the overall economic conditions for the group as a whole are worse.

Not surprisingly, the income of full-time year-round male workers was considerably higher than for female workers in all racial/ethnic groups in 1979. Again, non-Hispanic White and Asian men had the highest incomes, and African American, Latino, and American Indian men had lower income levels. Among Latinos, Mexican and Puerto Rican men had lower levels of earnings than other groups.

Overall, Latinos, African Americans, and American Indians were more disadvantaged than non-Hispanic Whites and Asians. For instance, the educational levels of Latinos were lower, and they were less likely to be professionals, to have their own businesses, or to earn as much as other groups. Among Latinos, Mexicans and Puerto Ricans were more socioeconomically disadvantaged than Cubans. Overall, women were in a worse economic position than men, with women of all racial/ethnic origins earning considerably less, and being less likely to work full-time or to have their own businesses. Although African American and Puerto Rican women were more likely to be professionals than were men, they were concentrated in female-dominated occupations with lower prestige and pay.

What distinguishes the particular disadvantaged position of African Americans, Mexicans, Puerto Ricans, and American Indians relative to other racial/ethnic groups? One of the primary factors is the long history of discrimination and oppression experienced by particular groups in the United States. This includes African Americans, with a history of slavery and pervasive discrimination, and Mexicans and American Indians, both conquered populations in the United States.

On the other hand, Cubans and Asians have fared better because they are immigrants from countries that have been somewhat selective in their migration experience. Migration from these countries has for the most part involved people of higher socioeconomic status compared to other immigrant groups.[6] The consequence of this is that these immigrants bring with them personal characteristics, motivation, and economic resources that ease their integration into American society.

What of the immigrant populations among the less successful groups, namely Mexicans and Puerto Ricans? Both Mexican and Puerto Rican migration is not as selective with respect to socioeconomic characteristics, in part because both groups cross less restrictive barriers when migrating (Ortiz, 1986). This is true for Mexicans because of their proximity to the United States and because of the existing Mexican community, which extends a kinship network to newcomers. It is also true for Puerto Ricans, who are U.S. citizens and for whom strong "push" factors cause them to leave Puerto Rico. In addition, both Mexican immigrants and Puerto Ricans enter communities that have historically experienced institutional discrimination. Consequently, they have not fared as well as Asians or Cubans.

Studies conducted to identify factors affecting the earning power and upward mobility of Latinos shed light on these processes. As one would expect, human capital characteristics play a significant role in the economic advancement of Latinos. Tienda (1983) found that education, work experience, English-language proficiency, and nativity influenced the earnings of Latino men. Moreover, Snipp and Tienda (1984) found no gender differences in the occupational mobility of Mexican Americans. Both men and women were equally disadvantaged by virtue of their concentration in low-skill, low-status occupations.

Institutional and political factors have also been associated with the upward mobility of Latinos. A study of earning differentials among male workers found that, compared to non-Hispanic Whites, Mexican Americans and African Americans experience: (a) greater discrimination, (b) greater structural obstacles to achieving success in the labor market, and, consequently, (c) lower returns on their human capital (Verdugo & Verdugo, 1984). Tienda and Lii (1987) concluded that more schooling did not narrow the earning differentials between non-Hispanic White men and men of color, suggesting that well-educated workers of color posed a threat to non-Hispanic Whites, who have typically dominated high-status occupations. Thus, competition and discrimination may be even more prevalent among the well educated.

There is evidence that the geographic stability of Latinos may enhance their socioeconomic status but drive down wage levels for some Latino groups. Earlier research concluded that the close personal ties valued by Latino families hamper geographic mobility and, therefore, upward mobility (Alvirez, Bean, & Williams, 1981). However, Keefe's (1984) research showed that as Mexican Americans became more upwardly mobile, their kin networks grew larger. Apparently, the support provided by the extended family structure contributes to socioeconomic success. However, Reimers (1984) found that, unlike other Latino groups, Mexican and Puerto Rican men were offered lower wages in states with large concentrations of Latinos. This finding helps explain the lower earning levels among these two groups.

Family Characteristics

In this section, family characteristics are examined, including marital status, fertility, female headship, family income, and poverty. Over the last 30 years, there have been dramatic changes in these characteristics, including lower marriage and fertility rates, fewer two-parent families, and reduced economic status for most families. Families of color have been particularly affected, especially African American and Puerto Rican families.

MARITAL STATUS

Table 2.6 shows changes in the marital status of women in each group between 1960 and 1980. For almost all groups, the percentage of married women has declined, whereas the percentages who are single, divorced, widowed, or separated (referred to as marital disruption) have grown. However, the increase in marital disruption

TABLE 2.6 Marital Status of Women by Race/Ethnicity, 1960-1980[a]

	Percent Married			Percent Never Married			Percent Disrupted		
	1960	1970	1980	1960	1970	1980	1960	1970	1980
Non-Hispanic White	64.0	60.1	57.5	19.0	18.4	21.2	17.0	21.4	21.4
African American	51.3	44.2	35.1	21.7	23.4	34.4	26.9	32.4	30.6
Asian	—	—	61.7	—	—	25.0	—	—	13.3
American Indian	55.1	54.3	48.0	29.1	22.2	28.6	15.7	23.4	23.3
Latina	—	58.2	52.8	—	23.2	27.5	—	18.7	19.7
Mexican	61.2	58.8	55.6	24.6	23.4	27.3	14.2	17.9	17.1
Puerto Rican	61.4	55.0	43.0	21.9	19.5	31.1	16.6	25.5	25.9
Cuban	—	58.5	54.5	—	18.7	22.3	—	22.8	23.2

NOTE: Dashes indicate that information was not available.
a. In 1960, based on those 14 years old and over; in 1970, based on those 16 years old and older; and in 1980, based on those 15 years old and older.

occurred primarily between 1960 and 1970, and the increase in the number remaining single occurred between 1970 and 1980.

Puerto Rican and African American women have experienced the greatest changes in marital patterns. By 1980, they had the lowest rates of marriage and the highest rates of being single, divorced, widowed, or separated, in contrast to other Latinas and non-Hispanic Whites. Mexican women, like non-Hispanic White and American Indian women, experienced a modest change in marital status. However, Mexicans have had a lower rate of marital disruption and a higher rate of remaining single than non-Hispanic Whites. Cuban women do not appear to have changed much during this period, although it is difficult to tell, since 1960 figures are not available for this group.

FERTILITY

Fertility among younger women is usually indicative of having children prior to marriage. Among younger women, African Americans, Puerto Ricans, Mexicans, and American Indians have higher fertility rates than non-Hispanic White and Asian women. Young African Americans and Puerto Ricans who have a child tend to do so prior to marrying, whereas young Mexican-origin women who have a child tend to do so within marriage (Darabi & Ortiz, 1987). Young Cuban women, on the other hand, have an especially low fertility rate, which is consistent with their older age at first marriage (Gurak, 1978). Fertility among older women reflects the total number of children a woman has in her lifetime. Older African American, Latina, and American Indian women have higher fertility rates than non-Hispanic White and Asian women. Among Latinas, Mexican women have the highest fertility levels, followed by Puerto Rican women, with Cubans having a fairly low fertility rate (Bean & Tienda, 1987; Gurak, 1978).

FEMALE HEADSHIP

Table 2.7 presents the percentage of families headed by women for each group over time. The percentages of African American and Puerto Rican families headed by women have increased dramatically and are the highest of all groups. For instance, the rate of female-headed families among Puerto Ricans almost tripled between 1960 and 1985 (from 15% to 44%) but subsequently declined by 1990

TABLE 2.7 Percentage of Families Headed by Women by Race/Ethnicity, 1960-1990

	1960	1970	1980	1985	1990
Non-Hispanic White	9.3	9.0	11.2	12.8	12.9
African American	21.7	27.4	37.8	43.7	43.8
Asian	—	—	11.0	—	12.3
American Indian	16.4	18.4	23.5	—	—
Latina	—	15.3	19.9	23.0	23.1
Mexican	11.9	13.4	16.4	18.6	19.6
Puerto Rican	15.3	24.4	35.3	44.0	38.9
Cuban	—	12.3	14.9	16.0	18.9

NOTE: Dashes indicate that information was not available.

(39%). Among Mexicans and Cubans, the percentage of families headed by women had increased to slightly less than 20% by 1990. Female headship has not increased so dramatically among non-Hispanic White and American Indian families during this period. Asian families have a slightly lower level of female headship than non-Hispanic Whites.

FAMILY INCOME

Table 2.8 presents median family income for all families from 1959 to 1989 (in 1979 dollars). For most groups, income increased substantially between 1959 and 1969, and then increased slightly between 1969 and 1979. From 1979 to 1985, family income decreased slightly for non-Hispanic Whites and to a greater extent for African American and Latino families. This is largely attributed to the downturn in the economy during the early 1980s. Asian families had the highest income levels of all groups in 1980.

Among Latino families, Cuban families had the highest income in 1989 ($18,000), followed by Mexican families ($13,000), with the lowest income level found among Puerto Ricans ($11,500). Mexicans are similar to other groups in that they experienced an increase in income levels between 1959 and 1969, a slight increase between 1969 and 1979, and then a decrease from 1979 to the mid-1980s. The income of Puerto Rican families declined continuously from 1969 to 1984 and then subsequently increased by 1989.

TABLE 2.8   Median Family Income for All Families, 1959-1989 (in 1979
Dollars), and for Female-Headed Families, 1979, by Race and
Ethnicity

			All Families			Female-Headed Families
	1959	1969	1979	1984	1989	1979
Non-Hispanic White	14,675	19,722	20,835	19,961	21,063	9,138
African American	7,872	12,012	12,598	10,623	11,832	6,448
Asian	—	—	22,713	—	—	9,370
American Indian	7,393	11,549	13,678	—	—	6,596
Latina/o	—	14,550	14,712	12,839	13,727	5,948
Mexican	9,530	13,786	14,765	13,090	13,024	6,627
Puerto Rican	8,629	12,208	10,734	8,680	11,670	4,593
Cuban	—	16,889	18,245	18,198	18,303	8,017

NOTE: Dashes indicate that information was not available.

Female-headed families had considerably lower income levels in
1979 than families in general. For most groups, the average income
level for female-headed families was about half that of all families.
Among Latino families, female-headed families had income levels less
than half that of all Latino families. Families headed by African
American, American Indian and Latina women had considerably lower
1979 income levels than families headed by women of other racial/
ethnic backgrounds. Puerto Ricans had the lowest income level of all
groups ($4,600), whereas Cubans had income levels ($8,000) more
comparable to non-Hispanic White female-headed families ($9,100).

Changing Status of Families: Conclusions

African American and Puerto Rican women have experienced the
most dramatic changes in marital and family status over the last 30
years. They are less likely to be married, more likely to head families
on their own, and more likely to have children at younger ages and
prior to marriage. In contrast, the percentage of women not married
or heading families has increased modestly among Mexican, Cuban,
Asian, and American Indian women. Moreover, Mexican and American Indian women tend to have more children than other women. For

all groups there has been an increase in the percentage of families headed by women, although the growth among non-Hispanic White, Mexican, and Cuban families is considerably less than among African American and Puerto Rican families. Non-Hispanic White and Asian families have higher family incomes and lower poverty rates than Latino and African American families. Among all groups, families headed by women have lower income levels and are much poorer than families in general.

Puerto Ricans have shown greater changes than other groups, particularly with respect to family characteristics and decline in economic well-being. As mentioned earlier, one factor influencing these changes appears to be the Puerto Rican migration to the Northeast, a region characterized by declining opportunities, specifically in low-skilled employment and advancement. It is also a region where Puerto Ricans are treated as a racial minority. The mid-1980s stands out as a period in which Puerto Ricans, and to a lesser extent African Americans, show particularly low levels of economic standing. This may to be due to the economic conditions during the Reagan years, which created more inequality than prosperity.

We have seen that there has been an increase in the percentage of families headed by women, and that families headed by women have considerably lower income, and are much poorer, than families in general. This phenomenon, the "feminization of poverty" (Pearce, 1978), reflects the deteriorated economic conditions of families after divorce or separation. It has occurred primarily among non-Hispanic White families, as non-Hispanic White men have always held a position of privilege relative to non-Hispanic White women and people of color. Within marriage, non-Hispanic White women hold more secure economic positions. However, when these unions are dissolved, their economic status is affected.

In contrast, minority families face very different economic conditions. Because minority families are much more likely to be poor, even with two parents present, marital dissolution or remaining single does not have as large a detrimental effect on their economic status (Bane, 1986).[7] In other words, because minority families are more likely to be poor before marital dissolution, they are only slightly more likely to be poor after marital dissolution. Consequently, the feminization of poverty does not have the same meaning for minority families as it does for non-Hispanic Whites. In general, minority families are considerably more vulnerable to economic hardship as a result of structural conditions and changes in these condition over time.

Although Latino families are clearly affected by some of the same dynamics faced by other families of color, they also have certain unique experiences. Latino families tend to be younger and have more children. In addition, as many are currently immigrant families, they must struggle to adjust to a foreign language and new culture. These struggles have been occurring in an era of fluctuating economic conditions, particularly in the 1980s and 1990s, and in an era of declining economic opportunities for less-skilled workers. This, coupled with the federal government's increasing reluctance to provide economic security for American families in general, suggests that Latino families stand to suffer even worse material conditions in the future.

The trends for Latino families described in this chapter demonstrate the unique social, economic, and familial characteristics that have shaped, and will continue to shape, the development of these families in the United States. Equally important, these data highlight intragroup differences and commonalities within the broader Hispanic category. This profile of Latinos as an ethnic minority group provides a context for understanding and interpreting the dynamic evolution of Hispanic families overtime.

Notes

1. In 1992, about 21% of all Latinos belonged to "other" national origin groups, including 14% from the Spanish-speaking Central and South American nations. The remaining 7% of Latinos are immigrants from the Dominican Republic and Spain, and Spanish-Americans and "Hispanos" (Hispanics who trace their ancestry to the original Spanish settlers). The "other" category also includes people identifying themselves generally as Hispanic or Latino without reference to national origin.

2. Because many recent immigrants from Latin America are undocumented, they may not be counted by the census. There is evidence, however, that the census counted many undocumented people (Passel & Woodrow, 1984), although certainly not all were counted. Thus the census information presented is somewhat biased.

3. Because Puerto Rico is a territory of the United States, Puerto Ricans living on the island are citizens of the United States and thus are not technically considered immigrants. However, given the distinct Spanish culture of Puerto Rico and the adjustment experiences of Puerto Ricans once they come to the United States, Puerto Ricans are more like immigrants and are considered foreign born for the purposes of this discussion.

4. Unmarried women without children tend to work less than unmarried women with children. Although this may seem counterintuitive at first glance, it is due to the fact that women without children tend to be younger and enrolled in school.

5. This is the closest indicator to earnings that is available in the census publications. Measures of income include earnings, farm and nonfarm self-employment income, interest and dividends, social security, public assistance, and other sources, whereas earnings include earnings and farm and nonfarm self-employment income. For full-time year-round workers, however, earnings should be fairly similar to measures of income.

6. Supportive empirical data on this are provided by Gardner, Bobey, and Smith (1985), who compared immigrants from two Asian countries to the population in the country of origin. They compared the educational levels of Filipinos and Koreans age 25 to 29 who immigrated during 1975 to 1980 to the population in the Philippines and Korea. The overwhelming majority of the Filipino (85%) and Korean (94%) immigrants were high school graduates, in contrast to a much smaller percentage in the Philippines (27%) and Korea (54%).

7. Bane's study documented this difference between African American and non-Hispanic White families using Panel Study of Income Dynamics (PSID) data. Unfortunately, this phenomenon has not been examined among Latino families because no data exist that allow us to test for it. PSID has only a handful of Latino families at present, and although a Latino subsample is being added to this survey, longitudinal data for Latinos will not be accumulated for at least 10 years. Consequently, it will be many years before we will be able to test issues that are now being examined with the African American and non-Hispanic White subsamples of the PSID.

Appendix

In gathering data for this chapter, the following elements from the decennial censuses were used:

U.S. Bureau of the Census. Census of Population, 1960

Characteristics of the Population, Volume 1. U.S. Summary, Part 1

Persons of Spanish Surname. Subject Reports, PC(2)-1B

Non-White Population by Race. Subject Reports, PC(2)-1C

Puerto Ricans in the United States. Subject Reports, PC(2)-1D

U.S. Bureau of the Census. Census of Population, 1970

Characteristics of the Population, Volume 1. General Population Characteristics, Chapter B. U.S. Summary, Part 1

Characteristics of the Population, Volume 1. General Social and Economic Characteristics, Chapter C. U.S. Summary, Part 1

Negro Population. Subject Reports, PC(2)-1B

Persons of Spanish Origin. Subject Reports, PC(2)-1C

Puerto Ricans in the United States. Subject Reports, PC(2)-1E

American Indians. Subject Reports, PC(2)-1F

Japanese, Chinese, and Filipinos in the United States. Subject Reports, PC(2)-1G

U.S. Bureau of the Census. Census of Population, 1980

Characteristics of the Population, Volume 1. General Population Characteristics, Chapter B. U.S. Summary, Part 1. PC80-1-B1

Characteristics of the Population, Volume 1. General Social and Economic Characteristics, Chapter C. U.S. Summary, Part 1. PC80-1-C1

In addition, the following items from Current Population Reports were employed:

Estimates of the Population in the United States, by Age, Sex, and Race 1980 to 1985. *Current Population Reports,* P-25, No. 965.

Women in the American Economy, Cynthia Teauber and Victor Valdisera. *Current Population Reports,* P-23, No. 146.

Hispanic Population in the United States, March 1985. *Current Population Reports,* P-20, No. 422.

Black Population in the United States, March 1988. *Current Population Reports,* P-20, No. 442.

Black Population in the United States, March 1990. *Current Population Reports,* P-20, No. 448.

Hispanic Population in the United States, March 1990. *Current Population Reports,* P-20, No. 449.

All are available from the U.S. Government Printing Office in Washington, D.C.

3

Variations, Combinations, and Evolutions

Latino Families in the United States

AÍDA HURTADO

L atinos of differing national origins have different histories, structural and cultural integration, and regional residence. Only recently has this heterogeneity been taken into account in the study of their family lives. For the last 20 years, research on Latino families has primarily focused on Mexican descendants (for extensive reviews see Miller, 1979; Mirandé, 1977; Staples & Mirandé, 1980; Vasquez & Gonzalez, 1981; Vega, 1990; Zapata & Jaramillo, 1981). During this time Mexican descendants made up the majority of Latinos, with Puerto Ricans consti-tuting the second-largest group. However, although the Mexican-origin group still constitutes the majority, there has been a dramatic increase in the Latino population, primarily through new immigration from Mexico and the rest of Latin America (U.S. Bureau of the Census, 1991). Most Latinos reside in California (7.7 million of the total national Hispanic population of 22.4 million). A recent statewide survey of Latino heads of households found that immigrants outnum-bered Latinos born in the United States (65% versus 35%, respectively) (Hurtado, Hayes-Bautista, Valdez, & Hernández, 1992).

The large number of Latino immigrants have joined neighborhoods populated by U.S.-born Latinos and older immigrants. Consequently, family patterns, cultural practices and values, and socioeconomic integration are in a state of transition for Latinos as a whole. Latinos of different national origins are intermarrying, which creates a commingling of cultures, histories, and socioeconomic backgrounds among groups that have considerable similarities. These recent developments have only been touched on in the current research on Latino families, as most studies still focus on Mexican descendants.

In this chapter, I review the research on Latino families from 1980 to 1992 to update the most recent reviews. I make reference to research prior to 1980 only to elucidate our understanding of the current work on Latino families. I use the term *Latino* to designate all groups whose ethnicity originates in Latin America (e.g., Mexicans, Puerto Ricans, Cubans, Central Americans). For purposes of accuracy, throughout this review I use the ethnic label used in the source reviewed. This is also the case with non-Hispanic Whites, who are referred to as Anglos in most of the research. In my own conclusions I use the terms *Chicano* to refer to U.S. citizens of Mexican descent, *Mexican* for immigrants, and *Mexican descendants* for both Chicanos and Mexicans. Because most research has focused on the Mexican-origin population, this review is heavily slanted toward this group, although whenever the studies permit, I do generalize their findings to Latino families.

I begin by reviewing the assimilation framework, which is the most widely used perspective in studying Latino families. I then turn to the underclass model, the current version of the deficiency model that flourished in the 1960s and was used to explain Latino families' lack of assimilation. However, the structural and social changes that took place from the 1970s to the present have affected all families, resulting in expanding definitions of *family* to include the characteristics of Latino and African American families. To a certain extent the changing definitions of family legitimated the ways Latino families accomplished their functions differently from Anglo, middle-class families. The functionalist reevaluation of Chicano families proved to be an important impetus to further study of Latino families and inclusion of gender and race as central to the analysis. However, there is already a critique of the functionalist reevaluation because of the assumptions about gender that adherents to this approach take in their studies. Chicana feminists have been at the forefront of this critique and have been instrumental in pushing forward the study of Latino family life.

One of the most promising research directions is the structural deficiency model, in which Latinos' socioeconomic position and history are an integral part of how their family lives are examined. I conclude by proposing several paths for future research.

The Effects of Assimilation on Latino Families

The predominant framework for understanding ethnic families in general, and Latino families in particular, has been assimilation. Generally, assimilation is defined as acquiring the language, values, and behaviors of the dominant group. Gordon (1964) specified seven dimensions to the assimilation process (cultural, behavioral, structural, identificational, attitude receptional, behavior receptional, and civic assimilation). This framework implies that Chicanos and other Latinos will make the same adaptations to structural changes as European immigrants at the turn of the century (O'Guinn, Imperia, & MacAdams, 1987). The assimilation framework, however, ignores the fact that Latinos and European immigrants started from a different economic base, as well as different cultural values and history (Ybarra, 1983). Although Latino families are also undergoing significant restructuring, it is not at all obvious that their adaptations are simply imitating the dominant group of Anglos. For example, Norma Williams (1990) found that Chicano families in Texas, regardless of social class, still provided for their members the regeneration of culture, values, and worldview. However, she noted that cultural values, as well as the content and frequency of cultural rituals, have changed considerably from generation to generation.

Latino families are not entirely bounded by tradition, as stated in the anthropological research of the 1950s (Heller, 1966; Madsen, 1973; Rubel, 1966). They are dynamic and must grapple with structural changes, such as the increased employment of women (Saenz, Goudy, & Lorenz, 1989; Zavella, 1984, 1987), the increased educational achievement of their children, and the consequences of migration within different Latino communities in the United States (Rogler & Cooney, 1984). However, these adaptations to change have been creative and built on their preexisting historical and cultural base. Williams (1990) found that most of her working-class respondents considered themselves religious and attended church, but they did not perceive religion to be central in the workplace or in the school, as most of their children attended public schools. Similarly, in a recent statewide survey of California heads of household, 90% of the 1,086 respondents agreed that women have a right to birth control and 71% agreed that women have a right to an abortion (Hurtado et al., 1992). Also, Jorgensen and Adams (1988) found that among Mexican American women, their attitudes about future fertility decisions had a stronger influence over their future behavior than adherence to their ethnic group's norms. This was true even for Catholic women.

Another way to examine assimilation has been to measure what is called traditional sex-role attitudes. From this perspective, Latinos have more rigid definitions of the appropriate behaviors for women and men, which result in a variety of outcomes. The most current empirical research consistently fails to show a relationship between sex-role attitudes and a variety of behaviors. For example, Ortiz and Cooney (1984) found no relationship between Hispanic women's labor force participation and their traditional sex-role attitudes, even for first-generation Hispanic women, who, as a group, adhered more closely to traditional views of sex-role behaviors. Instead, Hispanic women who had more education were more likely to be employed than those women with less education who were married with children. Similarly, Soto and Shaver (1982) found that the sex-role traditionalism of Puerto Rican women did not directly affect their psychosomatic symptoms, such as anxiety, depression, and hostility. Rather, assertiveness, a psychological characteristic not necessarily related to a specific ethnic group, was directly related to psychosomatic symptoms. Furthermore, with the same sample of Puerto Rican women, Soto (1983) found that the more educated women were less traditional than the less educated women, regardless of the number of generations in the United States. Even the most educated women in her sample, however, reported that their parents had been more strict than non-Puerto Rican parents regarding dating, curfews, and going out with friends.

The concept of *acculturation* has been used many times as a synonym for assimilation. Several acculturation scales have been validated on Latino populations and are based largely on an individual's English dominance (Cuellar, Harris, & Jasso, 1980; Padilla, 1980). Researchers who integrated this conceptual and empirical refinement in their studies still found that the internal functioning of families was not affected by acculturation; rather, the families' interaction with outside institutions (such as schools) changed as families become more acculturated. These findings make sense because the English language is necessary for families to interact with the institutions outside the home (Rueschenberg & Buriel, 1989). Three areas of family life that remained unaffected by acculturation were the ability of social support networks to enhance or to hamper the psychological well-being of dual-earner Mexican American families, the amount of the husband's power within a marriage, and how decisions get made in marriage (Cooney, Rogler, Hurrell, & Ortiz, 1982; Holtzman & Gilbert, 1987).

Even the intermarriage of Mexican Americans and Anglos does not seem to be an absolute index of acculturation. Mexican American spouses, some of whom are third generation in the United States, still identified as Mexican origin, spoke some Spanish, and taught Mexican culture and history to their children (Salgado de Snyder, López, & Padilla, 1982). More than two thirds of adolescents (69.8%) who came from interethnic families of Anglos and Mexican Americans still identified themselves as Mexican-origin, while the rest identified themselves as "American." A large number of the respondents spoke some Spanish (82.9%) and listened to Spanish-language radio (71.5%). Overall, adolescents from interethnic marriages were not conflicted about their "mixed" heritage, had very positive views about their Mexican background, and did not want to assimilate. Simultaneously, they did not express a preference for marrying someone of Mexican origin or for having best friends of Mexican descent.

Many researchers assumed that assimilation to Anglo values alone would determine whether Chicanas work outside the home. In her study of the impact of "Sun Belt industrialization" on 22 Chicanas and their families in Albuquerque, New Mexico, Zavella (1984) found that, contrary to an assimilation framework, women disclosed a strong commitment to their jobs and said that their employment had a significant effect on their family's finances. However, their overall values and ideology about family did not change completely to match Anglos. Rather, some aspects of their views about family changed and others did not. How and in what direction they changed was based on the women's particular work histories, job satisfaction, their monetary contributions to their families, and the demands at home. Furthermore, Saenz et al. (1989) found that unlike Anglo women, employment alone did not decrease depression for Mexican American women. Only Mexican American women with higher-prestige jobs reported lower levels of depression, whereas Mexican American women with low-prestige jobs reported higher levels of depression than those women *not* working. This difference between Anglo and Mexican American women may be related to the fact that Mexican Americans have more positive views of housewives than Anglos, which in turn may be due to the fact that Mexican American women's access to employment is limited to low-wage, low-prestige, repetitive jobs. However, both Anglo and Mexican American women were more satisfied with their marriages and reported less depression when husbands contributed their share to the upkeep of the household.

Baca Zinn (1982c) found significant differences *entre dicho y hecho* (between what is said and what is done) in her study of Chicano families. Wives who stayed at home did most of the household tasks and had less influence over family decisions than wives who worked outside the home. However, all husbands and wives believed that authority should rest in the husband/father of the family, regardless of wives' employment status. Baca Zinn (1982c) concluded that employed wives openly challenged their husbands' dominance at the behavioral level while still adhering to the "ideology of patriarchy." However, rather than attributing behavioral changes to increased assimilation by Chicana women in the workforce, she explained them as deliberate acts by Chicanas to protect their families from a society that discriminates and subordinates all Chicanos, not just women. This is a much more sophisticated conceptual development in deciphering the complexities of cultural and economic adaptation to subordination than a simple model of assimilation from Mexican culture to Anglo culture.

Many researchers still use the assimilation framework to account for behavioral and attitudinal changes in the family lives of Latinos. Unlike previous research, however, lack of assimilation is not portrayed as a negative characteristic but merely as a fact of social existence. The current assimilation literature identifies different dimensions of family life among Latinos and compares them to those of Anglo families. When differences between Latinos and Anglos are observed in the direction predicted by the assimilation framework, the change is attributed to Latinos becoming more like Anglos, and therefore becoming more "modern" than "traditional." Furthermore, any behavior that seems to move from "pathological" to "normal" is also attributed to Latinos becoming more like Anglos; whether it is Mexican American women voting more often than in the past or husbands contributing to household chores, all are explained as a result of acculturation to dominant Anglo culture (MacManus, Bullock, & Grothe, 1986).

The results in the research using the assimilation framework usually indicate that in some spheres there are "cultural changes" and in others there are not. The limitations of the assimilation framework become apparent when most researchers are unable to fully explain the contradictory pattern of results. For example, Triandis, Marín, and Hui (1984) found that non-Hispanics perceived less emotional support within the family and experienced less hierarchy and conflict in work roles than did Hispanics, but the authors were unable to explain this pattern of results, other than to suggest that Hispanics were more family oriented and less attached to their "work roles" than non-Hispanics.

Unfortunately, the assimilation framework often uses global ethnic categories, such as "Hispanic" versus "mainstream" population, without considering the internal heterogeneity of the Hispanic group, either by specific Latino-group membership, language, and socioeconomic status or number of generations in the United States. All of these factors have been found to be significant for many dimensions of Latino social life, such as identity, voting patterns, and ethnic socialization (Hurtado & Gurin, 1987; Hurtado, Gurin, & Peng, 1994; Hurtado, Rodríguez, Gurin, & Beals, 1993). In addition, the global category of Hispanic and the mainstream group often include African Americans and individuals with varying degrees of education and different work status (Triandis et al., 1984). Consequently, when familial "cultural" differences are found, it is difficult to know which of the many variables is causing the differences reported.

Puerto Ricans, in particular, illustrate the complexity of cultural adaptation. As citizens of the United States, they move freely between Puerto Rico and the U.S. mainland, undergoing a variety of cultural transitions in the process. Rogler and Cooney (1984) indicate in their intergenerational study of Puerto Ricans involved in this type of migration that:

> The new setting creates a set of life circumstances never before experienced by the immigrant Puerto Ricans, and New York City's [where the majority of Puerto Ricans migrate] immense size and structural complexity impose upon them new and unfamiliar patterns and demands, such as the need to learn a new language and relegation to the status of a minority group. (p. 5)

As an example of the cultural continuity/discontinuity between Puerto Ricans on the island and Puerto Ricans in the United States, Procidiano and Rogler (1989) found that Puerto Rican couples in Puerto Rico and New York City married similar partners based on their education, age, and culture-specific values, such as the degree of acceptance of familism and fatalism. Although Puerto Rican couples in Puerto Rico were more likely to endorse familism and fatalism, these values were still used by their New York counterparts in the selection of spouses. These researchers concluded that "the sociocultural dislocations, previously attributed to the migration experience, do not disrupt the social processes underlying marital homogamy" (p. 353).

However, cultural adaptation by Latinos is not a linear process determined by length of residence in the United States (Chapa, 1988). Instead, cultural adaptation varies by socioeconomic status, number of generations in the United States, and the ability to speak Spanish and English (Hurtado et al., 1993; Rogler, Cooney, & Ortiz, 1980).

Latino Family Life Unaffected by Assimilation

There are several areas in which Latinos indeed exhibit *intragroup* (between different Latino groups) and *intergroup* (between Latinos and Anglos) variation but not necessarily in a linear fashion, as predicted by the assimilation framework. These include ethnic identity, familism, and Spanish-language maintenance.

ETHNIC IDENTITY

Chicanos and other Latinos retain a strong sense of ethnic identity, regardless of the number of generations in the United States (Hurtado et al., 1992, 1993). Although the ethnic labels that are chosen may vary by generation and by language, overall ethnic identification remains. In fact, the pattern of ethnic identification for different Latino groups typically stems from their national origins, changing at most to a bicultural identification that includes the United States. For example, looking at Puerto Rican families who had migrated to New York, Rogler and Cooney (1991) found that although the parents and their adult children varied on how much they identified as purely

Puerto Rican, not one mother, father, or adult child identified only as North American.

Rogler et al. (1980) also found that structural integration, as measured by education, had an effect on the different components of identity for parents, but *not* for their adult children (whose educational achievement was related only to knowledge of English). For adult children of Puerto Rican parents, education was not related in a linear fashion to subjective affiliation; language spoken to family, friends, and neighbors; mass media language usage; or attitudinal cultural preferences. That is,

> ethnic identity among both parents and children is related to variation in education, from no schooling through high school graduation, but additional years of schooling beyond high school graduation are not significant. . . . The ethnic identity of those who had attended college, graduated from college, or went on to postgraduate training is not significantly different from the ethnic identity of those who had only graduated from high school. (p. 211)

Age of arrival in the United States is of greater significance than education for ethnic identification. Generally, the younger the child (preschool versus early adolescence), the more likely he or she is to have a bicultural identity. However, the endpoint of immigrant children's adaptation to the United States is not total rejection of their ethnic origins and complete assimilation to the Anglo mainstream; rather the endpoint is a stable biculturalism (Rogler et al., 1980). Similar results have been found with third-generation Chicanos (Hurtado et al., 1993). Moreover, ethnic identification is manifested as a strong sense of community and allegiance to Latino issues (Williams, 1990).

FAMILISM

Latinos, regardless of their national origins (e.g., Mexican American, Central American, Cuban American, Puerto Rican), report a strong commitment to family. Certain dimensions of familism are stronger than others with each successive generation in the United States. For example, regardless of acculturation levels, Latinos perceive a high level of family support and desire geographical closeness to their families (Keefe & Padilla, 1987; Sabogal, Marín, & Otero-Sabogal, 1987). Other dimensions of familism decrease with increasing levels of acculturation, for example, using family members as role models exclusively and needing to be the only source of material and emotional support to members of their extended family (Rogler & Cooney, 1991). However, even among the most acculturated individuals, Latinos' attitudes and behaviors are still more familistic than Anglos.

Several researchers have attributed the difference between the familism of Anglos and Mexican Americans to their different definitions of "sufficient interaction" between family members and to Mexican Americans' extended definition of family membership. Whereas Anglos do not consider it necessary to have frequent face-to-face interaction with kin or to live geographically close to them, Mexican Americans are more likely than Anglos to live near their families and less likely to rely on letters or long-distance phone calls to maintain family ties (Keefe, 1984). Moreover, Mexican Americans include among their kin *compadres* and *comadres* (godparents) and may also include other community members, for example, elderly persons who may hold positions of respect within their neighborhood, as part of the family (Rothman, Gant, & Hnat, 1985; Vidal, 1988).

Familistic attitudes are also manifested in the household structure of Latinos. On average, families of Mexican descendants contain 4.1 persons, 35% contain more than 5, and 1 in every 5 families has 6 or more persons (Angel & Tienda, 1982b). However, household structure also varies by the number of generations Latinos have resided in the United States. For example, Chávez (1985) found that compared to undocumented workers from Mexico, legal immigrants rarely lived in households with unmarried siblings, and they almost never lived with friends in the same household. The majority of legal immigrants lived in nuclear family households (71.4% of the sample from San Diego, California), while less than half of the undocumented immigrants (43.5%) had this type of living arrangement. Single undocumented immigrants marry and eventually have other kin join them, creating extended family networks.

Extent and type of familism is also influenced by the place where Latinos live. Researchers have consistently found that Puerto Rican families in New York, in San Juan, Puerto Rico, and in Miami have intense contact with their kin (Pelto, Roman, & Liriano, 1982). But Puerto Rican families in Hartford, Connecticut, exhibited great variation in the extent they relied on kin for material and social support.

Thus, Pelto et al. (1982) advocated studying Latino families within "ecological settings" to fully capture the different adaptations Latino families make in their surroundings.

Comparison between different racial/ethnic groups is also important in defining the phenomenon of familism. For example, Mindel (1980) found that in an inner-city sample of Anglos, Mexican Americans, and African Americans from Kansas City, Missouri, Mexican Americans were the most familistic both in attitudes and behavior, African Americans were in the middle, and Anglos were the least familistic. In addition, African Americans and Mexican Americans used extended family networks in different ways. Although African Americans had less interaction with their families than Mexican Americans, African Americans were more likely to use their kin for instrumental purposes, such as material aid, whereas Mexican Americans used their kin for more social and emotional support.

Although the manifestation of familism among Latinos has changed over time and geographical setting, a substantial body of research shows that Latinos not only "ascribe to familistic norms, but practice them" (Gratton, 1987). In fact, counter to what assimilation theory would predict, recent cross-sectional studies indicate that familism, and therefore social support, increases with each generation living in the United States (Keefe & Padilla, 1987; Ramirez & Arce, 1981). However, there are gender differences in the behavioral manifestation of familism. Thus, women in the family tend to be relied on for help on health matters, whereas men are relied on for home repairs and upkeep. Same-sex family members are relied on for financial issues and personal problems, and feelings of solidarity are greater with same-sex family members as well.

In a related study, women helped when the tasks were defined as "women's work," such as caring for the sick (Markides, Boldt, & Ray, 1986). Familism may in fact reinforce the gender subordination of women by placing a disproportionate burden on them, especially as they grow older. For example, Perez (1986) found that Cuban elderly in trigenerational households provided services such as child care and contributed whatever retirement income they had to the household. Furthermore, in certain areas of the country, such as San Antonio, Texas, trigenerational families constitute 40% of the Mexican American population age 65 to 85. Latino families living in trigenerational households are not uncommon, and appreciation of this fact will become increasingly important for understanding Latino family life.

SPANISH-LANGUAGE MAINTENANCE

Latino families experience considerable transition from Spanish to English language usage with each successive generation in the United States. Using cross-sectional data, Arce (1982) found that parents usually spoke Spanish to their own parents, Spanish and English to their siblings, and more English than Spanish to their own children. However, those children still had competence in Spanish, indicating a transition not into monolingualism in English, but to stable bilingualism in English and Spanish. The high maintenance of Spanish language within Latino families may be explained by their positive attitudes toward their language and by the desire to preserve it as one of the most important aspects of Latino culture (Hurtado & Gurin, 1987).

Research has also shown that Spanish competence, unlike other aspects of Latino culture, actually increases with structural integration. Hazuda, Stern, and Haffner (1988) found that Chicanos residing in the affluent Northside of San Antonio were more proficient in understanding, speaking, and reading Spanish than were residents of the less affluent Westside barrios.

Issues of Spanish-language maintenance within Latino families will become even more important than in the past as the number of Spanish speakers increases as a result of immigration from Mexico and Latin America.

Current Conceptualizations of Pathology: The Underclass Model

The underclass model is one of the most recent policy frameworks used to explain the position of racial/ethnic households in the United States (Schorr & Schorr, 1988). The current underclass model is a new and "improved" version of the assimilation framework: It extends the culture-of-poverty thesis that contends the poor have a different way of life than the Anglo mainstream of society and that these cultural differences explain continued poverty. There are three culprits in the underclass model's explanation for the poverty experienced by minority populations: culture, family, and welfare (Baca Zinn, 1989). The major argument is that the culture of Latinos (and of other racial/ethnic groups) is responsible for their lack of economic advancement because these groups' values are characterized by low aspirations, excessive masculinity, and the acceptance of female-headed families as the norm.

There is substantial evidence that the cultural deficiency version of the underclass model is seriously flawed (Tienda, 1989). For example, current empirical evidence refutes the notion that poverty is caused by cultural values and passed on from one generation to another (Baca Zinn, 1989). First, there is a high turnover of individual families in poverty. That is, although the number of people in poverty remains about the same, the poor people in one year are not necessarily the poor of the following year. In simpler terms, welfare families do not reproduce welfare offspring (Corcoran, Duncan, Gurin, & Gurin, 1985). Second, motivation cannot be linked to poverty. Such measures as parental sense of efficacy, future orientation, and achievement motivation have no effect on welfare dependency (Hill & Ponza, 1983). Economic opportunities are necessary for the expression of people's motivation. Ambition alone does not catapult individuals out of poverty. Furthermore, poverty is not the result of female-headed households but rather the result of the breakup of *poor* two-parent households (Bane, 1986). For Anglo families, marital dissolution does result in increased poverty among female-headed households. Put more poignantly, African American children in two-parent households have less income than Anglo children in mother-only households (Baca Zinn, 1989; Hill, 1983). Variations in welfare payments across states are not related to systematic variations in family structure, such as female-headed households and number of children (Darity & Meyers, 1984; Ellwood, 1988; Ellwood & Summers, 1986). In effect, the changing nature of the family in society at large has set the context for the reevaluation of the Latino family in particular.

THE CHANGING CHARACTERISTICS
OF NON-HISPANIC WHITE FAMILIES

Non-Hispanic White families have changed dramatically since the early 1960s, when the lack of assimilation that resulted in the cultural deficit model flourished as the preferred explanation for Latinos' and other racial/ethnic groups' lack of economic advancement. Families from the dominant culture no longer look the way they did in the 1950s or early 1960s. Massive cultural and economic changes have modified Anglo families to look more like racial/ethnic families: more female-headed households, higher rates of divorce, more children living in poverty, and higher school dropout rates (Staples & Mirandé, 1980). As Baca Zinn (1990) observes,

> As social and economic changes produce new family arrangements, a family pluralism, if you will, has broadened the definition of what constitutes a family. Although many of these family alternatives appear new to middle-class Anglo Americans, they are actually variants of family patterns within ethnic communities. Presented as the new lifestyles of the mainstream, they are, in fact, the same lifestyles that have in the past been deemed pathological, deviant, or unacceptable when observed in Black families. (p. 79)

Married Anglo women are now participating in the labor force at a rate that, until recently, was seen exclusively among women of color (Smith, 1987). The consequence has been Anglo women's decreased fertility and changes in marriage patterns. Anglo women marry later, have fewer children, and live alone or as heads of their own households (Hartmann, 1987). Different family arrangements include nonmarital cohabitation, single-parent households, extended kinship units and expanded households, dual wage-earner families, commuter marriages, gay and lesbian households, and collectives (Baca Zinn, 1990). Of foremost importance in advancing these changes has been the feminist movement, the gay movement, and the changing labor market.

The Functionalist Reevaluation of Chicano Families

The dramatic changes in structure experienced by dominant families happened primarily during the 1970s and early 1980s, providing a practical and theoretical aperture for reexamining all racial/ethnic families. Most scholars undertaking this "revisionist scholarship" were Chicanos. Their focus was exclusively on Chicano families because Latino immigration at this time had not reached its current rate. Revisionist scholars unwittingly followed Parsons and Bales's (1955) functionalist approach to the study of families. From a functionalist theoretical framework, the "modern" nuclear family—the husband working while wife stays at home model—is viewed not only as an inevitable consequence of "modernization," but as the institution best suited to perform society's most vital functions: the socialization of children and the stabilization of adult personalities. (Pierce, 1984, p. 93)

Chicano scholars asserted that there were cultural variations in how these functions were carried out (Mirandé & Enriquez, 1979; Montiel, 1970). Chicano families, like Anglo families, indeed carried out these functions, but they performed them within the context of Chicano culture.

In general, scholars in ethnic studies took the lead in providing a functionalist reevaluation of racial/ethnic families in the United States. They approached the project by documenting how the family characteristics of Chicanos were the result of specific historical events and cultural processes. The experience of conquest, in particular, resulted in cultural adaptations to subordination that included a strong sense of family and collective commitment to their group for economic survival. Perhaps one of the most important outcomes of the functional reevaluation of Latino families was to highlight that although Latino families live in poverty, they do not have many of the characteristics delineated in the underclass model, such as high divorce rates (Moore, 1989). Their traditional family characteristics, however, have not resulted in increased economic advancement (Hayes-Bautista, Hurtado, Valdez, & Hernández, 1992). The underclass model assumes that the gendered division of labor, with men being the providers and women the homemakers, is the preferred familial arrangement to solve poverty (Baca Zinn, 1982a; Comas-Diaz & Duncan, 1985). Latinos fit this model to a certain extent, but the overriding goal to keep their families together has forced Latina women to underplay their concerns.

The Feminist Critique of the Functionalist Approach to Studying Chicano Families

The functionalist reevaluation of Chicano families, however, was reactive. At the core of this analysis was the rebuttal of previously derogated characteristics, such as familism, mutual aid, and cooperation. The functionalist reevaluation did not result in elucidating the internal dynamics of Chicano family life, but instead perpetuated the stereotypical views of Chicano families by simply recasting the previously described negative characteristics as positive ones. However, revisionist scholars did make an enormous contribution by beginning to delineate how the negative characteristics attributed to Chicano families might be ways to cope with structural barriers, such as racism and labor force discrimination, rather than cultural deficits. Nonetheless, many questions remained unanswered because they fell outside the functionalist analysis and therefore might present a "dysfunctional" picture of Chicanos' internal family dynamics. Of foremost importance is the position of women within Latino families.

Chicana feminists have been at the forefront of the critique of the functionalist perspective on Chicano families (Andrade, 1982; Baca Zinn, 1980, 1982b, 1982c; Pesquera, 1984; Ybarra, 1982b). Their work has challenged the notion that Chicano families are exempt from sexism because Chicanas have power within the domestic sphere:

> Her [the Chicana's] domestic role is not passive. She is charged with the essential familial functions . . . transmission of values and beliefs to the next generation and the provision of needed warmth, support and affection for family members. . . . Men have power and authority relative to outside institutions and women are responsible for the daily affairs of the family. (Mirandé & Enriquez, 1979, pp. 116-117)

The assertion that Chicanas are separate but equal within Chicano families, however, was challenged by researchers who focused on the internal dynamics of Chicano families. For example, Chicanas' and other Latinas' authority to participate in family decisions increased as a result of working outside the home, not as a result of Latino men in these families voluntarily relinquishing power (Baca Zinn, 1980; Cooney et al., 1982; Pesquera, 1984; Ybarra, 1982b). Furthermore, Chicanas' and other Latinas' position in the labor force placed them in a disadvantaged relationship to men so that their ability to make life decisions about marriage, children, and career was severely limited. Their experience of "triple oppression" because of class, race, and gender is not adequately accounted for in the functionalist reevaluation of the Chicano family (Segura, 1984).

Women's Issues Within the
Context of the Latino Families

Overall, our understanding of Latino/Chicano families has been most advanced in the study of gender relations. Researchers have begun to portray an accurate picture of Latino family life by focusing on Latinos' conceptions of womanhood and manhood and their relationship to structural variables such as participation in the labor force. This approach has resulted in focusing on family phenomena such as marital decision making (Baca Zinn, 1980; Cooney et al., 1982; Rogler & Cooney, 1991; Ybarra, 1982b), gender subordination within the family (Comas-Diaz, 1988; Pesquera, 1984), conceptions of masculinity (Mirandé, 1988b; Baca Zinn, 1982a) and femininity (Comas-Diaz & Duncan, 1985), and the role of fathers in the socialization of children (Bronstein, 1984; Mirandé, 1988b; Nieto, 1983). The focus on gender averted the persistent conceptual cul de sac where Latino families are either a tangle of pathology or an undifferentiated human mass of collective values. Instead, gender studies view Latino families as a relational unit where power between men and women is negotiated and a unit where structural forces, such as racism and labor market segmentation, affect family members. Furthermore, the most recent scholarship on Latino families refuses to categorize the family as "either a refuge or an institution determined by relations of production, [but as] both" (Baca Zinn, 1983, p. 142).

As a result, a considerable amount of research now examines the distribution of power within Latino households (Cooney et al., 1982; N. Williams, 1990; Zavella, 1985). For example, N. Williams found that both men and women took it for granted that significant changes had occurred between generations. Even those working-class husbands who had expressed traditional views of marriage expected their wives to work outside the home and depended on their spouses' incomes to sustain their standard of living, as well as advance their aspirations of upward mobility in the educational and the occupational spheres.

Researchers have also begun to examine how Latina women exert their authority over their bodies. Amaro (1988) found evidence to counter the stereotypes that Mexican American women are dominated by Catholic doctrine, passive in fertility decisions, and desirous of large families. Instead, she found that the women in her sample (83.1%) used contraception (even though most of them [81.6%] were

Catholic) and did not want more children (66.7%); some (11.1%) wished that they had fewer children, and almost all the women (91.1%) felt that the woman (not the man) should make the final decision whether to use contraception or not. These results were independent of the women's acculturation levels.

Obviously, there are salient contradictions between the competing economic demands that force women into the labor force and then demand that they remain loyal to outmoded norms for proper "female" conduct. Women are more likely to feel the contradiction when they join the public realm, such as when they enter the labor force or when they become politically involved. For example, in her study of Chicana cannery workers, Zavella (1985) found that husbands complained that their wives' political organizing at work took too much time and resulted in their wives neglecting their families.

The contradiction between economic and educational accomplishment and "proper" conduct for women is especially salient for Latinas who pursue higher education. Chicanas who are strongly ethnically identified and would prefer to marry within their own group are more likely to experience psychological stress and to perceive their educational achievements as threatening Chicano men. Chicanas who either are not ethnically identified or are willing to marry outside their ethnic group do not experience stress as a result of their educational achievements (Gonzalez, 1988). Zambrana and Frith (1988) also found that Mexican American women's professional satisfaction is not related to whether they are single, with a partner only, with children only, or with partner and children. In fact, the women who experienced most professional stress were single women, and the women with partners and children experienced the least. The most *personally* satisfied, however, were the women with partners only. These authors (1988) propose that this group of women are benefiting from the loosening of the norms requiring them to have children and instead enjoy their careers and their family lives with their partners.

To be sure, family now has a broader definition, but there are still racial meanings that create a hierarchy in which some family forms are privileged and others are subordinated (Baca Zinn, 1990). Therefore, much of the latest research on Latino families, produced mostly by scholars in ethnic studies, proposes a framework that integrates class, race, culture, and gender to fully understand the family lives of Latinos.

Structural Deficiency Model

The emergent structural deficiency paradigm explains the diversity of family structures as related to but not causing the social location of people of color. Latino families, like other ethnic families, developed their adaptations in a historical context of labor exploitation. Social institutions were organized to support Anglo families and their family structure, which encouraged and rewarded women for staying at home (with all the disadvantages that entailed). However, the social function of Latinos and other racial/ethnic groups was primarily to provide a source of cheap labor, regardless of the consequences for family life. Under these circumstances a diversity of family structures developed simultaneously (Griswold del Castillo, 1984). In this view, the characteristics of racial/ethnic families are adaptations to structural limitations and sources of strength, rather than of deviance. More important, the differences are not necessarily caused by cultural differences, but rather they are adaptations and resistance to the economic facts of group membership. The most recent research from this perspective focuses on how particular family adaptations are the result of culture *and* class. Furthermore, as Baca Zinn (1990) indicates:

> With respect to single-parent families, teenage childbirth, working mothers, and a host of other behaviors, Black families and other racial/ethnic families serve as barometers of social change and as forerunners of adaptive patterns that will be progressively experienced by the more privileged sectors of American society. (p. 79)

Indeed, several studies have already shown that when social class is held constant, there is little variation in the family dynamics of Mexican American and Anglo families on several dimensions.

To be sure, disentangling the effects of race, class, culture, and gender is a promising direction for future research on families. No longer will research results be attributed to particular racial/ethnic groups; rather, the focus will be on the social contexts that produce specific family patterns.

Future Directions for Research

Three areas of Latino family life have remained virtually unexamined: sexuality, intermarriage among different racial/ethnic Latino groups other than Anglos, and the elderly. Issues of sexuality and the negotiation of sexual orientation, such as how Latino gays and lesbians are treated within Latino families and Latino communities, have not been the focus of Latino family research. Similarly, how does ethnicity influence the subjective meanings of masculinity and femininity (Baca Zinn, 1982a). References to sexuality are made when related issues are under study (Amaro, 1988), but there are no studies in the social sciences per se in the area of sexuality and Latino families (Almaguer, 1991). For example, the fact that Latino families restrict their daughters' sexuality is used as an indicator of Latino families' traditionalism in comparison to Anglo families (Soto, 1983). Or normative restrictions on sexuality are mentioned when they have implications for the psychotherapies used with Latina women (Espín, 1984). Family scholars, however, have not specifically focused on how Latino families negotiate sexuality. Theoretical analyses of sexuality among Latinos are based on historical, literary, philosophical, and autobiographical materials (see, among others, Alarcón, 1981; Almaguer, 1991; Arguelles & Rich, 1984; Bruce-Novoa, 1986). However, the empirical base for the study of sexuality within the context of Latino families is virtually nonexistent (Almaguer, 1991; Amaro, 1988).

Intermarriage is also another important area for future research. The focus of most work has been on marriages between Anglos and Mexican-origin individuals. However, future research will have to address intermarriage between individuals from different Latino groups and its implications for ethnic identification and ethnic socialization of children. Recent work suggests that perhaps there is an emergent ethnic identity that is indeed *Latino,* rather than based on a specific Latino group such as Puerto Rican, Mexican, Salvadoran, and so on.

The intergenerational family is not uncommon among Latinos, and little is known of how family dynamics are enhanced or hampered by the presence of more than one generation in the household. Sotomayor (1989) proposes three major functions that elderly family members can perform in an intergenerational household:

1. The socialization of younger household members
2. The provision of emotional support
3. The transmission of Latino culture and language

However, there are insufficient empirical studies to assess whether, in fact, these functions are accomplished in intergenerational families and whether Latino families are different from other racial/ethnic families in the United States.

Conclusions

There has been considerable advancement in our understanding of Latino families. The evidence is overwhelming that all groups of Latinos have a strong commitment to maintaining their language, culture, and ethnic identity. Furthermore, regardless of their national origins, all groups of Latinos want their children to maintain their cultural traditions and language, regardless of the number of generations in the United States. Although Latino groups vary in their knowledge and degree of exclusive identification with their ethnic group, no study of ethnic identification and cultural maintenance has found individuals who identify exclusively as Anglo or as North American (Hurtado et al., 1993; Rogler et al., 1980). Cultural and language transition does occur, but it takes the form of a stable biculturalism rather than complete assimilation into the dominant mainstream. Furthermore, whereas actual cultural knowledge and skills in reading and writing Spanish may decline with each subsequent generation in the United States, a strong ethnic loyalty remains, which may be mobilized to reacquire some of the cultural awareness lost in younger generations (Padilla, 1980). In conclusion, levels of acculturation and/or assimilation are unrelated to levels of ethnic identification, language maintenance, shared decision making in marriage, and husbands' power within the home (Cooney et al., 1982).

Immigration from Latin America is likely to continue and research indicates that its status as documented (or undocumented) affects the structure of households, child care arrangements, and labor force participation (Chávez, 1985). The continuing influx of immigrants to the United States from Mexico and other Latin American countries reminds U.S.-born Latinos of the differences in socialization processes in the United States and the rest of Latin America. Future research will have to have at its core an understanding of the sociodemographic realities of the Latino population. Immigrant status (documented versus undocumented) and number of generations in the United States are important in determining the internal dynamics of family life.

Scholars have developed a strong theoretical argument for why it is necessary to take into account race, ethnicity, and social class in the study of families. Unfortunately, with very few exceptions, racial/ethnic families are still compared to Anglo families without attention to class variation. Furthermore, research on Latino families has for the most part not adequately documented *intragroup* variation in family structure and culture. Future research on Latino families will also have to disentangle the effects of class and membership in different Latino groups.

In conclusion, the internal diversity of the Latino group by national origins, history, immigration patterns, and sociodemographic characteristics has implications not only for scholarly work but also for the social policy developed from this work. Social policies effective for Mexican descendants in the Southwest may be disastrous for Puerto Ricans in the Northeast. Massive immigration and internal migration have important consequences for Latino families in the United States. This situation, however, is not unprecedented, and it represents the latest cycle in this country's history. Research that focuses on the family lives of Latinos may help us understand how families of all racial/ethnic backgrounds change in response to changing social situations and cultural influences.

4

The Status of Latino Children and Youth

Challenges and Prospects

JULIE SOLIS

L atinos represent the fastest growing segment of the U.S. population under the age of 21. By 2030, the number of Latino children and youth will reach 9.6 million—more than double their number in 1980, 4.7 million (Duany & Pittman, 1990). Latino families have adapted to their circumstances in ways that reflect sources of strength that need to be built upon, rather than sources of weakness that need to be eliminated (Baca Zinn, 1990; Hayes-Bautista, 1989).

This chapter reviews the status of Latino children and youth within the contemporary context of Latino families. It emphasizes the unique circumstances of Latino youth and children in three areas: education, employment and economic mobility, and marriage and childbearing decisions. These three areas are integrally related and constitute focal social concerns for both Latino families and social institutions. When possible, attention is given to differences found among Latino subgroups—namely, Mexican-origin, Central and/or South American, Puerto Rican, and Cuban—because differences among these groups often are greater than overall differences between Latinos and non-Latinos. The key effects of nativity, generation, and language are elucidated whenever possible, although research on Latinos has generally not included intragroup analyses.

TABLE 4.1 Percentage of the Population Under the Age of 21, by Latino Group, 1992 (in thousands)

Group	Total Number	Percent Under 21	Number Under 21
Mexican	14,062	43.2	6,075
Puerto Rican	2,352	39.8	936
Cuban	1,041	21.6	225
Central/South American	3,084	33.5	1,033
Other Hispanic Origin	1,557	33.1	515

NOTE: The percentages were calculated from data compiled by the U.S. Bureau of the Census (Garcia, 1993, p. 13).

Children and Family Characteristics

In 1992, Latinos under the age of 21 numbered almost 8.8 million (almost 40% of the total Latino population). In contrast, only 27.6% of non-Hispanic Whites were under the age of 21 (Table 4.1). An examination of the proportion of children and youth in each of the major Latino groups shows that the Mexican-origin and Puerto Rican groups have the highest concentrations of individuals under the age of 21, followed by Central and South Americans, and last by Cubans (Garcia, 1993).

POVERTY AND FAMILY CHARACTERISTICS

Over the past 30 years, all Latino groups have experienced the same trend toward marital instability that has been evident in non-Hispanic White and African American groups (Bean & Tienda, 1987). In 1988, 23% of Latino households were headed by a woman, compared to 43% of African American households and 13% of non-Hispanic White households. Among Latino groups, households headed by a woman were most common among Puerto Ricans (44%), followed by Central and South Americans (24%), then Mexicans (19%) and last Cubans (16%) (Duany & Pittman, 1990). From 1980 to 1988, the proportion of Latino children and adolescents living in single-parent families increased from 25% to 34%.

In 1991, almost 29% of all Latinos (6.3 million) were living in poverty. In the same year, the poverty rate for families with children under 18 was 40% for Latinos, 15% for non-Hispanic Whites, and 44% for African Americans (U.S. Bureau of the Census, 1993e). The prevalence of poverty among Latino children can be attributed to a number of factors. First, a growing number of Latino children are being raised by their mothers alone. Second, a large proportion of Latino children have young parents, a phenomenon that is due in part to the growing number of teen births. Latino teenagers are twice as likely as their non-Hispanic White peers to have parents younger than 30 years of age. In 1988, 17% of Latino teenagers had parents younger than 35 years of age, compared to 27% of their African American peers and 11% of Hispanic White teenagers (Duany & Pittman, 1990). Third, Latinos tend to have a relatively large number of children per family. About one half of Latino families, compared to one third of non-Latino families, had four or more members.

Finally, the parents of many Latino youth have low levels of education, low levels of income, and high levels of unemployment (data that follow are from Duany & Pittman, 1990; U.S. Bureau of the Census, 1990b). With respect to education, only 42% of Latino adolescents have parents who are high school graduates, compared to 66% of African American and 80% of non-Hispanic White teenagers. In terms of income, 54% of Latino youth live in families that earn less than $20,000 a year, compared to 60% of African American and 24% of non-Hispanic White youth. In the area of unemployment, 31% of Latino teens live in households where parents are unemployed or looking for work, compared to 36% of African American teens and 14% of non-Hispanic White teens. The unemployment rates are even higher for female-headed households: 56% for Latinas, 47% for African American women, and 29% for non-Hispanic White women. Clearly, the effects of poverty are devastating to the overall well-being of Latino families and children.

ROLE OF THE FAMILY

An important dimension of the psychosocial development of Latino youth and children is the role of family and social support networks. A number of studies have documented the high value that Latinos of various national origins place on family support. Even highly accul-turated Latinos are much more familistic than non-Hispanic Whites (Sabogal, Marín, & Otero-Sabogal, 1987). With respect to the younger generation, it has been found that Mexican American young adults feel a stronger pull toward family than their peers. Health, family functioning, and life satisfaction among Latino family members has been related to the effectiveness of available social support, including spousal support. A study of dual-earner Mexican American families with young children found that, particularly for the wives, highly effective social support mechanisms contributed to high life satisfaction, positive attitudes toward work and family, and low perceived role conflict (Holtzman & Gilbert, 1987). Vega et al. (1986) found that low-income Mexican American families with school-age children manifested family health functioning through four life course stages. Compared to middle-income non-Hispanic White parents, low-income Mexican American parents were more adept at trying new ways of dealing with problems and shifting responsibilities from one person to another. Another study (Schumm et al., 1988) examined satisfaction with a variety of family relationships among intact families, both rural and urban, in 14 states. Generally, both Latino parents and their adolescent family members were more satisfied with family life than their non-Hispanic White counterparts.

Familial influences on the development of Latino ideological orientations have also been studied. Compared to non-Hispanic White adolescents, Mexican American youth appear more inclined to adopt the religious and political beliefs, as well as the occupational preferences, of their parents, regardless of socioeconomic status (Abraham, 1986). A study of five generations of Mexican American children found that identification with American norms and political orientations prevailed in the first and second generations (Lamare, 1982). However, in the third generation, notable declines in political assimilation and acculturation became evident. By the third generation, Mexican American children expressed skepticism about traditional American political culture, which the authors speculate can lead to a deeper sense of alienation in subsequent generations of Mexican Americans. The literature on Latino familism clearly demonstrates the pivotal role that support networks play in the psychosocial development of Latino children and youth.

DEVELOPMENTAL ISSUES

Poor social, environmental, and economic circumstances affect the growth and development of children, placing them at high risk for physical and developmental problems. Given the low socioeconomic status of many Latino children, attention to risk factors that affect them is critical. Risk factors of importance to infants and children include genetic, prenatal, perinatal, neonatal, postnatal, environmental, psychological, and socioeconomic indicators. In general, research on risk factors related to children has focused on the effects of physiological factors. More research is needed concerning the social and psychological factors that increase the risk status of Latino children (Siantz, in press).

Research on the cognitive and psychosocial development of Latino children has been extremely limited and has tended to take a rather narrow focus. Bilingualism and its relationship to intelligence-test performance, academic achievement, and self-concept have been the major focus. Other investigations have examined cognitive styles and prosocial behaviors, such as cooperation and altruism, among Latino children (Padilla & Lindholm, 1983). Much of the past research has been problematic, as Latino children are generally judged according to standards that use non-Hispanic White children as the reference point (Knight & Kagan, 1977; Knight, Kagan, Nelson, & Gumbiner, 1978). More recent research (Oakland, de Mesquita, & Buckley, 1988) has examined the effect of cognitive style (field dependence versus independence), as well as mental age, linguistic, and sociocultural variables, on reading achievement among Mexican American children. It found that cognitive style-matching was not important. Rather, the student's intelligence and English-language competencies were far more important to reading development.

Surprisingly, even less research has been done on the social and personality development of Latino adolescents. Most of the research on Latino youth has focused on deviant behaviors, such as substance abuse, dropping out of school, and gang-related activities. Issues related to normal development and nondelinquent behaviors have been essentially unexamined.

Educational Status

Some progress has been made in the educational status of Latinos. During the past 20 years, the proportion of Latino adults with a high school diploma has increased from 1 in 3 to 1 in 2. However, most would agree that the rate of improvement has been haltingly slow. Today, Latinos drop out of school at a rate higher than any other group. Studies have shown that Latinos drop out of school at two and a half times the rate of non-Hispanic White students. Latino dropout rates in many school districts throughout the country reach well over 50% (Delgado-Gaitan, 1988).

Since the mid-1970s, Latino high school graduation rates have improved only slightly, whereas African American high school graduation rates have increased steadily (data that follow are from Duany & Pittman, 1990). From 1975 to 1986, the graduation rates of 18- to 24-year-olds increased from 58% to 60% for Latinos and from 65% to 76% for African Americans. A substantial number of Latinos terminate their education even before entering high school. Among Latinos 16 to 24 years of age who lacked a high school education in 1988, 32% had a sixth-grade education or less, compared to only 5% of non-Latinos. Another 34% of Latinos had completed between 7 and 9 years of schooling, compared to 36% of non-Latinos. Thus, at least half of Latinos who fail to graduate from high school never even started it. The likelihood of eventually attaining a high school diploma is higher among dropouts who are close to completing high school than among those who have several years to go. However, only 34% of Latino non-high school graduates were within 2 years of completing high school, compared to 59% of non-Latinos.

Furthermore, in 1986, Latino youth (12- to 15-year-olds) were about 2.5 times as likely as non-Hispanic Whites to be two or more grades behind in school (Duany & Pittman, 1990). By age 17, almost 40% of Latino youth were 1 year behind expected grade level and another 17% were 2 or more years behind. The rate of grade delay among Latinos has been on the increase and is slightly more than African Americans (Duany & Pittman, 1990). Grade delay increases the likelihood of dropping out of school. Bean and Tienda (1987) found that gender, place of birth, and marital status affected school completion. Generally, young men were more likely to drop out than young women. This finding counters other research showing that dropout rates are higher among females than males (Chávez, Edwards, & Oetting, 1989). In addition, foreign-born youth tend to drop out at a higher rate than U.S.-born youth. The event of marriage was highly related to the probability of being a dropout. In addition, living independently or with relatives and living in poverty were associated with higher rates of high school noncompletion.

Along with high dropout rates, Latino youth are at risk for low educational achievement in other ways (data that follow are from

Duany & Pittman, 1990). According to the 1988 testing results of the National Assessment for Education Progress (NAEP), the reading, math, and science skills of Latino and African American 17-year-olds are roughly comparable to the skills of non-Hispanic White 13-year-olds. Racial and ethnic differences in advanced skills are also evident, due in part to the underrepresentation of students of color in advanced courses. For example, among 1987 high school graduates, about 50% of non-Hispanic Whites, compared to about 30% of Latinos and African Americans, took Algebra II. Latinos are much more likely to be placed in watered-down general or vocational classes than are Asian and non-Hispanic White students. In 1987, Latinos and African Americans each accounted for 40% of the remedial class population, with the remaining 20% made up of non-Hispanic Whites. With respect to participation in gifted and talented programs, 2.4% of both Latinos and African Americans and 5.4% of non-Hispanic Whites were enrolled in 1986. In addition, Latino high school graduates are much less likely than other groups, except African Americans, to attain advanced degrees. An examination of the advanced attainment levels of 1980 high school seniors shows that 21% of African Americans, 30% of Latinos, 40% of non-Hispanic Whites, and 50% of Asians had attained postsecondary degrees or licenses by 1986. Over the 6-year period, 41% of Latinos, 36% of African Americans, 31% of non-Hispanic Whites, and 10% of Asians had never enrolled in any postsecondary courses.

Family income is a major predictor of college enrollment, and this certainly holds true for Latinos (data that follow are from Children's Defense Fund, 1989; Duany & Pittman, 1990). Attainment of a college degree by 1986 occurred among only 5% of low-income Latino seniors who left high school in 1980, compared to 18% of high-income Latino seniors. However, even high-income Latino seniors had the lowest college attainment rates of all groups. The proportion of high-income seniors who had attained college degrees by 1986 was 18% for Latinos, 26% for African Americans, 40% for non-Hispanic Whites, and 46% for Asians.

GROUP DIFFERENCES

Little recent data examines differences in educational attainment by national origin and cultural and demographic factors (gender, language, place of birth, and marital status). However, Bean and

Tienda (1987) conducted analyses of the 1980 census data in two areas: school delay and school dropouts. The authors examined the age-grade delay patterns among Latino youth living with their parents in 1980 and enrolled in school up to and including the 12th grade, thus excluding school dropouts and students living separate from their parents. Among U.S.-born Latinos, the average school delay rate was much higher for Mexicans and Puerto Ricans (about 10%) than for Cubans and Central/South Americans (about 6%). Regardless of national origin, foreign-born Latinos were at least twice as likely as their U.S.-born counterparts to be held back, with an average delay rate of about 20%. Regardless of place of birth, young men showed a higher incidence of delay than young women. The highest rates of delay were found among foreign-born students who speak little or no English. With respect to the effects of language on school delay, Bean and Tienda (1987) found that it is individual English ability that matters. Among Mexicans, Central/South Americans, and other Hispanics, poor English skills increased the likelihood of grade repetition, irrespective of place of birth. Cubans exhibited the ability to overcome language barriers eventually, which reduced the likelihood of grade repetition, despite high levels of Spanish maintenance. Contrary to popular belief, the household language environment of the student was unrelated to school delay.

Looking at the school noncompletion rates of Latino youth, ages 18 to 25, in 1980, the average dropout rates for Mexicans and Puerto Ricans were much higher than for Cubans and Central/South Americans. Mexican-born youth and Puerto Ricans from the island had the highest noncompletion rates of all. Among Mexicans, foreign-born students were twice as likely as U.S.-born students to drop out of school. Similarly large differences in school noncompletion rates were found between U.S.-born Puerto Ricans and Puerto Ricans from the islands. Even though Cubans and Central/South Americans have the highest percentage of foreign-born and the highest rates of Spanish maintenance in the home, they have not been kept from achieving levels of schooling close to those of non-Hispanic Whites. In general, resources such as income and parental education have been more readily available to Cubans and Central/South Americans than to Puerto Rican and Mexican-origin populations, differentially influencing their options in society (Bean & Tienda, 1987).

As in the case of school delay, English-language proficiency was an important predictor of school noncompletion (data that follow are from

Bean & Tienda, 1987). Among all Latino groups except Cubans, the likelihood of dropping out of school increased at lower levels of English ability. The effect for Cubans was in the expected direction but was too weak to be statistically significant. The effects of language were particularly strong for Central/South Americans. As with the issue of delay, the home language environment was not related to the propensity to complete school.

FACTORS RELATED TO ACHIEVEMENT

Much research has been conducted to determine the factors that contribute to the school success and failure of Latino and other students of color (Chávez et al., 1989). Research on determinants that account for sociocultural influences is also plentiful (Delgado-Gaitan, 1988). However, the effects of factors strongly related to minority status, namely, experiences of discrimination, self-concept, and personal aspirations, have not been adequately investigated. Research on factors related to educational attainment and achievement among Latino youth are reviewed in three areas: (a) political/institutional factors, (b) cultural/linguistic factors, and (c) psychosocial factors.

In regard to political/institutional factors, it has been widely documented in the literature that Latino students do not receive the academic support necessary for educational success (Delgado-Gaitan, 1988). In fact, researchers have suggested that the low attainment levels of Latinos, such as high rates of grade repetition, are the result of discriminatory school system policies rather than language and socioeconomic factors that hamper the ability of Latinos to perform well in education settings (Nielson & Fernández, 1981). Two major demographic trends regarding Latino students support the discriminatory school policy thesis (data that follow are from Children's Defense Fund, 1989). First, Latino students, like African Americans, are found primarily in central cities where the quality of schools is often poor. In 1987, the vast majority (91%) of Latino youth lived in metropolitan areas compared to 82% of African American youth and 74% of non-Hispanic White youth. Within metropolitan areas, Latino youth, like African American youth, were twice as likely as non-Hispanic White youth to live in central cities—55% compared with 23%. High school dropout rates are highest in the inner-city schools. In 1986, only 52% of inner-city Latinos had completed high school.

Second, Latino students are attending segregated schools at a rate that appears higher than African Americans. Latino attendance in segregated schools has increased markedly. From 1972 to 1986, the proportion of Latinos attending predominantly minority schools increased from 57% to 72%. In contrast, the proportion of African Americans attending segregated schools declined over time to 63% in 1986. Although there are exceptions, schools that serve racial/ethnic minorities are generally inferior in quality to schools that serve non-Hispanic Whites. Qualitative differences are evident in the level of course work; the level of teacher education and experience; the amount of actual instructional time, equipment, and facilities; per-student expenditures by each school district; and teacher expectations (Children's Defense Fund, 1989).

In regard to cultural/linguistic factors, popular belief contends that home bilingualism hinders the school performance of Latino students and that the cultural ambience of Latino homes is the source of educational problems for Latinos. Much of the research examining the effects of language and generational status on Latino achievement has found the opposite to be true (Buriel & Cardoza, 1988). The interplay between cultural and linguistic factors has produced a complex pattern of relationships with respect to Latino achievement levels. With respect to generational status, one would expect levels of educational attainment to increase with each passing generation. However, a growing body of research indicates that third-generation Latinos are lower achievers than their first- and second-generation counterparts (Buriel & Cardoza, 1988). Studies on the effects of language have shown that limited English proficiency, not the language of the home, has a negative effect on achievement. In fact, research has shown that Spanish proficiency has a positive effect on achievement (Duran, 1983; Whitworth, 1988).

An analysis of data from the *High School and Beyond Survey* (U.S. Department of Education, Office of Educational Research and Improvement, 1988) study revealed the complexity of the relationship between achievement and language, generational status, and personal attitudinal factors. Buriel and Cardoza (1988) examined the relationship of Spanish-language background to achievement among three generations of Mexican American high school seniors. The study found that regardless of generational status, the most important predictor of achievement was personal aspirations. Furthermore, the study found that Spanish-language usage had no relationship to achievement for first-generation students and a mixed relationship to achievement for second- and third-generation students.

The investigators offer two theoretical explanations for their findings. According to the cultural integration hypothesis, Mexican immigrants place a high value on achievement, upward mobility, and learning the English language. First- and second-generation children are exposed to these values within an environment that is predominantly Spanish-speaking. In subsequent generations, immigrant values may be replaced by middle-class motivations for continued success. The ghettoization hypothesis (Nielson & Fernández, 1981) is offered to explain the circumstances of third-generation students whose families have not experienced upward mobility over the generations. In this scenario, parent and child feel much less optimistic than recently immigrated families about their own chances of success. Among later generations of this type, stated aspirations remain high, but realistic expectations of achieving them are low.

Last, the study of the role of psychosocial factors clearly illustrates the importance of familial beliefs and value systems in relation to Latino aspirations toward achievement (Buriel & Cardoza, 1988). Latino parents who value schooling, believe in their child's ability to succeed, and participate actively in their schooling give their child a better chance at academic success. According to Buriel and Cardoza, research has shown that mothers play the most influential role in the achievement of their children. Romo (1984) compared the perceptions of Mexican immigrant and nonimmigrant families regarding education. The data showed that compared to immigrant families, families born in the United States demonstrated higher expectations of the school system, which, fueled by experiences with discrimination, led to high levels of skepticism and alienation that were not evident among immigrant families. Delgado-Gaitan (1988) proposed that schools train parents regarding the culture of the school and that they reflect the cultural values of Latino parents in the school curriculum so that parents can participate in their child's schooling in a supportive manner.

INFLUENCE OF PEERS ON ACHIEVEMENT

The influence of peers throughout the education process, particularly in late childhood and adolescence, is another important psychosocial factor. The literature regarding the role of peers tends to focus on its negative impact on Latino achievement and its association with deviant behaviors. The literature suggests that association with deviant peers (which tends to lead to deviant acts) occurs within the context of a dysfunctional family environment and the absence of religious involvement (Barrett, Simpson, & Lehman, 1988). Oetting and Beauvais (1987) postulated that school adjustment problems can lead to peer cluster formations that are highly likely to encourage substance abuse. The substance abuse, in turn, decreases educational performance and leads students to distance themselves from peers and teachers who might have a positive influence. In support of this theory, Chávez et al. (1989) found that compared to matched controls, both Mexican American and non-Hispanic White high school dropouts were more likely to use alcohol and drugs, to be victims or perpetrators of violence, and to have experienced a serious illness within the preceding year. However, lower rates of drug use were found among the Mexican American male dropouts than among the non-Hispanic White male dropouts. Also, the Mexican-origin female dropouts were less likely than the non-Hispanic White female dropouts to be victims of violence.

Overall, Latino youth who have been involved with the legal system have high rates of substance abuse (Watts & Wright, 1990) and lower levels of self-esteem (Calhoun, Connley, & Bolton, 1984) than Latino youth who have not been adjudicated criminally. Mitchell and Dodder (1980) found that the performance of illegal acts among Mexican American college students was more strongly related to peer association than among non-Hispanic White college students. The authors concluded that peers play a role in validating and justifying deviant behaviors, which also tend to be less serious than non-peer-motivated deviant behaviors. Accordingly, a study of Mexican American youth in a drug abuse prevention program found that the reduction of problem behaviors, such as substance use, school problems, or legal involvement, was most influenced by a decrease in the use of drugs by peers (Barrett et al., 1988). In fact, the reduction of problem behaviors was also related to family support during treatment and commitment to religious involvement. Self-esteem did not affect problem behaviors but did relate strongly to family support. Thus, ties with family and religion are important to healthy patterns of functioning among youth.

Finally, it is important to note that findings regarding the effects of parental socioeconomic status on achievement have been mixed. Bean and Tienda (1987) found that parental education and work status predicted educational achievement, whereas Caraveo-Ramos and Saldate (1987) found that family occupational status was not an important predictor of achievement for Mexican American college students.

Improving the educational status of Latinos presents complex problems yet there is promise for the future. The continual influx of immigrants brings with it the potential for tapping and nurturing high achievement levels. However, the political and institutional barriers to high-quality education for Latino youth and children are formidable. Certainly much needs to be done to prepare Latino youth and children for the workforce realities of tomorrow.

Employment and Economic Mobility

Clearly, Latino youth are not acquiring the skills and knowledge to compete in a labor market that is changing and growing more complex. Regardless of educational status, Latino youth and young adults exhibit employment trends that resemble or outmatch their non-Hispanic White counterparts. A racial and ethnic comparison of labor force participation patterns shows that in 1988, Latino males, ages 16 to 24, were working (or looking for work) at the same rate (about 75%) as young non-Hispanic White men, compared to 62% for African American young men. Of those Latino youth who were employed, 75% were working full-time, whereas 66% of employed African American and non-Hispanic White youth were working full time. The youth unemployment rate was 14% for Latinos, 24% for African Americans, and 9% for non-Hispanic Whites. This suggests that Latino youth found jobs relatively easily. Gender differences are evident, however. Young Latinas were much less likely to be employed or looking for work than young Latino males. Among young women, the labor force participation rate in 1988 was 55% for Latinas, 51% for African Americans, and 67% for non-Hispanic Whites.

According to the *High School and Beyond Survey*, Latino males work more hours while attending school than any other group. This survey also found that among Latino male dropouts, at least 41% left school for economic reasons. It has also been shown that of all youth who have dropped out of school, Latino youth are the most likely to be employed. Among the students who left school in the 1987-1988 school year, 55% of the Latinos, 49% of the non-Hispanic Whites, and 23% of the African Americans were employed in 1988. However, among students who completed high school but did not enter college, only 60% of Latinos and African Americans, compared to 75% of non-Hispanic Whites, were employed. Among youth who were enrolled in college, Latino rates of employment exceeded African American rates but lagged behind rates for non-Hispanic Whites.

The overall labor force participation rates of Latino groups do not vary considerably; however, their employment rates do (data that follow are from Duany & Pittman, 1990). In terms of the labor force participation of 20- to 24-year-olds in 1988, the rates for non-Hispanic Whites (79%), Central/South Americans (78%), Mexicans (75%), and Cubans (75%) were comparable. However, only 66% of Puerto Rican young adults were working or looking for work. At least 75% of non-Hispanic White, Cuban, and Central/South American young adults held jobs in 1988. In contrast, only 66% of Mexicans, 58% of Puerto Ricans, and 54% of African Americans, ages 20 to 24, were employed.

On average, the earnings of working Latino males, ages 15 to 19, were higher than those of working non-Hispanic White males of the same age in 1987 ($4,118 and $3,378, respectively). However, among 20- to 24-year-olds, Latino males earned about $1,700 a year less than non-Hispanic Whites. Mean annual earnings among young adults in 1987 varied considerably according to ethnicity. Cubans and non-Hispanic Whites had the highest annual average earnings (about $9,000), followed by Puerto Ricans (about $7,800), then Central/South Americans (about $7,700), and last Mexicans ($6,690). African Americans had the lowest annual earnings ($5,433). It is interesting to note that Puerto Rican young adults have lower labor force participation rates but higher median earnings than Mexican young adults (Duany & Pittman, 1990).

Several studies have found that Latino youth and young adults are not equipped with the support and know-how to overcome the political and institutional barriers they encounter in the workplace. An analysis of data from a national longitudinal study of high school students (Holsinger & Fernández, 1987) found that from 1972 to 1976, job aspirations declined at a greater rate among Mexican Americans than among non-Hispanic Whites. The authors attributed this finding to obstacles that were experienced by Mexican American young adults, including job discrimination, lack of access to adequate labor market information, inadequate job search skills, and the inability to finance additional training and formal schooling. An analysis of data regarding two-parent families from 14 states found that job satisfaction among Mexican American young males was more heavily influenced by occupational status than by income status (Hawkes, Guagnano, Acredolo, & Helmick, 1984). This finding is attributed to the high value that Mexican Americans place on the less material dimensions of personal and family status. The authors concluded that a mismatch between occupational status aspirations and actual education plans and goals leads to status inconsistency effects among Mexican American adolescents, thereby contributing to a sense of alienation and frustration. Another study of Mexican American college graduates found that career progression was related not only to personal factors, such as high school grades, work ethic, and the need for achievement, but also to structural variables (Gould, 1982). The extent to which career development support was available for Mexican American young adults in the industry that employed them directly affected their degree of career progression.

Adolescent Marriage and Childbearing

A phenomenon of significance to Latinos is the increasing number of adolescent marriages and childbearing with and without a partner (data that follow are from Duany & Pittman, 1990). Latino youths have higher marriage rates than African Americans or non-Hispanic Whites their age. Among 18- and 19-year- old females in 1988, 24% of Latinas had married compared to 5% of African American and 12% of non-Hispanic White women. Among 18- and 19-year old males, rates of marriage for Latinos and non-Hispanic Whites were virtually the same, about 4%. In 1987, there were 473,000 births to women younger than 20, of which 66,000 were Latinas. An examination of the proportion of all births to women under the age of 20 in 1987 showed that about 10% of non-Hispanic White births, 16% of Latino births, and 23% of African American births were to this age group. By 1990, these rates had increased by about 0.5% for each group (U.S. Bureau of the Census, 1993e). The rate of marriage among Latina adolescents who have given birth has steadily decreased. From 1980 to 1987, the proportion of births to Latina adolescents who were married declined

TABLE 4.2 Births and Marital Status of Hispanic Women Under 20, by Subgroup, 1987

	Mexican	Puerto Rican	Cuban	Central/ South American	Other Latina
Percent of total Latino births to women under 20	66	12	1	6	16
Percent of all births to women under 20 by subgroup	17	20	6	8	18
Percent of births to married Latinas under 20	49	23	57	38	34
Percent of births to married Latinas 18-19 years of age	59	30	66	44	40

NOTE: The data were compiled by the Children's Defense Fund (Duany & Pittman, 1990).

from 57% to 43%. The rate of births to married teens is similar among Latinos and non-Hispanic Whites. In 1987, the proportion of married teens who had given birth was 48% for non-Hispanic Whites, 43% for Latinos, and 9% for African Americans (Duany & Pittman, 1990).

Considerable differences are found among Latino groups with respect to the proportion of births among women younger than 20 and of births among teens who were married in 1987 (Table 4.2; data that follow are from Duany & Pittman, 1990). Births to women under 20 are predominantly to Mexican-origin women (66%) and to Puerto Ricans (12%). Teen births account for about one fifth of all births to both the Mexican-origin (17%) and Puerto Rican (20%) populations. By 1990, slight but similar increases were found in the number of teen births within each Latino subgroup (less than 1.0%). Rates of marriage among teens who gave birth were lowest among Puerto Ricans and Central and South Americans and highest among Cubans and Mexicans. Mexican rates of birth to married teens were slightly higher than non-Hispanic White rates, both in terms of total births (49% vs. 48%) and births to 18- and 19-year-olds (59% vs. 57%). Cuban rates of birth of married teens are greater than the rates for Mexican-origin and non-Hispanic White youth.

School-age pregnancy and childbearing together constitute one of the most intractable problems in our society. The United States has the highest school-age birthrate of the industrialized nations. One in 10 young women aged 15 to 19 become pregnant each year. A number

TABLE 4.3 Cumulative Rates of Sexual Activity, Pregnancy, and Childbearing to Women Under 18, by Racial and Ethnic Group, 1985

	Latino	Non-Hispanic White	African American
Percent sexually active	40	42	59
Percent pregnant	NA	21	41
Percent gave birth	14	7	26

NOTE: The data were compiled by the Children's Defense Fund in 1985 (Pittman & Adams, 1988).

of adverse medical, social, and economic consequences have been associated with school-age childbearing and parenting. Furthermore, the children of school-age mothers tend to repeat the pattern set by their parents (Erickson, 1990).

An examination of the dynamics of teen reproductive behavior requires the understanding that an adolescent goes through a series of decision-making steps from the initiation of sexual activity through parenting. Decisions must be made about when to initiate sexual activity, whether or not to use contraceptives once a decision is made to become sexually active, and whether or not to become a parent if pregnancy should occur. Differences in decision making at each of these steps account for racial and ethnic differences in childbearing practices among teens. One cannot say that childbearing patterns are simply due to racial and ethnic differences in sexual activity (Pittman & Adams, 1988).

Of all racial and ethnic groups, Latina adolescents are the least likely to be sexually active but are more likely to give birth (Table 4.3). Latinas are also less likely to be sexually active before marriage than other groups. An analysis of data from the 1982 National Survey of Family Growth found that the rate of premarital sexual activity was 30% for Latinas, 36% for non-Hispanic Whites, and 55% for African Americans. This was also confirmed by local studies in Los Angeles County, which found that Latina adolescents tend to initiate sexual activity at a later age (Aneshensel, Fielder, & Becerra, 1989; Erickson, 1990). In contrast, the sexual activity levels of Latino male adolescents resemble those of non-Hispanic White adolescent males.

The relatively high birthrates of Latinas, compared to non-Hispanic Whites, can be attributed, in part, to their family planning practices. Although Latina adolescents are no more likely than non-Hispanic

White adolescents to get pregnant, when they do become sexually active, they are less likely than non-Hispanic Whites and African Americans to use contraceptives early on or to use them at all. Thus, the risk of pregnancy among Latinas is magnified by their lack of contraceptive use. In addition, Latina teens are less likely than non-Hispanic Whites and African Americans to have an abortion once pregnant. Thus, their birthrates are slightly higher than non-Hispanic White teens, who are more likely to terminate their pregnancies (Aneshensel et al., 1989; Becerra & de Anda, 1984; Erickson, 1990; Leibowitz, Eisen, & Chow, 1986). However, the Children's Defense Fund (1991a) reported that from 1982 to 1988 use of contraceptives at first intercourse among Latina teens more than doubled, from 22% to 54%, mainly because of a large increase in the use of condoms (from 13% to 42%).

A few studies have examined differences in the sexual and fertility behavior of U.S.-born and foreign-born Latina adolescents. According to these studies, foreign-born Latinas, as compared to U.S.-born Latinas, were more likely to be sexually conservative regarding the number of sexual partners and age at first intercourse. They were also more likely to have planned their pregnancies and to be married or living with a partner. On the other hand, they were less likely to have knowledge of or experience with birth control and more likely to begin their prenatal care later in pregnancy or not at all. As a group, a larger percentage of foreign-born Latina teens reported their intention to be housewives and mothers as compared to U.S.-born teens (Becerra & de Anda, 1984; Rapkin & Erickson, 1990). The more acculturated teens did not want to give up school to be full-time mothers.

Although pregnancy is one of the reasons for school dropout among Latinos, evidence suggests that it is not a primary cause. Felice, Shragg, James, and Hollingsworth (1987) found that, compared to non-Hispanic White and African American pregnant adolescents, Mexican American pregnant adolescents were more likely to have dropped out of school prior to becoming pregnant and more likely to be married at the time of conception. A large number of factors contribute to both the dropout rate and the pregnancy rate among Latinas. These factors include the low education level of Latino males, the high ratio of males to females, lag in grade level for age, and Latina attitudes regarding traditional family sex roles.

Cultural attitudes play an important role in the dynamics of reproductive behavior among Latino adolescents. A study of high school students in Los Angeles found that, compared to African Americans and Asians, Latinos were more likely to consider people under 21 years of age as ideal for marriage and childbearing (Erickson, 1990). Among less acculturated Latinas, there is a tendency to endorse traditional female roles and to seek the special status that is afforded pregnant women according to cultural norms (Kay, 1980). Among more acculturated Latinas who come from dysfunctional families or the drug and gang culture, pregnancy and marriage may be viewed as a more attractive alternative to their current lifestyles (Erickson, 1990).

The roles of the family and father of the child also have important cultural implications. A number of studies have shown that Latino adults generally hold conservative views about sexual behavior and find issues regarding teenage sexuality highly controversial (Martinez, 1981; Moss, 1987; Namerow & Philliber, 1983). Although the adolescent's parents may be initially shocked and angered about the pregnancy, they eventually provide support and look forward to the birth. Research has also shown that compared to pregnant non-Hispanic White adolescents, pregnant Latina adolescents are more likely to be in long-term relationships, and their partners are more often supportive of the pregnancy and employed or enrolled as full-time students (de Anda, Becerra, & Fielder, 1988; Felice et al., 1987; Kay, 1980).

Fertility studies regarding Latinos have shown that fertility decreases as women become more acculturated, that is, as they increase their levels of education and speak less Spanish (Bean & Swicegood, 1982; Sorensen, 1988). This may be true of first-generation Latinas whose traditional lifestyles are compatible with American norms and expectations. These complex issues present formidable challenges to improving the behavioral risk and health status of Latino youth. Clearly, early childbearing is associated with a number of factors related to the poverty status of Latino youth: low educational attainment, low income, low-paying jobs, and unemployment, regardless of marital status (Burke, Gabe, Rimkunas, & Griffith, 1985; Duany & Pittman, 1990).

Summary and Conclusions

Clearly, Latino youth must overcome a number of obstacles to improve their chances of socioeconomic advancement. Many of the barriers, however, find their roots in discriminatory practices that make it more difficult for some Latinos to acquire the skills needed to compete effectively and for other Latinos to obtain the high-status occupations commensurate with their skills and work experience. Improving the status of Latino youth involves a fundamental restructuring of the way things are done in this country.

Some of the psychosocial issues of importance to Latino youth that require further examination are:

1. The major stressors that affect males and females
2. Sources of social support
3. Decision-making processes regarding events that affect their life chances
4. The importance and utility of role models (Padilla & Lindholm, 1983)

Latino children and youth truly lie at a crossroads. In many respects, traditional cultural strengths have kept Latino youth healthy, optimistic about the future, and active in the labor force. However, ingrained patterns of poverty and discrimination have dulled aspirations over time and have contributed to a growing and pervasive sense of alienation and frustration. The longer that institutional reforms are delayed, the more intractable the problems of Latino children and youth become.

PART II

PROGRAM AND PRACTICE

5

Including Latino Fathers in Parent Education and Support Programs

Development of a Program Model

DOUGLAS R. POWELL

The task of designing a parent education and support program that is appropriate for Latino fathers is hindered by the absence of research on fathers in Latino families and by parent-education program traditions based on the needs and experiences of middle-class mothers of European American origin. It is only recently that the contributions of fathers in general, and Latino fathers in particular, to children's development have been taken seriously. Growing awareness of the distinct influences of fathers on children has led to questions about how best to design educational programs aimed at supporting the fatherhood role.

This chapter examines issues involved in designing and implementing a parent-education and support program that includes low-income Latino fathers. It describes lessons learned from the experiences of a program development project in Los Angeles, designed to generate a program model that would be responsive to the needs and circumstances of Latinos. The project includes interview data from a small set of 29 immigrant, Mexican-origin fathers. Known as Nueva Familia, the program was launched by MELD, an organization in Minneapolis,

Minnesota, that has developed an innovative program model of parent education and support. The program was carried out in health clinics in the Los Angeles area. A grant from the Carnegie Corporation of New York supported the program development and evaluation work, and grants from the James Irvine and Stuart foundations supported program operations.

The Context:
Parent Programs and Latino Fathers

The two major barriers to developing programs for Latino fathers—the female-oriented traditions of the parent-education field and the absence of information on Latino fathers—exist largely as a function of well-established cultural assumptions about the role of mothers as the primary parent and fathers as peripheral to family childrearing responsibilities.

BIASES OF THE PARENT-EDUCATION MOVEMENT

The conventional methods and content of parent-education and support programs reflect the interests and orientations of White, non-Hispanic, middle-class mothers. Because mothers have been viewed as the primary caregivers of their children, the literature on parenting and on educational programs for parents has given scant attention to fathers. Mothers have been the main focus of research on parental effects, and they are the intended recipients of publications and other programmatic efforts to strengthen the parenthood role.

In organized programs for parents, most participants and most staff are women, and typical program methods are defined by women's ways of knowing and relating (Bowman, 1992). Among the major barriers faced by fathers in learning about parenting are these deterrents identified by a sample of mostly well-educated White non-Hispanic fathers of young children (Johnson & Palm, 1992):

conventional stereotypes of fathers (e.g., detached breadwinner) and the
    strong socialization patterns associated with these stereotypic images;
information about parenting directed heavily toward women;
time limits due to job involvements; and
the social isolation of men.

Throughout the long history of parent education in the United States, there have been scattered attempts to work with lower-income populations of color (Schlossman, 1976). Since the late 1960s, parent education has been widely and eagerly pursued as a strategy for improving the cognitive and social functioning of children considered at risk due to the low-income status of their families. Efforts to extend conventional methods and content of parent education to populations other than middle-class White parents generally have not been successful. The lessons learned from these experiences have led to the following:

1. Growing interest in the social contexts in which parents attempt to rear young children
2. Alternatives to the paternalistic role of program staff as experts
3. Strategies of adapting program designs to accommodate the characteristics and needs of local communities (Powell, 1988b, in press)

Much of the current interest in program responsiveness stems from criticisms of the practice of imposing dominant culture norms on minority populations (Sigel, 1983), including the assumption that low-income and minority mothers are incompetent (Baratz & Baratz, 1970). Today there is an increased interest in mechanisms that enable programs to be responsive to populations of color (Powell, 1990; Rogler, Malgady, Costantino, & Blumenthal, 1987) and growing recognition that programs found to be effective with middle-class parents cannot be assumed to be successful with lower-income populations (Schorr & Schorr, 1988). Strategies for providing parent-education and support programs that work effectively with fathers are the subject of several recent volumes (Minnesota Fathering Alliance, 1992; Levine, Murphy, & Wilson, 1993), and research on educational programs for fathers is beginning to be available (e.g., McBride, 1990). Growing awareness of gender differences in communication styles (e.g., Tannen, 1990) and other aspects of interpersonal relationships has contributed to interest in program designs that accommodate men.

These developments are promising, but much remains unknown about the roles of fathers in parent-education and support programs, especially in initiatives serving lower-income Latinos. Furthermore, mothers continue to be the main target of most existing and proposed parenting interventions. For instance, a Children's Defense Fund report on Latino youth (Duany & Pittman, 1990) argues that "early efforts that target the special needs of Latinas are particularly critical"

(p. 30) because Latinas head a significant proportion (23%) of all Latino households and because high school dropout rates of young Latinas are coupled with relatively high birthrates.

Perspectives on Fathers in Latino Families

There is a limited amount of research on Latino fathers when compared to research on non-Hispanic White males and on African American males, and much of the literature is based on anecdotal evidence. Thus, it is difficult to make comparisons across studies of Latinos or to provide even global generalizations about roles and orientations.

Two contrasting images of fathers' roles in Latino families are found in the available literature. The traditional view casts the Latino father as a dominant, authoritarian figure in the family. Oscar Lewis's (1960, 1961) ethnographic studies in rural and urban Mexico portrayed the father as maker of all major decisions and master of the household. Relations with children were deemed to be distant emotionally, and severe physical punishment was used to maintain the respect of children and wife (see Mirandé, 1988a). In the traditional view, men are fearful of nothing and forthright in asserting sexual dominance over women (Madsen, 1973). Women are seen as docile, submissive, and dependent. Similar portrayals were offered in a study of Puerto Rican culture (Sanchez-Ayendez, 1988).

Machismo ranks high in the traditional image of Mexican culture. In a recent volume on Latinos, Shorris (1992) noted that machismo is "the making of a man" (p. 437), which little boys learn "at home, in school, and in the street" (p. 436). There are debates in the literature regarding definitions and determinants of machismo, however. One set of questions pertains to the prevalence of, and distinctions between, false versus authentic forms of machismo (see Mirandé, 1988a). The false form entails excessive demonstrations of masculinity (e.g., fixation on phallic symbolism), which may serve to mask deeply ingrained feelings of inferiority. In contrast, positive approaches to machismo are emphasized in definitions that recognize the value of strength in adverse situations and uncompromising positions on matters of great personal importance (Mirandé, 1988a).

Another set of questions focuses on the extent to which male dominance represents a cultural pattern or response to structural factors in society. Male dominance may take on greater significance when social stratification systems exclude members of a minority population from important public roles (Baca Zinn, 1982a). On the other hand, male authority in Latino families may be a cultural value that transcends societal boundaries (Mirandé, 1988a).

An alternative view of the father in Latino families suggests a more egalitarian approach to decision making and greater levels of father involvement in childrearing than commonly associated with the traditional view (see Mirandé, 1988a, 1991). The alternative and more egalitarian perspective on family decision making is supported by research on California migrant farm families (Hawkes & Taylor, 1975) and by an investigation of division of household labor within Mexican American families in Los Angeles and San Antonio (Grebler, Moore, & Guzman, 1970).

Latino fathers' relations with their children also may be more involved than the traditional perspective suggests. In an observational study of 78 parent-child dyads in 19 two-parent families of lower and middle socioeconomic levels living in a small mountain city in Mexico, Bronstein (1984, 1988) found that fathers were more emotionally nurturant and more playfully involved with their children than mothers were. Mothers were more nurturant than fathers in a physical sense; for example, they offered food, helped with grooming, and showed concern for safety and health. There were no differences between mothers and fathers regarding authoritarian control behaviors (e.g., scolding, criticizing). Fathers used direct control strategies and provided instruction significantly more often with sons than with daughters, but mothers tended to treat sons and daughters similarly. This latter pattern has been found in studies of parent-child interaction in other cultures. Bronstein's findings are in contrast with the image of the Mexican father as aloof and likely to maintain an authoritarian relationship with his children and with his wife, suggesting that Mexican fathers' patterns of relating to their 7- to 12-year-old children are similar to those of U.S. fathers with infants and preschool children.

Most likely the important question here is not which view represents the most accurate portrayal of Mexican fathers, but how elements of these differing perspectives might influence a father's interest and participation in a parent program. Because there is considerable diversity within a given population, evidence generally can be found to support a number of contrasting views. The design of parent programs requires an understanding of the extent to which different orientations to fathers' roles are prevalent and intertwined in a particular population.

Lessons Learned From the
MELD Nueva Familia Initiative

MELD of Minneapolis, Minnesota, launched an initiative in Los Angeles to develop a parent-education and support program for low-income Latino families with young children. Plans called for the Nueva Familia program to be based on an adaptation of the MELD model of providing information and support to parents of very young children (prenatal through age 2). The model is a modified peer, self-help approach, employing long-term peer discussion groups facilitated by lay persons who receive extensive training and supervision. Printed curriculum materials that include practical information on child development and parenting are provided to parents as one of the bases of group discussions. There is attention to both child and parent development. The model emphasizes informed decision making about childrearing practices, and it does not promote or endorse a particular approach to childrearing.

Founded in 1973 by Ann Ellwood, the MELD program has been implemented in numerous sites throughout the United States and abroad. The original model was implemented with middle-class couples expecting their first child. There are versions of the program for adolescent parents, deaf parents, parents of children with special needs, and Hmong parents.

In the Nueva Familia initiative, MELD worked in collaboration with two Los Angeles area health clinics to develop and provide program services to parents. Group sessions were the primary mode of program delivery, supplemented by home visiting. This chapter describes lessons learned from two sources: (a) interviews on parents' program preferences and family roles conducted prior to program implementation and (b) experiences in implementing the program design in low-income, urban communities in greater Los Angeles. Although relatively small, the sample of fathers interviewed at the preprogram phase of the project is unique in that little systematic information exists on immigrant Latino fathers and, furthermore, comparable interview data were collected from their spouses/partners.

Fathers' Program Preferences
and Roles in the Family

PROCEDURES

The information about fathers' program preferences and family roles described in this chapter was secured from a sample of 29 Mexican men and their spouse/partners living in the Los Angeles area. They were recruited for the study following procedures similar to those used for securing clients for a voluntary program aimed at low-income expectant parents and parents of very young children. Previous research has indicated that voluntary programs serve self-selected populations (Powell, 1988a), and therefore it was determined that a nonprobability sample of prospective program users recruited through customary program outreach procedures would yield information more generalizable to a volunteer program population than a probability sample that included individuals unlikely to participate in a volunteer program.

Information about the study was disseminated through 10 health clinics and Women, Infants, and Children (WIC) programs serving Latinos in two greater Los Angeles geographic locations populated largely by individuals of Mexican origin. Interviewers used the following methods to make contact with potential study participants:

1. Informal presentation of study purposes and procedures in the waiting rooms of health clinics and programs
2. Follow-up (in person or via telephone) of a potential participant referral made by a health program worker
3. A telephone call from a potential participant to the interviewer in response to a printed study description disseminated at health program sites

The vast majority of study participants were secured through the first two methods. Most contact initially was with women, and typically the interview with the father occurred after his spouse/partner had participated in the study. The following criteria were used to select study participants:

1. Family enrolled in or eligible for participation in WIC, a federal health program targeted at low-income populations
2. Mexican ethnic identity as defined by birthplace in Mexico and residence in Mexico until age 11 or older

   3. Twelve or fewer years of formal schooling
   4. Eighteen years of age or older
   5. One of three categories of child age: spouse/partner in second or third
      trimester of first pregnancy, parent of one child under the age of 1 year,
      or parent of two or more children under 4 years of age

The sample described in this chapter is divided between parents
expecting their first child ($n = 11$) and parents of infants/toddler-age
children ($n = 18$).

It required considerable persistence to recruit and interview the 29
fathers. Of the 58 Mexican women we interviewed, 45 were residing
with a spouse/partner, but interviews were secured with slightly more
than one half of these men. A minority of the 17 not secured for an
interview refused to participate in the study or were not available in
spite of repeated and varied attempts to contact them, including visits
to the residence. Most of those not interviewed maintained demand-
ing schedules that included two or three jobs and sometimes night
classes (English as second language). This employment pattern is not
uncommon (Shorris, 1992). Findings regarding the program preferences of the larger set of 58 Mexican women in comparison to a
sample of 63 Mexican American women are reported elsewhere
(Powell, Zambrana, & Silva-Palacios, 1990).

Interviews were conducted by Latinos matched to study participants by gender. All interviews were conducted in Spanish, using
interview forms generated through back translation. This procedure
is an alternative to direct translation from English to Spanish. Direct
translation can yield culturally or linguistically inappropriate interview items (Zambrana, 1991). To avoid this potential problem, the
development of interview items for the present study was done by
bilingual individuals of Mexican origin who had experience in working with Mexican communities and who paid close attention to
colloquial words, symbolic meaning, and word structure.

SAMPLE CHARACTERISTICS

The sample for the study of program preferences comprised 29
fathers who were born in Mexico. They had been living in the Los
Angeles area a median of 6 years and at their current address for a
median of 1 year. The average age was 26.8 years (standard deviation
= 6.3). The men were an average of 19.4 years old when they moved

to the United States (standard deviation = 4.6). The median years of formal education was 8; 31% had 6 years or less of formal education, and 20% had 12 years. Nearly all of the men (90%) were employed, generally at low-paying jobs, a median of 40 hours a week; only 11% worked less than 40 hours a week. All resided with their child's mother, and 83% were married to their child's mother. The spouse/partners had a median of 9 years of formal education, and a majority (76%) were not employed outside the home. Overall, spouse/partners had been residing in the Los Angeles area less time (median of 4 years) than the males.

Households had an average of 6.5 members (standard deviation = 1.9), most of whom were relatives. Most of the couples (83%) had relatives living in the Los Angeles area, and a median of 2 relatives in the Los Angeles area could be counted on for help. Most (70%) attended church services on a monthly or more frequent basis.

Spanish was the primary or only language used in communicating with others. About 90% talked with their spouse/partner mostly or exclusively in Spanish, but a smaller percentage (69%) talked with their children mostly or exclusively in Spanish. About 28% of the fathers indicated they could speak English very or pretty well, and 24% indicated they could read English very or pretty well. Slightly fewer of their spouse/partners indicated they could speak (21%) or read (17%) English very or pretty well.

PREFERRED PROGRAM METHODS

As shown in Table 5.1, a combination of parent group and home visiting was the program mode preferred by a majority of fathers. With regard to a parent group, the clear preference was for a meeting attended by both mothers and fathers; 7% preferred a group comprising fathers only. Accordingly, most wanted their spouse/partner to attend all or some meetings. Most fathers had not had experiences in other types of groups or classes other than school, and most preferred to be familiar with at least some group members prior to participation. Fathers appear to be most comfortable with program staff who are professionals or experienced in rearing children. These information sources were deemed to be the most helpful. Reading material was rated as least helpful.

These patterns were consistent with results of a sample of 58 immigrant Mexican mothers, who in general responded as follows:

TABLE 5.1 Fathers' Preferred Methods for a Parent Education Program, in Percent ($n = 28$)

Preferred program setting:	
Group	32
Group and home visit	61
Home visit	7
Prefer familiarity with group members	82
Want spouse/partner to attend:	
All meetings	58
Some meetings	42
Want other family members to attend:	
All meetings	30
Some meetings	52
Prefer group with both fathers and mothers	93
Most helpful information source:	
Person with specialized training	54
Parent who has reared child(ren)	29
Other parents with same-age child	11
Reading material	7
Least helpful information source:	
Person with specialized training	7
Parent who has reared child(ren)	4
Other parent with same-age child	43
Reading material	47
Preferred frequency of program contact:	
Twice weekly	21
Weekly	32
Once every other week	18
Monthly	29
Have had previous experience in a formal group	14

1. preferred a program with both group and home-visiting components;
2. wanted group meetings with both fathers and mothers present;
3. preferred spouse and extended family members to attend all program meetings;
4. viewed individuals with special training as the most helpful source of childrearing information;

5. deemed reading material as the least helpful information source;
6. strongly preferred prior familiarity with other program participants; and
7. had not had prior experience in a group or class outside of school (Powell et al., 1990).

PREFERRED PROGRAM CONTENT

Concerns in two major areas were examined as possible program content: childrearing matters and topics regarding the family and its relations with the environment. Descriptive responses are presented in Table 5.2.

It is clear that fathers have concerns about childrearing topics. Each of the topics rated by fathers of infant/toddlers was a concern a lot or most of the time to more than one half of the fathers. More than one half of prospective fathers had a concern about all but two of the topics rated by respondents (labor/delivery and breast- vs. bottle-feeding). There was a tendency for more mothers than fathers to have a higher intensity of concern; the difference was statistically significant for couples with infant/toddlers ($t = 2.72$, $p < .01$, two-tailed) but not for couples who were expecting their first child.

With regard to concerns about the family and larger environment, the major concerns of fathers appeared to be direct consequences of poverty and language-minority status. Most fathers (50% or more) indicated that there were problems dealing with adequate money, affordable housing, a good-paying job, and English-language abilities. Their spouses/partners identified similar problem areas, as shown in Table 5.2.

The percentages in Table 5.2 represent respondents who indicated an area was a minor problem, somewhat of a problem, or a serious problem. It was unusual for respondents to indicate that an area was a serious problem. Only about one fourth of the fathers (24%) rated one of 13 items as a serious problem (adequate money), and a similarly small percentage of spouses/partners identified 3 of 13 items as a serious problem (24%, not enough money; 24%, finding or keeping an affordable place to live; and 31%, not speaking enough English to be understood). There were statistically significant differences (two-tailed t tests, $p \leq .05$) between males and females on only 2 of the 13 items (not enough money and not speaking enough English to be understood). There were no statistically significant differences between mothers and fathers regarding level of concern about family and environmental topics.

TABLE 5.2 Percentage of Fathers and Mothers With Concerns About Child and Family Functioning

Child Concerns	Fathers	Mothers
Pregnant with first child (_n_ = 11)		
How baby is growing	55	82
Eating right foods	73	55
Losing baby	54	91
Labor and delivery	36	64
Taking care of baby in first weeks	73	73
Breast- vs. bottle-feeding	18	64
Infant/toddler (_n_ = 18)		
Eating/diet	64	100
Safety/protection	82	78
Health/illnesses	68	100
Medical care	63	90
Clothing	59	67
Toilet training	55	100
Discipline	82	94
Helping child have better life than parent	86	90

Family Concerns	Fathers	Mothers
All parents (_n_ = 29)		
Health problems in family	45	39
Not enough money	72	79
Finding or keeping a safe place to live	41	43
Finding or keeping a place to live you can afford	58	55
Finding or keeping a job	52	44
Relatives drinking too much or using illegal drugs	36	44
Relations with spouse/partner	41	34
Relations with family members who live with you	14	21
Relations with relatives who do not live with you	28	7
Not speaking enough English to be understood	69	72
Seeing family members treated badly because they are Latinos	28	10
Relations with government agencies, clinics, hospitals	21	12
Fear of deportation of me or members of my family	38	52

The pattern of not identifying serious problems may reflect respondents' use of Mexican poverty conditions as a reference point. Life

TABLE 5.3 Fathers' Perceptions of Appropriate Husband and Wife Roles:
Percentage of Fathers Who "Strongly Agree" or "Agree" (*n* = 29)

Statement	Percent
A wife should do whatever her husband wants	58
Married women have the right to continue their education	93
Men should share the work around the house with women, such as doing dishes, cleaning, and so forth	86
A wife should vote the way her husband wants	61
Women should take an active interest in politics and community problems	79
Husbands should make all the important decisions in a marriage	69

difficulties in the United States may be assessed as not serious when viewed in relation to experiences in Mexico. Alternatively, the measurement strategy for identifying serious problem areas may have been limited culturally. The interviewer's request that respondents indicate "how much of a problem" various items have been in the past 3 months may have conflicted with cultural traditions that call for information about family matters not to be shared with strangers and that place a high value on self-reliance. For males in particular, the prospect of admitting a serious problem may have been experienced as an affront to manhood.

ROLE IN THE FAMILY

Responses to a series of questions about husband-wife relations point to a mixture of traditional and more egalitarian roles in the couple relationship. As shown in Table 5.3, a majority indicated that wives should do what husbands want, husbands should make all major decisions, and wives should vote in accordance with a husband's wishes. However, a sizable percentage of fathers did not agree with these statements, and most indicated that men should share in housework responsibilities. In general, spouses/partners supported these tendencies; none of the differences reported in Table 5.3 was statistically significant.

Respondents were asked to indicate who usually carried out five child-care tasks: feeding, diaper changing, putting baby to bed, comforting baby, and playing with baby. Not surprisingly, only a small percentage of fathers were the primary provider of these types of care (under 10%, except for the 14% who typically put the child to bed). However, these tasks were not the exclusive domain of one individual in the family; for all tasks except changing diapers, more than one half of both male and female respondents indicated responsibility for the task was shared among a number of individuals in the family.

SUMMARY

The traditional view of the role of fathers in Latino families—the macho patriarch—implies that Latino fathers would not be good candidates as participants in a program focused on parenthood. However, the data presented here suggest the traditional role is not universal, and, although there is some tendency for fathers to express less concern about childrearing matters than their spouses/partners, interest in their children is strong. Thus, the idea of participating in a parent program should not be excluded. It would appear that programs most likely to be accessible psychologically to fathers would be embedded within the father's social network. Familiarity with other program participants and the involvement of spouse/partner and other family members are desired. Program attention primarily to childrearing issues and secondarily to issues that facilitate a stronger role for Mexicans in the dominant culture—especially decent-paying jobs and removal of language barriers—would seem to be compatible with the agenda of Mexicans.

Fathers' Program Participation

The key lessons learned about father involvement in the Nueva Familia program development phase in Los Angeles fall into four areas: ambivalence about involving fathers in the program, methods of recruiting and working with fathers, the program roles of fathers vis-à-vis staff, and the function of group sessions as a bridge to the dominant culture.

AMBIVALENCE TOWARD FATHERS

An assumption of the original program plan for Nueva Familia was that men would be involved in the program. MELD is unique nationally in the parent education field because of its long-standing experience in attracting and sustaining the involvement of fathers in discussion groups.

However, the idea that men could be recruited successfully for the Nueva Familia program was questioned persistently from the beginning of the project. At the first training session for Los Angeles staff, for instance, host agency officials reported that involving fathers "is a nice idea but it won't work" and that "most men don't care" about childrearing. Also, a male who considered the possibility of assuming the role of group facilitator in collaboration with his wife eventually decided that he did not wish to be involved in the program because it represented "woman's work."

Initially it was decided that women would be the target of recruitment efforts because their involvement would be easier to secure than the participation of men. An early promotional brochure about the program issued by one of the host agencies indicated (in Spanish) that "fathers will attend on an intermittent basis."

The two health clinic sites differed significantly in their approach to men. In one of the groups attended almost exclusively by women, a group facilitator frequently discussed the need for Latinas to free themselves from male domination. She believed that Latin women "need to reeducate their husbands" about the inappropriateness of women being subservient to men. At the same site, an evening group composed of couples was successfully launched, with leadership from a female group facilitator. At the second site, a male served as the primary staff person and group facilitator, and fathers were a part of the groups operating at this site.

The Nueva Familia program experience of ambivalence toward the involvement of men in parent programs is consistent with other reports in the literature. In a descriptive analysis of the roles of men in early childhood programs, Levine et al. (1993) noted that mothers often had very mixed feelings about the idea of involving fathers or other males in early childhood programs. Rarely discussed in programs, this ambivalence may stem from bad experiences in their own lives with fathers, husbands, or other men and/or fears about giving up their domain as the individual with primary responsibility for children and family life; childrearing functions may be a core element of personal identities.

METHODS OF RECRUITING
AND WORKING WITH FATHERS

Mothers' and fathers' participation in the Nueva Familia program was interdependent in two ways. Among some women, attendance at group meetings seemed to be partly a function of spousal approval and the nature of relations with their husbands/partners. Women's attendance levels were negatively correlated with stress in the husband/partner relationship ($r = -.25$, $p < .02$). Some prospective female participants indicated they could not attend group meetings because their husbands did not approve of their participation in the program, and during the preprogram interview work, several women informed interviewers that they needed their husbands' permission to be interviewed.

On the other hand, it appeared that father involvement in the program came about via their partners/wives. A father would rarely attend a session without his spouse/partner. Moreover, many men periodically accompanied their spouse/partner to the meetings in a manner that connoted "guest" status. Often the program participation intentions of men were not clear; they would attend with their spouses/partners erratically and contribute in a minimal way to group discussions. It is interesting to note that in a Head Start program operated by the Texas Migrant Council, Mexican-origin fathers eventually became involved in the program because they tired of waiting in the truck while their wives attended group meetings (Levine et al., 1993).

About one half of men associated with Nueva Familia attended one or two sessions only (58% at one site, 50% at another site). This attendance pattern is similar for women; slightly more than 50% of all parents recruited to the parent groups attended one or two sessions only.

The highest level of father participation occurred in the couples' group noted earlier. Both attendance and verbal contribution levels were high. An analysis of group observation records for 16 sessions of the couples group indicates about 30% of verbal contributions to the meetings were made by fathers. About 39% of verbal contributions were made by staff and 31% by mothers. Observation reports indicate this group was characterized by a near constant give-and-take between leader and parents—the sessions appear to be more of a group conversation than a one-way lecture with few verbal utterances from parents (see transcript of observation report in subsequent section of this chapter).

A number of factors may account for the success of the couples group, including father roles in the sessions (see subsequent section) and the style of helping offered in the group meetings. The tone of the couples group set by the female leader was information- rather than feeling-based and respectful of parents' experiences and opinions. Staff presentations were concrete, practical, and participatory. It was common to take blood pressure readings, for instance, and the goal and substance of activities were clearly defined. The helping style of the couples' group is consistent with Bowman's (1992) suggestions about appropriate methods of working with fathers. He indicated that many fathers want information, not a "bull session," and may view exercises as gimmicks.

Whether this approach to groups is sufficiently responsive to women is an open question. In the Nueva Familia experience, one facilitator whose groups typically did not include men indicated a group session may "become more academic" if men were present. The groups that were all-women or nearly so were qualitatively different than the groups with higher levels of male participation. In the female-dominated groups, discussion of feelings was emphasized, and interpersonal issues dominated the content.

According to some recommendations in the literature, fathers are best served with a program designed exclusively for fathers. The Avance program serving Mexican American families in San Antonio, Texas, for instance, recommends a "men only" concept for classes, because men will open up better and not be intimidated by the presence of women. In the Nueva Familia program, the preprogram interview data, as described earlier, did not support the idea of fathers-only and mothers-only groups, and indeed a fathers-only group was not attempted. In view of the above-described pattern of father participation coming about via spouse/partner, it is not clear that a fathers-only group could have materialized.

ROLES IN THE PROGRAM

It is often asserted that male staff are a requisite to the program participation of men. Numerous programs have found that the employment of men, especially "graduates" of the program, provides role models who implicitly give permission to other men to be involved in the program. For instance, in Avance, the male van driver is a program graduate who has established close relationships with fathers (Levine et al., 1993).

The MELD Nueva Familia program experience suggests that the roles men are able to assume in a program may be as important as the placement of men in staff positions. Recall that in the program site where a father served as the primary staff person, the participation of fathers was uneven in terms of attendance levels and verbal contributions to group meetings. There were indications that the male staff member preempted the father participants by being the leader of songs and organizer of nearly all activities. In contrast, in the couples' group where a woman was the primary staff person, fathers were highly involved in group meetings through attendance and contributions to discussions. Moreover, the fathers "owned" the ritual of leading the group singing at the conclusion of a session. Thus, it would appear that careful attention needs to be given to father roles in a program; securing male staff alone may not be sufficient.

It is not easy to challenge traditional gender roles by placing men in positions typically held by women. In an early childhood program serving a predominantly Mexican American population in Texas, for instance, mothers stopped coming to parent meetings after a male teacher was hired to work in the 3-year-old classrooms. Husbands did not want their wives to be in the presence of this "other man," and thus a program's efforts to address gender-role stereotypes in the selection of early-childhood staff met unforeseen problems (Levine et al., 1993).

PROGRAM AS BRIDGE

Much of the content of group discussions in the Nueva Familia program was a contrast between life in Mexico and in the United States. Clearly, the program was functioning as a bridge to a culture the program participants did not understand. Although the group facilitators differed significantly in their stances toward the utility and importance of Mexican traditions, the group meetings were similar in their emphasis on helping participants learn the ways of parenting and living in urban Los Angeles.

Men seemed particularly eager to engage in group content focused on life as an immigrant in the United States. For example, the film *El Norte*, shown at one of the sessions, is the story of a brother and sister who fled their native Guatemala to find many hardships in the United States; seeing the film prompted one father to tell about his frightening experiences living under a freeway for several days with a group of men who were crossing the border illegally. At another session, a father told of his work at a U.S. turkey farm, where conditions were reportedly deplorable for both turkeys and workers, and where he suspected that seriously ill turkeys were being sold. At the same session, parents discussed what they miss about their native country (e.g., good times in their neighborhoods, better-tasting fruits) and shared a favorite dish at a carry-in dinner.

The following excerpt from a transcript of a group observation report demonstrates the high level of father involvement in two salient matters—baby care and vasectomies. For fathers in the group, it appears the latter topic is approached in a novel way in the dominant U.S. culture and thus the group functions as a forum for helping participants understand (but not necessarily accept) U.S. custom. The excerpt also illustrates the facilitator's respect for the fathers' perspectives and experiences while at the same time maintaining a commitment to the integrity of knowledge about vasectomies.

Nine parents were in attendance (five women, four men). There were self-introductions because some parents did not know one another. A father inquired about the status of a couple that had attended 2 weeks earlier but was absent from the present meeting. The facilitator explained that the mother had high blood pressure and was close to delivery.

The facilitator indicated that the group would talk about baby's bath. She distributed two sets of papers on bathing and brought out a small plastic pan with a doll in it. She asked for volunteers to bathe the baby, telling the group to look at the papers to see if the volunteer bathed the baby correctly. No one volunteered. She asked a father if he would volunteer, telling him she would provide directions. He agreed.

During the bathing demonstration, the father indicated he had seen his mother give baths to his nephews, and that she had washed the baby's head first. The facilitator asked what he was going to use to wash the baby's body. He said shampoo. The facilitator told him there is a special kind of soap for babies.

The father described his steps in bathing the baby. There was discussion of whether to use talcum powder on a very young baby. The father indicated he would use talcum powder on an older baby. The father described how he would dry the head, then the back.

The facilitator told the father's wife, "You're lucky!" Father said, "Don't tell her that, she's going to want me to bathe [the baby] all the time!" The facilitator replied, "And why not? At times it's good to do it." The father dressed the doll. The facilitator told him, "Now you know you can do it well. And now, baby should be hugged so it can feel loved." Parents applauded the father. "He gets a 10," said the facilitator.

A mother was recruited to bathe the doll. There was discussion of proper care of the navel and making sure the baby does not fall from the table. The facilitator told of her own 2-month-old falling after a bath. There was discussion of cleaning the baby's eyes, ears, and head (cradle cap).

The facilitator introduced the topic of circumcision by noting its inclusion on the handout. A father reported he'd been told it's "bad for you. In Mexico it was said to be dangerous." There was discussion of reasons for circumcision and the amount of pain experienced by the child. A father indicated he's "never had that done and I don't have any problems." There was discussion of a father's report that there is a circumcision procedure for females, too. There was further discussion of the purpose of circumcision, with fathers talking about men and hygiene and asking questions about financial costs of the procedure.

The facilitator said, "Do you know what I've noticed? The men are the ones who worry about circumcision." A father reported that in Mexico a rumor was circulating that liquid was taken from the spinal cord to sterilize boys. The facilitator described the procedure for sterilizing women. The facilitator and the parents then discussed the possibility of women getting pregnant after a sterilization procedure was conducted.

A father commented on why men do not get sterilized. Another father said, "Maybe American men do it, but not to me." Psychologically you "cease to be a man," he said. There was laughter.

The facilitator reported that men continue to function sexually after a vasectomy. A father said, "They're left like oxen." The facilitator countered, "It's not the same," indicating the testicles are cut off when oxen are sterilized but not when men are. There was discussion of men's experiences with sterilization procedures with animals in Mexico. A father said the animals get fat. "Maybe that's what happens to men. Americans at the beach . . . when beautiful women go by they don't pay attention to the fat men!"

A father indicated sterilized men "are lower than animals." The facilitator said the father had "an erroneous idea." The father said, "You're not going to convince me. If my wife told me I had to [have a vasectomy] I would separate from her." The facilitator emphasized again that the testicles are not removed. A father indicated "it hurts animals a lot" and described an uncle in Mexico castrating a cat because he had fathered too many kittens. Another father reported, "I've done that to pigs, so they'll get fat." The facilitator discussed fears associated with sterilization, described other birth-control methods, including birth-control pills, and then refocused discussion on bathing the baby.

Concluding Comment

The lack of preplanning in the development of community-based programs is a major pitfall of work with Latino populations. As noted by Zambrana (1990), it is important to ask a community what it perceives to be the most urgent problem. Data collection efforts before and during the implementation of a program can be seen by communities as effective ways to document client needs, identify successful program dimensions, and describe strategies that do not work well. Systematic planning prior to the development of programs for Latino communities is particularly important because typically there is a lack of trust concerning the intentions of program developers. This is a result of a history of "hit-and-run" programs in many communities and a perceived lack of equal power and respect in program development work (Zambrana, 1990, p. 7). Too often the implicit message of program developers to a prospective host community is one of superiority in problem definition and solution. This fear or lack of trust in many Latino communities is further complicated by residents' involvement in multiple jobs, making it difficult for prospective program participants to accommodate services that are offered during usual business hours.

The need for preplanning is particularly critical for programs designed to serve ethnic minority populations (Laosa, 1990) and to include father participation. Bowman (1992) recommends that program designers assess the ways in which a meeting environment is friendly to fathers. He notes the "experiences of awkwardness, intimidation, bewilderment, and embarrassment" that some women experience upon entering a traditional male setting "may be close to the experiences of many men coming to a parent group" (p. 103).

The lessons learned in the MELD Nueva Familia program contribute to our understanding of the conditions under which programs are responsive to low-income Mexican-origin fathers. In contrast to stereotypes about machismo in Latino cultures, the Nueva Familia experience suggests fathers can be good candidates for participating in a parent-education program. Designing programs that are accessible to fathers requires extraordinary sensitivity to the following:

1. The implicit and explicit assumptions of program staff regarding commitments to working with men
2. The interdependency of husband and wife involvements in a program, with a view of one as an informal facilitator or gatekeeper of the other's participation
3. The program styles of helping that are compatible with men's problem-solving strategies and ways of relating to others
4. The implications for women of involving men in a parent program
5. The provision of unique and respectful roles for fathers in program routines
6. Content that addresses survival issues for low-income immigrants in dominant U.S. culture

6

Central American Refugees in Los Angeles

Adjustment of Children and Families

CLAUDIA DORRINGTON

This chapter describes the community conditions and family needs of Salvadoran and Guatemalan refugees in Los Angeles. The data were drawn predominantly from in-person interviews with 50 Central and North American respondents affiliated with 13 organizations that were established after 1979 to specifically address the concerns of the incoming refugee population. Respondents were selected on the basis of their knowledge of and long-term work with the refugee communities; they included 15 Salvadorans and 6 Guatemalans who had been in the United States an average of 10.5 years. Among the remaining respondents, 20 were non-Hispanic White North Americans, 5 were U.S.-born Mexican Americans, and 4 were foreign-born Latin Americans (Dorrington, 1992).

Data were obtained in three major areas:

1. Sociodemographic characteristics of the refugee population
2. Types of family and child problems that exist for the Central American community, including those problems perceived as unique to the Central American community
3. The types of interventions that were found to be most successful

The following sections provide an overview of Central American immigration to the United States, background literature on the psychosocial context of their migration, characteristics of the refugee community, and the adjustment of families and children within the context of a "hostile" environment. The final section focuses on programs and interventions that might be helpful in addressing the multiple needs of the refugee families and their children and in easing the adjustment process.

Central American Immigration to the United States

Until 1980, Latinos of Central American origin constituted a relatively small group within the larger U.S. Hispanic population. The mid to late 1970s saw the beginning of rapid growth in the Central American communities, especially in the larger urban areas such as Los Angeles, Washington, D.C., Houston, and New York. This was primarily caused by two events: a large-scale refugee exodus following the onset of civil war in El Salvador in 1979, and a violent escalation in Guatemala's 30-year civil conflict during the early 1980s. Although it has been suggested that the increase in Central American migration to the United States since 1979 is a continuation of previous immigration patterns, in actuality it is a relatively new phenomenon, with a gradual increase during the 1960s[1] and a marked increase after the mid to late 1970s (Hamilton & Chinchilla, 1991; Immigration and Naturalization Service, 1953-1954, 1976-1990, 1991; Torres-Rivas, 1985). By 1980, the foreign-born Central American population was still relatively small, with just over 94,400 Salvadorans and 63,000 Guatemalans nationwide (U.S. Bureau of the Census, 1990a). Within 10 years, the Salvadoran and Guatemalan communities had increased fourfold (to 472,885 and 232,977, respectively) with almost 60% of the newcomers residing in California (U.S. Bureau of the Census, 1992).[2]

Despite the mounting evidence of targeted persecution of individuals and groups in El Salvador and Guatemala during the 1980s and the displacement of many people by warfare, the United States declined to afford refugee status or asylum to those fleeing these two nations.[3] Until passage of the Temporary Protected Status provision for Salvadorans in the 1990 Immigration Act, all the refugees were officially viewed as economic immigrants.

Consequently, during the late 1970s and 1980s, most Central American refugees were entering the country undocumented. Available data suggest that the demographic profile of Salvadorans and Guatemalans who left their countries after 1979 is similar to that of legal immigrants and of mass migration movements involving the uprooting of entire populations as a result of war or natural disaster. The large number of women and children distinguishes the population from the economic-motivated migration usually associated with undocumented immigrants. Just over half of the U.S. Salvadoran and Guatemalan communities are women, and most of the population resides in family units with children under the age of 18.

Although the Salvadorans and Guatemalans experience many of the circumstances of other disadvantaged communities within the United States—poor living conditions, incomes below the poverty level, racism, and social alienation—their arrival under "refugee-like-conditions" has made them particularly vulnerable (U.S. Committee for Refugees, 1989). Predominantly undocumented, they have had to contend with the constant fear of apprehension and deportation to nations where their lives were at risk. As refugees, they also have considerable social welfare needs stemming from both their past traumatic experiences and their current living conditions. Furthermore, because they are undocumented, the Central Americans are excluded from the formal political processes and have fewer political rights, restricted access to the labor market, and very limited public social service entitlements.

As a culturally diverse and mainly non-English-speaking group, the Central American refugees face discrimination and exploitation and also have to contend with adjustment to a new social and cultural environment in a society that has not officially welcomed them.

Central American Families: The Psychosocial Context

The available literature provides evidence that the Central American refugee communities face extensive psychosocial problems. Studies conducted among nonpatient samples demonstrate high levels of stress, anxiety, and depression, as well as evidence of posttraumatic stress among both adults and children. Additional major problems highlighted in the literature (Arroyo & Eth, 1985; Berryman, 1983; Cervantes, Salgado de Snyder, & Padilla, 1988; Cordoba, 1986, 1992;

Hamilton & Chinchilla, 1986; Leslie & Leitch, 1989; López Garza, 1988; Padilla, Cervantes, Maldonado, & Garcia, 1987; Peñalosa, 1986) include the following:

Lack of financial and material resources
Unemployment and underemployment
Loss of employment status
Inadequate and overcrowded housing
Lack of English-language skills
Experiences of racism and hostility
Marital and family conflict
Isolation from family and ethnic community
Concerns over the loss of cultural heritage

At the same time, several studies attest to the self-sufficiency and resourcefulness of the Salvadoran and Guatemalan refugee communities in this country (Cordoba, 1992; Peñalosa, 1986; Rodríguez, 1987; Wallace, 1986). A study by Rodríguez (1987) among Central Americans in Houston noted that Salvadorans in particular

bring a level of community organizational experience not typically found among undocumented Mexicans. . . . [This is] an important resource for constructing, or participating in, small organizations that help the migrants' incorporation into the host society by providing temporary housing, job information, English classes, etc. (p. 5)

Rodríguez also reported that, unlike the Salvadorans, Guatemalans of Hispanic origin were not evolving their own community support networks. In contrast, however, the indigenous Guatemalan refugees of rural origin have developed strong community networks to assist each other. The indigenous communities interacted mainly among themselves and conducted activities to maintain group cohesion and cultural identity.

Central Americans in Los Angeles:
The Community Setting

The Central American community in Los Angeles began to grow rapidly after 1978. Although there is some evidence that a small immigrant enclave existed in the West-Central area of the city before then (Peñalosa, 1986), it was only after the onset and escalation of warfare and civil rights abuses in the region, and the resulting influx of refugees, that this area became known as "Little Central America" or even "Little San Salvador." By mid-1982, a reporter described the Pico-Union area as follows: "In a neighborhood that in the last two years has taken on the looks, sounds and smells of a Central American town, there are more than 200,000 Salvadorans living on a narrow corridor of aging buildings along Pico Boulevard" (Lindsey, 1982).

Overall, the data from this study support the findings of previous studies, which indicate that the experiences of refugees in Los Angeles are shaped by their historical experiences and motivations for leaving their homelands, their attitudes toward being in this country, and the legal and political climate and generally hostile reception that Central Americans received on arrival.

Although many of the respondents likened the socioeconomic conditions experienced by Salvadoran and Guatemalan families to those of other Latino groups in the United States, several unique factors were identified. Predominant among these was the reason for migration, that is, the experience of civil war, oppression, and trauma. Whether in flight from direct persecution or intolerable economic conditions greatly exacerbated by warfare, most of the Salvadorans and Guatemalans who arrived in Los Angeles after 1978-1979 can be viewed as political refugees. Until very recently, and then only in the case of Salvadorans, they could not return to their countries of origin with any guarantee of safety. The refugees were fleeing a situation of terror, and many had been directly persecuted and traumatized in their own countries and/or en route to the United States. Loss of family and friends, homes, and livelihoods under violent conditions and direct persecution or torture characterized the experiences of the first refugee arrivals and many of those who followed. One Salvadoran respondent, a community organizer, believes that "90% of the Salvadorans have suffered some loss in our families. Perhaps 45% of the people have been victims of torture and persecution." The effects of this trauma remained with the community and were expressed in multiple ways. Another Salvadoran respondent explained:

Many people arrive here with posttraumatic stress syndrome . . . because they were persecuted or tortured, suffered an assassination or disappearance of family members, and came with this fear which is expressed in many ways. It's expressed in depression, loss of appetite, the people cry, continue having the same fear, they believe that here they will be persecuted too. You identify people in uniform and the police here with those of the Salvadoran army and you don't trust them.

Overall, the Salvadorans and Guatemalans who arrived after 1978-1979 were characterized by respondents as refugees and in, a few cases, as economic refugees—individuals who had lost their jobs or land, whose lives had been disrupted, or who had been displaced as a result of armed conflict in their regions. Direct or indirect persecution was seen as the primary motivation for the exodus.

Refugees experienced adverse situations, not just in their home-lands or en route to the north but also after their arrival. Unlike other legally recognized refugee groups who share comparably traumatic histories—for example, the Vietnamese—Salvadorans and Guatema-lans did not receive the assistance or official refugee status that would have given them access to resources they desperately needed, such as health care or temporary economic assistance through welfare. Thus, many have experienced the difficulties of other undocumented immi-grants in achieving some form of economic stability or standard of living above the poverty level in a labor market where they were vulnerable to discrimination and exploitation. The fear of deportation and forced return to countries where their lives were in danger was seen by respondents as a further differentiating factor. The problems repeatedly identified—and recognized as being common to many other groups in the United States, in particular the undocumented—include poor living conditions, unemployment or underemployment, and discrimination. The multiple stressors faced by the refugee com-munities after arrival were described by one respondent as

> having left their country, coming to a new place, a new life, a new city, not speaking the language, being in a position of no power, no privilege, no access to anything, being treated [with] basic discrimination and racism all the time, and classism. People who did have training of [some] kind or schooling end up working in the garment industry, cleaning people's houses, in the service class. Struggling around housing, not having adequate housing, with kids going to school and not under-standing the system. I mean you name it.

The respondents further differentiated the Guatemalan community in Los Angeles from other Latino groups and from the Salvadorans.

Among the refugees who arrived during the past decade were many indigenous Guatemalans who constitute groups with their own unique cultures, languages, customs, and beliefs and who have long experienced discrimination in their country of origin. A Guatemalan respondent expressed some of the differences and problems as follows:

> Another problem is the problem of the indigenous, which could be compared with the Peruvians, who also have this problem. We have a lot of indigenous refugees with a culture that is different from the Latino. There are 23 different languages spoken in Guatemala. . . . Among them [indigenous Guatemalans], there are differences, different ways of life, dress, ways of speaking. . . . 60% of Guatemalans are illiterate. This figure is much higher among the indigenous; 80% of them don't know how to read or write, and some of them don't know how to even speak Spanish very well. . . . These people are the most likely to be exploited here.

Guatemalans and their historical experiences are seen as different in ways that do not necessarily lend themselves to acquiring the same level of visibility and support that the Salvadorans have been able to engender, particularly during the early 1980s. With the exception of the K'anjobal indigenous Indian community, many of whom reside in the West-Central area of Los Angeles, the Guatemalans are more dispersed around the city. Furthermore, respondents said that class and ethnic divisions prevalent in Guatemala were transferred to the United States and hindered collective action. Within the smaller, less concentrated, and more culturally diverse Guatemalan community, community organizing and the mobilization of support and resources from the larger society have been more difficult and on a smaller scale. As noted by one respondent:

> Unlike other Central American communities in Los Angeles, the Guatemalan community is very dispersed, with recently arrived people going to live with family members in various parts of L.A. county. This has been a great influencing factor [in terms of] the lack of consolidated support for the refugees, as well as difficulties in organizing the community.

The historical experience of the Guatemalans, a protracted war and repression since the 1950s, has affected multiple generations. The people have "suffered long periods of distrust and uprootedness; the strength of their culture for coping is being diminished inside and outside of Guatemala," noted one respondent. Like Salvadorans, Guatemalans are community- and family-oriented, maintaining close connections as a means of coping under adverse conditions. However, with the Guatemalan dispersion in Los Angeles, in the words of the same respondent, "their natural coping behaviors are broken down. Many are isolated and that makes an already stressful experience worse." Respondents report that the Guatemalans' isolation, as well as their long history of living under conditions that generate fear and distrust, has motivated many to seek safety and greater obscurity rather than confrontation and visibility within the United States:

> [The Guatemalans] are very different from Salvadorans and even Mexicans. They are probably the most reserved people in the region. . . . The Guatemalans are much less assertive, more discreet, more reserved, more authoritarian, more conservative and protective of family, indirect, and take longer to trust—as learned in order to survive.

However, despite the inherent differences between the two refugee groups, the respondents reported that Guatemalans and Salvadorans have several significant factors in common: the traumatic experience of war and oppression, a wide range of basic social and material needs stemming from both their current living conditions and their past experiences, and the experience of involuntary exile from their countries of origin. This experience of forced exile, longing for return, and belief that the exile would be short-lived were seen by most respondents as factors that have influenced the refugees' experience and activities in the United States. To a certain extent this "mentality" of temporary exile was seen as problematic by both North American and Central American respondents, especially with regard to long-term adjustment. Several of the respondents reiterated this theme in different ways:

> They didn't plan to come here, they don't want to be here, and this causes many problems for them.

> There was much resistance among the Guatemalans once they were in Los Angeles. They wanted and planned to go back to Guatemala. They didn't want to learn English, they were suffering from a tremendous loss of status.

And there's a lot of resistance to living here. I know Salvadorans who have been here for 10 years who don't speak English. It's not that they can't, they just won't. They stick with their friends and don't want to incorporate into this society.

The mentality of temporary exile initially shaped the purposes and activities of the refugee communities' organizing efforts to address their social and political needs. A primary collective organizational purpose was related to social change: promoting activities that would result in improved conditions in Central America, allowing the refugees to return as soon as possible, and assisting the people who remained in the region. Activities also focused on the rights, protection, and social needs of the refugees in this country, but direct services established by the refugees themselves were not initially designed with a view to permanent settlement but with a view to meeting immediate basic needs for shelter, clothing, and health care. Services addressing longer-term adjustment and settlement—literacy, English-language proficiency, and economic development—for the most part came later.

Building Community:
Strengths and Barriers

Study respondents agreed that the Salvadorans who arrived during the 1980s were predominantly of urban origin, representing all social classes: students, workers, teachers, some professionals, and a few clergy. Less than 40% were considered to be of rural origin, in contrast to the Guatemalan refugee population, which was described as predominantly of rural origin. Over half of the Salvadorans were women; quite a few of them were widowed, and others did not know whether or not their husbands were alive. Most adults were under the age of 30. Average families had four to five children but not necessarily all in the United States. In some cases complete family units came together, and in others half the family was left behind. One family member, male or female, might arrive first, later assisting others to join them. In general, the data suggest that the refugees had very limited material resources as measured by income levels. Unpublished data on a sample of 2,500 Salvadoran and Guatemalan clients show that the average monthly family income from all sources was less than $622 for an average family size of five members.

Although they lacked material resources, Central American refugees, particularly Salvadorans, brought with them a variety of community organizing and leadership skills and experiences that were vital to their survival and self-sufficiency in Los Angeles, according to most of the respondents. Of particular importance was the presence of individuals with past leadership experience and expertise, as well as large numbers of people who had been involved, in one way or another, in grassroots organizing in their countries of origin, whatever their formal education.

The experience of severe trauma can paralyze people's ability to move on in their lives and to deal with day-to-day stressors, let alone adjust to a new environment under conditions of poverty and social rejection. Yet for a considerable number of Salvadoran and Guatemalan refugees, the trauma experienced and the conditions that family members continued to face in their homelands inspired activism rather than passivity. Many of the refugees, especially those arriving during the first years of the influx, came with experience and skills in community organizing, an understanding of political processes, and strong ideological commitments, accompanied by a strong commitment to build their own community and achieve self-sufficiency.

Students and professionals from various fields were among the first groups of refugees to flee their countries. However, they faced limits on the extent to which their skills could be used in the United States. Professional licensing requirements, lack of English language, cultural differences, and undocumented status were all reported as inhibiting the full use of these skills. Respondents said that many highly educated and skilled refugees experienced the additional stress associated with downward social mobility and loss of status when they were unable to secure employment in their field of expertise and were forced to seek entry-level jobs in the service sector or in factories in order to survive.

On the other hand, for the refugee population of rural origin, the lack of fit between their farming skills and the demands of the U.S. labor market in an urban setting has made it especially hard to find employment. As reported by the respondents, lack of formal education, low literacy levels, lack of English (or Spanish-language skills in the case of the indigenous Guatemalans), and lack of knowledge about the social systems of their new environment have all served as serious obstacles to finding employment. Overall, most respondents reported that unemployment or underemployment, low-paying jobs in poor working conditions, workplace discrimination, and employer exploitation have been the most serious problems faced by the refugee communities since their arrival. This has resulted in widespread poverty and poor and overcrowded living conditions, placing the community at risk for a wide range of psychosocial problems. As the respondents observed, inherent in these economic problems has been the undocumented status of many of the refugees throughout much of their stay in this country. Interrelated to both the economic difficulties and undocumented status has been the refugees' lack of access to resources that could have eased their socioeconomic conditions and difficulties associated with adjustment to a new culture, including access to public social services, health care, transportation, and adequate housing.

The refugee population's strong ideological commitments, commitment to mutual assistance, and past experience served to unite and motivate members to work toward meeting their own needs through the mobilization of Central and North American resources and the establishment of their own organizations, which sought to address both political and social service needs. However, as the war continued in their countries of origin, the poverty of community members, the day-to-day struggle for survival in Los Angeles, family commitments, and the lack of legal refugee status all contributed to the difficulties of sustaining broad-based involvement. Most respondents reported that just meeting basic material needs—food, clothing, and shelter— has been a constant and dehumanizing struggle for many refugee families. Several of the respondents referred to the refugees' plight as essentially one of "no power" or "no status" in a hostile and inhospitable environment that denied them entry and forced them to continue to live in poverty and fear.

A consistent view among respondents was that socioeconomic conditions for the refugees have essentially not changed or have further deteriorated during the last decade. Through its organizing efforts, the community has achieved significant changes, predominantly legislative and political, such as provision of Temporary Protected Status (TPS) for Salvadorans under the 1990 Immigration Act and a reduction in U.S. military aid to the Salvadoran and Guatemalan regimes. The need to devote energy and scarce resources to political and legal goals, the self-determined priorities of the refugees who initially sought to return to their homelands as soon as possible, left few remaining resources to be channeled into economic development or badly needed social services. Only since the signed peace agreement in El Salvador in January 1992, and a brief hiatus in the problems associated with undocumented status for a portion of the Salvadorans, have some of the community's self-established social service organizations been able to turn their attention to services that go beyond addressing basic survival needs and look toward community development.

Over time, respondents have noted changes in the needs and problems faced by different segments within the refugee community, in the needs of new arrivals (as opposed to those who have been here for as long as 12 years), and, within this group, in the issues that concern those who want to stay and those who want to return to their homelands. Over 10 years after the first Central American refugees began arriving, many Salvadorans and Guatemalans have become an established part of the community in Los Angeles and other major U.S. cities. As the war continued, respondents reported that fewer and fewer of the refugees seen by their organizations spoke of returning to their homelands. Despite a certain reluctance to stay here, the prospect of returning home became more daunting, especially for families with children born or raised here.

The Adjustment of Families in a "Hostile" Environment

The difficulties associated with past trauma, culture shock, and adjustment to a new culture have resulted in diverse psychosocial problems for many refugees. Respondents reported that refugees have exhibited a tremendous resilience and ability to cope in the face of adverse conditions, and many have adjusted to their new environment with few or no signs of difficulty. However, respondents have also observed numerous difficulties, ranging from poor physical and/or mental health to family instability, as family members have sometimes resorted to substance abuse or domestic violence, seen here as maladaptive coping responses under severe stress.

Second only to the problems of poverty and unemployment, respondents reported that problems stemming from adjustment difficulties and past traumatic experiences, including persecution, torture, loss or disappearance of family members, the witnessing of violence to others, displacement, and/or loss of all material resources, have been most evident in the refugee community, even many years after their arrival. Flight from their homelands, although it alleviated certain immediate dangers, did not erase the effects of these traumatic experiences. Many refugees continued to experience the same fears in the United States, exacerbated further by fear for the safety of friends and family left behind, by a real fear of deportation, and in some cases by threats on their lives by fellow compatriots reportedly linked to death squads in Central America. These fears were evidenced in a natural mistrust of people outside their community and a fear and suspicion of U.S. authorities.

The experience of trauma has been manifest in various ways. Predominant among these is a reportedly high number of adults and children who report symptoms of stress and mental health problems, including depression, anxiety, posttraumatic stress disorder, and psychosomatic illness. Factors observed as having contributed to these difficulties are isolation, loneliness, and "survivor guilt," particularly related to having lost family members or having left them behind, and in many cases, a natural tendency to suppress the emotional responses to and memories of the traumatic events.

Physical health problems and lack of access to adequate health care were cited by most respondents as another major problem facing the community. For many of the newly arriving refugees, the major health problems included infectious diseases, lack of immunization, and problems stemming from poor nutrition and a lifetime of health care neglect reportedly due to inadequate services in their countries of origin. For the newly arriving Central American children, the most commonly reported health problems were parasites and amoebas, skin infections, and physical underdevelopment resulting from malnutrition, as well as lack of immunization. Continued poor living conditions in the United States have only served to exacerbate preexisting health problems or contribute to poor health status. In addition, barriers to accessing adequate health care services in this country have left the community vulnerable to ongoing health care neglect and inadequate information on prevention.

A final major problem area pertains to issues of adjustment to a new culture and loss of culture of origin. The process of adjustment has been shaped by several factors, including, among others, the status of involuntary exile, the intention to return home as soon as possible, and the unreceptive response of the host country. Consequently, respondents observed that many in the refugee community were initially reluctant to make adjustments that might have aided in the accommodation of their new environment. In addition, maintenance of their cultures of origin has been of primary importance. Lack of language skills and knowledge of the system and culture, as well as value conflicts between the different cultures, are all reported as having posed problems for the refugee families. However, Central Americans themselves have identified the loss of culture of origin as one of their most serious concerns.

Refugee families are particularly concerned with maintaining and/ or transmitting their language and culture to their children. It is important for the adults that their children not only maintain their Central American culture but also remember their country's history and the struggles of their parents' generation. However, this has posed many difficulties for parents whose children were either born here or adjusted much faster to their new environment, owing to a combination of their youth and external pressures to adjust, including discrimination and the desire to be accepted. According to respondents, the children are rejecting a culture that has not been validated in the United States. However, they have tended to adopt the culture of other Latinos, specifically that of the Chicano and Mexican community, the largest Latino group in Los Angeles.

The Children's Experience

Respondents generally agreed that the adjustment experiences of the Salvadoran and Guatemalan refugee children have been variable, depending on their age at the time of migration, the level of family support available to them in the United States, the past and present experiences of their parents or adult caretakers, their reception in the school system and host community in general, and their own experiences in their countries of origin, including their cultural, political, educational, and socioeconomic backgrounds. Inevitably, the children share certain adjustment experiences common to other immigrant children: language and cultural barriers, discrimination, and conflicts between the norms and values of their culture of origin and those of the new environment. As illustrated by one respondent:

Depending on how young they were when they came, I think that children in the North American context, depending on where they are sent to school, experience some feelings of isolation because of the language barriers. But as they stay here over a number of years they become much more quickly acclimated than do their parents. That's true probably of the Mexican community as well. Sometimes that affects also the relationship between the child and the parent. The child has the power of the English language, whereas the parent still only speaks Spanish. Sometimes that is a problem.

In general, respondents note a disruption and/or change in family relationships, created not only by war and migration but by the demands of the new environment and the adjustment process. Children tend to adjust faster than their parents in learning the language and in assuming some aspects of the new culture. The children frequently assume adult roles, acting as translators and negotiating the system:

I see a lot of situations where (the parents) will take a young child to get their gas installed, to ask why their services were shut off, to pay the bill. . . . So it's the children here who learn to read and write for their parents who brought them. . . . In that sense the children play a different role from other children because they are secretaries or assistants to their parents in order to function.

More distressing to the community, however, is the actual breakdown of close family ties characteristic of the Salvadoran and Guatemalan cultures of origin:

The relationships within the family are lost, the relationships between the parents change a lot too, and the children feel this change. In their countries of origin the relationships are more intimate, the family is united, but not here. Here the child has to detach himself, the father and mother both have to work, and nobody has time for the children. Basically they have to look after themselves alone.

Family relationships have been disrupted in part by the harsh demands of economic survival but also in part by family dissension that emerges as a result of exposure to conflicting cultural values:

As a parent one has a culture that is very distinct from that of this country. Thus, there exists a certain clash between children and their parents. Especially when they are adolescents, they want to live in the style of here, in the way of life of this country, and we want a distinct culture. We want to impose our culture and they want to impose theirs. . . . Here there is more freedom (for example) the young women go out alone. This is a culture shock for the parents.

Another area of conflict is that it is expected and acceptable behavior for parents to discipline their children through the use of corporal punishment. In the United States, such disciplinary methods may be interpreted as child abuse. As one respondent noted:

The parents really want to keep a tight hand on what's happening to their children . . . but some kids lose the respect they've had for their parents. . . . Through the TV, school, and so on children learn to be more aggressive, asking more, they have a different role in the family—more power in a sense when they speak the language and their parents don't. They have different models, see other roles, how other children behave. Parents think differently, they think it is necessary to punish. Children see more freedom, and parents see just more need to protect their children.

For many years after their arrival, parents dream of returning to their homelands. At the same time, they see their children becoming a part of a different culture: "A parent wants to take the children back, but they just don't adjust there—in the very country where they come from."

Respondents consistently reported that the adjustment of Central American children to living in Los Angeles has been shaped by their past exposure to the traumas of war and/or the traumas experienced by their parents or adult caregivers. In the children's new home, the reality of their past has been frequently denied or negated. The stark contrast between a refugee child's experience and that of his North American counterparts was described by one respondent as follows:

Let me tell you a story of a 10-year-old boy who lived in the province of Guazapa [a war-torn area in El Salvador]. He was accustomed to finding bodies in the river, seeing dead bodies in the streets. This was part of his daily experience at age 10. This is not the experience of 10 year olds here. So there's problems [for the children] with knowing who they are. They have a lot of wisdom in a sense and a lot of awareness, probably more than a child should have, a lot of maturity. . . . There's just a lot of denial here of those experiences, or people have never heard of El Salvador or Guatemala, which is a lot different than for, say,

Russian immigrants. Every American citizen knows where Russia is. The [Central American] children have the sense of not being known at all.

This "sense of not being known at all," not being accepted, understood, or heard, may in part explain the reported desire of many Salvadoran and Guatemalan children in Los Angeles to deny their own pasts and their own cultures in a bid to find a place for themselves in their new environment. The newly arrived refugee children, especially those in their teens, experience an initial loss of cultural and personal identity. Frequently respondents reported that the children encounter a denigration of their cultures of origin by their non-Central American peers, their schools, teachers, and the larger social environment. Their parents, who are also affected by discrimination, are frequently unable to counteract the negative messages received by their children. Subsequently these messages are internalized. One respondent gave the example of a 15-year-old, now apparently a gang member, who arrived here when he was 8. When asked about Guatemala, the country of his birth, he responded,

I don't want to go to Guatemala, there are only "Indians" there. Why would I want to go there? It's so ugly. I've seen photos of the people who walk in the streets, they're so ugly. . . . I don't want to return there. I want to became a North American citizen as soon as I can. I have nothing to go to Guatemala for.

A general consensus among respondents is that the parents do not always have the knowledge, time, or sufficient material resources to develop activities and programs that might effectively reinforce cultural pride in their children. Consequently, "the young people are in the most danger of becoming marginalized from both their country and the U.S. societies."

Respondents reported that many refugee children demonstrate "incredible internal resources" and "abilities to cope" with traumatic pasts, economic hardship, and the stressors of their parents and the adjustment process, including understanding a new language, a new school system, and diverse cultural values. Many others are not coping as well. As one respondent put it, "It's like they fall off a cliff." The "fall" is into the realm of gang activity as core gang members involved in substance abuse, violent crime, and theft. Or, if not actually manifest in overt behavioral problems, the fall is into the realm of depression, social isolation, and withdrawal. However, this fall is precipitated by loss of self-esteem, low school achievement in an alien system, loss of cultural identity, conflict between two cultures, and/or lack of familial or parental support due to death, absence, or the parents' own struggles with day-to-day survival. Moreover, for many Central American children, it is also precipitated by past exposure to the trauma of violence, warfare, and loss of family members in their countries of origin.

For Central American families, life in Los Angeles means their children face a different type of violence. Respondents generally agree that "many times parents do not know how to guide their children" in the face of problems such as gangs, drugs, and racism, characteristics of large urban centers in the United States and problems that the refugees "didn't have to face at home":

> They come from a country with much violence, therefore they are relieved to have left behind this type of violence in their country. But here they encounter another type of violence, such as the gangs and drugs. This is an abrupt change and it costs them a lot to adjust and to leave behind one violent reality only to come and have to adjust to another. . . . They thought they were coming to a peaceful place, but no, in the streets here they encounter much violence as well.

> I never thought that Los Angeles was a healthy place for the Central American Refugees. If they get jobs they are exploited. Their living conditions are usually terrible. Their young, especially boys and girls around 11 to 13, are getting into drugs and other things that never would have been options for them where they were living. It has caused such a great deal of anguish and distress among the parents who thought they were saving their children only to find them being abused in other ways. I think [this is true] especially among the indigenous of Guatemala, who have suffered a great deal because Los Angeles is just not Central America. It's a foreign country and not even a nice one at that. So they have been at everybody's mercy. I think they feel like they belong to nobody.

The conditions of life for the refugee families who remain in Los Angeles—isolation, discrimination, poverty, unemployment, lack of services, family disruption, and the children's vulnerability to gangs and drugs—are seen as essentially unchanged since the time that they first began to arrive. By necessity, the refugee community has had to direct its limited material resources to building organizations that could address its most essential needs, such as an end to the war and legal recognition in this country. Nonetheless, as the respondents consistently agree, members of the refugee community are very cognizant of the social problems facing their families here and also of interventions that would begin to address these issues in a culturally relevant manner.

Implications for Community Building: Services to Strengthen Families

Services and interventions that might aid the refugee families in their ongoing struggle with adjustment and resettlement in a hostile new environment are drawn from the respondents themselves. The Central American community contains many of the resources necessary for the delivery of services that would aid families in their relocation and adjustment, including leadership skills, community organizers, professionals and paraprofessionals, and the knowledge and ideas essential to creating innovative and culturally relevant services. All respondents in this study frequently noted the Central Americans' self-reliance and their high level of motivation to address concerns within their own communities. What is lacking for the most part is adequate fiscal support and the necessary political "will" from mainstream society to establish services or to expand and develop resources already within the community. Some of the community's most pressing needs can be resolved only through major national policy changes that address their legal status and access to the labor market in this country, community economic development, and universal access to appropriate health care and education.

The necessary elements of successful refugee and immigrant resettlement services have been well documented in the research literature. Many of these elements remain relevant to the needs of the Central American community, with a primary ingredient being major participation by the refugees in the development and implementation of their own services. Respondents in this study consistently reported that involvement in community development and organizing has served as an important intervention in itself, providing a sense of belonging, opportunities for empowerment, access to support from others with common experiences, and work that actively assists others in the community. As one respondent stated, "The whole process of becoming a voice for your people is therapeutic and helpful" when coping with past traumatic experiences. It provides a new sense of purpose and a positive connection with one's homeland when estranged in an alien environment. Beyond this, it is a forum where members of the community can use and develop their skills. These skills do not always "fit" those sought by the larger society.

Several of the multiservice organizations that were established in Los Angeles as well as other parts of the country during the early 1980s were developed "for" and "by" members of the Central American refugee community itself. The community also reached out to the mainstream, generating multi-ethnic collaborations and coalitions. These organizations share certain characteristics with the traditional settlement-house movement, specifically the movement's dual purpose: providing "immediate services and basic [social] reform" (Trolander, 1987, p. 1). However, Central American organizations also bring their own strengths and cultural characteristics that have their roots in Latin America. The most successful of these organizations have been those that provide models of empowerment designed after the organizational model of Paulo Freire[4] and the *base communities* or *Christian base communities* found in certain Latin American countries.[5] Such organizations not only provide models of empowerment but actually empower members of the community, for example, through their participatory decision-making structures, their community-organizing and political lobbying efforts, and their outreach community educational programs. These programs include teaching English and Spanish literacy, health education, and education about U.S. institutions and systems. Others teach non-Central Americans the sociopolitical history, culture, and social conditions of the refugee communities (Cordoba, 1992; Dorrington, 1992).

Most respondents agreed that these organizations need to expand services to address other wide-ranging psychosocial concerns of the Central American refugee families. Resource constraints, rather than lack of effective intervention strategies, have hindered development in this area. Programs proven effective in addressing adjustment-related issues include both cultural maintenance activities and group services for parents and youth. Reportedly successful and popular cultural maintenance programs have included language of origin and literacy teaching, cultural events and celebrations, and activities that promote knowledge and involvement in the history, traditions, and arts of the Central American peoples. Such programs provide a forum for addressing the problems of isolation, alienation, and loss of culture, identity, and pride that the refugees experience; the programs serve to bring family members together in shared activities. Successful group services have included programs that focus on specific themes. For example, some groups educate refugees on the expected stresses associated with past trauma and resettlement. Other groups focus on issues that are meaningful to parents raising children in a new sociocultural environment, such as addressing parents' questions and concerns about the school system, gangs, and drugs, and child discipline versus child abuse within the U.S. cultural context. Similarly, youth groups have apparently been more successful when they have centered around a particular activity, for example, artwork or music. Such groups also serve as informal support groups for adults and youth, who begin to share their own experiences of past trauma and loss and the current difficulties in their lives. Addressing difficulties such as family conflict and separation serves to ameliorate some of the psychological stresses common to political refugees. Flexibility, accessibility, a level of informality, and exclusivity or confidentiality, which are necessary for creating a "trust-based" environment, are all seen to be important characteristics of group services that might effectively aid Central American refugees.

Clearly, however, more intensive psychotherapeutic treatment programs are also required for refugee survivors of torture and others who may suffer from more debilitating symptoms as a result of past trauma, such as posttraumatic stress disorder or depression and anxiety related to adjustment difficulties. Despite wide recognition of the need, one of the most neglected social service areas in the refugee community, respondents generally agreed, is in the area of mental health. However, this is not necessarily a top priority within the refugee communities themselves, which are less familiar with Westernized concepts of mental health and treatment. The predominant concerns for the refugees since their arrival have been day-to-day economic survival and the achievement of social change goals that would alleviate conditions in their homeland. Even when available, the mental health services have not always been culturally appropriate.

The U.S. system of social service delivery is for the most part seen as alien, unresponsive, and incompatible with Salvadoran and Guatemalan cultures. Furthermore, only limited resources have been made available to the community to provide appropriate services. On the other hand, although many refugees have been understandably reticent to talk about their past experiences in traditional North American therapeutic settings, the public testimonies of trauma and persecution made by other refugees have served to mobilize resources and support from the North American population, particularly within the religious sector, and to further the community's social change agenda. Nonetheless, respondents consistently agree that psychological problems and stress have had a negative effect on refugee family adjustment and family relationships, manifesting themselves in problems such as physical abuse, drug and alcohol abuse, and marital discord, divorce, or separation. Community education on the potentially negative effects of past trauma and stress on family well-being can serve in part to decrease the stigma associated with the use of mental health services. Furthermore, mental health programs to enhance family relationships need to be provided within a larger organizational setting that offers a broad range of services, including education, legal assistance, cultural activities, material and employment assistance, and health care.

The strengths of the Central American refugee community itself provide the answers to the most effective intervention strategies. The mere expansion of a purely Westernized model of service delivery is not the answer. However, the non-Central American communities, particularly elements within the public and private social service sectors, have the opportunity to play an important supportive or "enabling" role (Trolander, 1987). By providing fiscal and material support, the larger society can assist in maintaining and promoting the expansion of existing Central American multiservice organizations and the development of new service centers. In addition, it can promote the further development of skills within the refugee communities by easing access to educational institutions.

Educators, policymakers, and social service workers can encourage validation of the Central American cultures and inform their work by making themselves aware of the unique histories, cultures, and life conditions of the Central American peoples. To date several Central American organizations have been able to maintain a culturally appropriate service environment and act as "advocate leaders" who "attempt to secure for their community those services that mainstream society has put beyond their reach, without sacrificing emphasis on ethnic identity" (Melville, 1991, p. 107). Their dual purposes—social change and direct service—and their multiservice approach provide settings reminiscent of the settlement-house movement but with empowerment of the refugee communities and cultural relevance as the guiding principles. "Nuestra experiencia es nuestra escuela," one Central American respondent stated, literally "Our experience is our school." This symbolizes the importance the communities place on self-determination and on shaping their own solutions to the problems of family adjustment in a new environment.

Notes

1. The 1952 Immigration and Nationalities Act (the McCarran-Walter Act) remains the basis of U.S. immigration policy. However, the 1965 amendments removed the National Origins Quota System, which had been in effect since 1921 and had created a ceiling on the number of immigrants that could enter from the Eastern and Western hemispheres. This removed an obstacle to Central American migration. A 20,000 limit from each country in the Western hemisphere was introduced in 1976, a limit that had been in effect for the Eastern hemisphere since 1965 (Aleinikoff & Martin, 1985).

2. The actual numbers of Salvadorans and Guatemalans in the United States can only be roughly estimated. Due to the number of refugees who arrived undocumented, 1990 census data are likely an undercount. In 1988, the U.S. Committee for Refugees (1989) estimated that a possible 1.5 million Central Americans had entered the United States under "refugee-like-situations" since the end of the previous decade. Estimates of the Salvadoran and Guatemalan population in 1985 ranged from 600,000 to 1,050,000, with Salvadorans in the majority by a ratio of 4:1 (Aguayo & Fagen, 1988; Montes Mozo & Garcia Vasquez, 1988; Ruggles & Fix, 1985).

3. Civil rights abuses, political assassinations, persecution, and torture in El Salvador and Guatemala have been well documented by various sources (American Civil Liberties Union, 1984a, 1984b; Americas Watch Committee, 1984; Amnesty International, 1988; Comite Pro-Justicia y Paz de Guatemala, 1987; Lawyers Committee for International Human Rights, 1984; Manz, 1988a, 1988b; Montes Mozo & Garcia Vasquez, 1988; Stanley, 1987; World Council of Churches, 1985, 1988, 1989). An estimated 74,000 civilians were killed in El Salvador, most of them by the military or military-supported "death squads," between 1979 and 1990. Over 75,000 Guatemalans were killed between 1978 and 1984 alone.

4. Paulo Freire, a Brazilian pedagogue, developed a model of community empowerment based on the use of educational strategies designed to develop a critical consciousness in the individual and the community at large. The model has been used widely in Latin America, particularly within the Christian base communities and other community-based organizations, to teach literacy and other skills combined with education on social issues.

5. Base communities or Christian base communities frequently embrace the methods of liberation theology, that is, analysis of reality, reflection, and action. They began to be established in Brazil and Central America in the late 1960s and throughout the 1970s in rural and urban poverty areas. The base communities were led by Catholic priests, brothers, and nuns, as well as lay people, and encouraged extensive community participation in understanding common problems and seeking a common solution and response (Crahan, 1988).

7

Latino Youth and Families as Active Participants in Planning Change

A Community-University Partnership

MARILYN AGUIRRE-MOLINA

PILAR A. PARRA

In this chapter, the authors describe the first two stages of a community-university project designed to engage a low-income Latino community in a process of social change with an initial focus on the prevention of alcohol and other drug problems among youth in the community. The chapter has two main purposes. The first is to briefly describe the establishment of a joint community-university partnership with Latino youth and their families, which was initiated in 1986 in the East Coast city of Perth Amboy. The Perth Amboy Community Partnership for Youth (PACPY) is a comprehensive community-based prevention strategy that integrates all key sectors of the community (parents, schools, health and social service agencies, city

AUTHORS' NOTE: The UMDNJ-Robert Wood Johnson Medical School, Department of Environmental and Community Medicine—Perth Amboy Community Partnership for Youth is funded by USDHHS-Public Health Service Substance Abuse and Mental Health Services Administration for Substance Abuse Awareness, grant No. 5H80 SP01479 and USDHHS-Public Health Service, Office of Minority Health, grant No. MPD-000522-01-1. The authors would also like to thank Claudia Dorrington for her editorial assistance.

government, local merchants, and the media) to form a partnership for prevention.

The second purpose of the chapter is to discuss the project's evaluation procedures and to present the methods and results of its first household survey conducted among Latino families. This first survey (of three) gathered baseline data on youth and family attitudes toward risk behaviors and perceptions of community change; the purpose was to subsequently evaluate the effectiveness of the project's preventive strategies. The survey was conducted among a random sample of Latino families in Perth Amboy (the intervention community) and in a selected area of Jersey City, which serves here as a comparison community.

The design of the project is based on a set of principles that entails an active role for community groups and individuals. It is well documented that effective efforts to reduce the social and health problems of Latinos and other low-income groups cannot occur without their active participation (Bernard, 1989). Bernard's description of communitywide prevention methods illustrates those strategies that are most effective in working with communities. The strategies include

> the systematic application of prevention strategies throughout the community in a sustained, highly integrated approach that simultaneously targets and involves diverse social systems such as families, schools, work places, media, governmental institutions, and community organizations. (Bernard, 1989, p. 126)

These strategies, combined with the principles of health promotion, increase the effectiveness of interventions designed to prevent a range of health and social problems and address the underlying risk factors. The emphasis is on processes that enable individuals and communities to increase control over the determinants of health and thereby improve their own health status (Aguirre-Molina, Ramirez, & Ramirez, 1993). Central to this approach is the community's effective participation in the definition of the problems, in decision making, and in actions to change and improve the determinants of health.

Community development is the ultimate goal of the prevention strategies employed to reduce risk factors and address the variables that contribute to their occurrence. Community development, as defined here, is the process of involving the community in the identification and reinforcement of those aspects of everyday life, culture, and political activity that are conducive to health.

The Children's Defense Fund, in recommendations aimed at helping Latino youth escape poverty, also stressed the importance of community participation in making long-term changes (Duany & Pittman, 1990). The focus of change is a reduction in certain risk factors, for example, poverty, family disruption, and intergenerational cultural conflict. These risk factors jeopardize the future of young Latinos in the community and contribute to a number of social and health problems among youth, including the occurrence of alcohol and other drug use, school dropouts, and adolescent pregnancy. Emphasized are interventions that establish close working relationships among the major social institutions that play an important role in young Latinos' lives. These institutions include family, school, and work, as well as Latino religious and community-based organizations. With regard to alcohol and drug use, evidence clearly indicates that single-system, single-strategy prevention efforts have a high likelihood of failure (Jessor & Jessor, 1977; Perry, 1986; Perry & Jessor, 1985). Alcohol and other drug problems are interrelated with other social problems. It is impossible to isolate these problems from the context in which they occur.

In order to provide a context for the initiation of the PACPY project, the next section presents a risk profile of Latino youth and their alcohol and other drug use patterns. A specific profile of the Latino population in the Perth Amboy community is presented in the project evaluation section. Both the risk profile and the profile of the Latino community in Perth Amboy, as well as the survey results, served to inform the work of the partnership.

A Risk Profile of Latino Youth

Latino youth represent the fastest-growing group of young people in the United States. By the turn of the century, they will constitute a significant proportion of the workforce and prospective leaders, making their achievements critical to the nation's future. However, to obtain equitable access to educational, employment, and economic opportunities, as well as to alleviate health and social problems, many young Latinos and their families require assistance (Duany & Pittman, 1990). This assistance is required because of the conditions of life and the accumulative social risk factors in many Latino communities, such as poverty, low-quality schools, and unsafe environments.

ALCOHOL AND DRUG-USE PATTERNS

Until recently, little has been known about alcohol and drug use among Latino youth. Most studies were based in school settings and used aggregate identifiers, such as Spanish-origin or Hispanic, to describe this population (Maddahian, Newcomb, & Bentler, 1985, 1988a, 1988b; Welte & Barnes, 1987). Other studies were limited to small or geographically linked samples (Espada, 1978; Maddahian et al., 1988a, 1988b; Velez & Ungemack, 1989) or focused on only one subgroup of Latinos (Bettes, Dusenbury, Kerner, James-Ortiz, & Botvin, 1989; Stroup-Benham, Trevino, & Trevino, 1990). In the last decade, an increase in epidemiological data on Latinos has contributed to the understanding of the patterns of tobacco, alcohol, and drug use among selected Latino subgroups. Two major surveys have been conducted. These are the Hispanic Health and Nutrition Examination Survey (HHANES), conducted between 1982 and 1984 by the National Center for Health Statistics, and a survey conducted by the Alcohol Research Group (ARG) during 1984 and 1985.

Since 1990, the annual "Monitoring the Future Report" (which has been surveying high school seniors nationally since 1976) began to report data by ethnicity (Bachman et al., 1991). However, these data are restricted to two groups, Mexican American and Puerto Rican/Latin American, and they do not control for intragroup variability. Nonetheless, an analysis of these data showed that young Latinos appeared to be at higher risk for alcohol and other drug use than any other racial and ethnic group (Caetano, 1983; Gilbert & Alcocer, 1988; U.S. Department of Health and Human Services, 1986, 1990). Cultural values and norms, in combination with adverse environmental and economic circumstances, place Latino adolescents at high risk for developing alcohol-related problems (Markides, Krause, & Mendes de Leon, 1988).

A number of studies have indicated that Latino 8th and 10th graders who were current drinkers imbibed more than their non-Hispanic White counterparts and substantially more than African American youth (Chávez & Randall, 1991; Windle, 1991). The decreases in alcohol use by the 12th grade, as observed in these studies, are most likely attributable to the high dropout rate of Latino youth by 12th grade. Further, these studies revealed that adolescent Latino females are approaching similar patterns of alcohol use. In fact, Mexican American girls are beginning to experiment with alcohol at approximately 13 years of age (Bachman et al., 1991; Linsky, 1985; Mora & Gilbert, 1991).

Of specific importance is the role of alcohol in the overall pattern of substance use among adolescents in general and Latinos in particular. Latino youth, more than any other group, use multiple drugs in addition to marijuana, the drug most commonly used by all adolescent drinkers (Morgan, Wingard, & Felice, 1984). A longitudinal study by Maddahian and his colleagues (1985) found that over a 5-year period, Latinos exhibited a general "upward mobility" in multiple drug involvement.

ENVIRONMENTAL INFLUENCES

It has been well established that the risk of alcohol/drug use increases disproportionately with the number of risk factors present in the community (Dryfoos, 1990; Hawkins, Lishner, Catalano, & Howard, 1986; Newcomb, Maddahian, & Bentler, 1986). Adolescent alcohol and other drug problems appear to be linked with family factors, inner-city schools, and deteriorated neighborhoods. The neighborhoods that are home to many Latino youth are characterized by poverty, unemployment/underemployment, and racial discrimination. These characteristics have a significant influence on alcohol and drug use patterns among Latino youth (Rogler, 1991).

Investigators have also identified other major environmental risk factors. Studies have found that a disproportionately large number of retail alcohol outlets are located in Latino neighborhoods and that the alcohol and tobacco industries employ aggressive marketing strategies to target Latino youth (Davis, 1987; Maxwell & Jacobson, 1989). As a result of these environmental and social conditions, Latino youth are at increased risk for school failure; use of alcohol, tobacco, and other drugs; adolescent pregnancy; and other related difficulties (Children's Defense Fund, 1990). The reduction of any of these behavioral risk factors requires the implementation of a culturally tailored and comprehensive preventive program. A preventive approach must move beyond the simple, single-focus, education programs that are commonly employed. Cultural factors, environmental factors, and community participation become crucial elements to incorporate in any intervention.

The Perth Amboy Community Partnership for Youth

"LA COOPERATIVA": DEVELOPMENT
OF A COMMUNITY PARTNERSHIP

The Perth Amboy Community Partnership for Youth (PACPY) was initiated in 1986. Although PACPY was launched by a university medical school (the UMDNJ-Robert Wood Johnson Medical School, Department of Environmental and Community Medicine), it has been driven by the community itself. Health promotion, as operationalized in the PACPY partnership, involves close cooperation among all sectors of the community. Thus mobilizing active participation by representatives of all the major systems in Perth Amboy was one of the first essential tasks of the project. Participants included Latino parents and youth, school personnel, human service providers, municipal government representatives, and representatives from churches and community organizations. These various sectors of the community were involved, either through advisory committees or direct participation in the services offered by the partnership. They have also been involved in identifying and defining the needs and problems of the community and in determining the goals of the partnership.

Although Latinos made up 41% of Perth Amboy's population in 1986 and 84% of those attending city schools, their presence within the community's decision-making infrastructure was limited. Latinos lacked a voice and presence in institutions such as the community school board or the city council. There was only one Latino elected official at the time the partnership began. This lack of visibility further contributed to the neglect and marginalization experienced by Latinos in the community. In the fall of 1986, in response to these conditions, a group of concerned Perth Amboy parents, community residents, and professionals from surrounding institutions met to discuss ways they could cooperate to address the numerous problems faced by Latino families and young people. The outcome of this, and the meetings that followed, was the formation of "La Cooperativa," a collective with the goal of cooperation for the common good of the Perth Amboy Latino community.

Although all members of La Cooperativa are important participants, two of the founders have become spokespersons for the group—a local priest and a Latina faculty member from the medical school. This was not only the beginning of the Perth Amboy community's partnership for prevention, but the beginning of the Latino community's collaboration with a major medical institution. The experiences of the last 7 years demonstrate how a grassroots community group can work in collaboration with a major academic institution without compromising the community's priorities.

Underlying the work of La Cooperativa are the principles of community empowerment. Thus, the early work of La Cooperativa was driven by community volunteers and student interns, who undertook a number of important tasks. The most important was the organization of community-led study circles. The study circles were the vehicles by which community members identified the problems they felt needed priority attention. In addition to poverty and unemployment, the key problems identified by the community were alcohol and other drug problems among young people and adults, adolescent pregnancy, the school dropout rate, and parent-child conflict. The community was most concerned with the lack of a unified Latino community voice advocating for change. This led La Cooperativa to the realization that the community needed a major intervention to initiate change, under the direction of Latinos themselves.

The study circles were the impetus for La Cooperativa to seek funding for a formal intervention to address the problems identified by the community. A major goal of the intervention, as determined by the group, was to prevent the occurrence of risk factors for alcohol- and other drug-related problems among Latino youth through a culturally tailored, multifaceted, preventive program that addresses the underlying causes of the problems. In 1988, the Latina faculty member of the medical school wrote and received funding for the formation of a community coalition to organize for social change and empowerment. Additional grants were obtained to build and strengthen the intervention, to evaluate the program, and to collect outcome data on the intervention. The evaluation process and preliminary data obtained are described in the evaluation section.

PACPY AND COMMUNITY DEVELOPMENT

The ultimate goal of the partnership, however, is sustained community development. Several key strategies used to reduce risk factors for Latino youth in the community were designed with this in mind. Three primary activities of the partnership address this broader objective. First, the partnership provides support for community action to modify the total environment and strengthen resources for healthy living. For example, community organization activities encourage participation in local activities, such as local and school board elections. In Perth Amboy, this resulted in the election of the first Latino mayor. Unlike former mayors, he is responsive to the needs of the community. Community organization activities also resulted in the candidacy of a local Latino activist for the school board.

Second, the partnership works to reinforce and expand social networks and social supports within the community. One example has been the organization of Latino parents in a Parents' Action Committee. The committee has been effective in addressing a number of school and community issues affecting members' children. In addition, an alliance of service providers was formed. The focus was on networking to reduce the severe fragmentation of services in the community, a fragmentation that has negatively affected the Latino population.

Finally, PACPY works to develop the material resources available to the community. Resource development has been conducted in two ways: first, by obtaining outside resources (such as grants, contributions, and volunteers) to help advance the community agenda via the partnership; and second, by working with existing community services to make them both more accessible and accountable. Partnership members have reached out to service providers and those with resources, to make them more aware of and accessible to Latinos in the community. As a result, the Department of Recreation, the Department of Labor, and other city departments have become more responsive to creating and expanding services for Latinos.

The next section of this chapter presents some of the methods and procedures used to evaluate the effectiveness of this community-university partnership. An important component of this project has been to build in mechanisms through which the interventions can be evaluated. It is hoped that the outcome will be a community-based prevention model that can be replicated in other comparable communities. Specifically, the next section presents:

1. the methods and data collection procedures;
2. the sociodemographic profile of the Latino community in Perth Amboy, as compared to a similar community in Jersey City that did not receive any intervention; and

3. the results of the first of three household surveys of Latino families. The surveys have been conducted on a bi-yearly basis in order to evaluate the project over time.

Other methods, which are not reported here, were also used to evaluate the interventions. These include in-depth interviews with key informants and a smaller sample of Latino families in the community, process evaluations, and documentation of all intervention procedures.

Project Evaluation: Methods and Procedures

METHODS AND DATA COLLECTION PROCEDURES

Two major methodological strategies were used to gather baseline information: examination of census data and a household survey. Using 1980 census data and supplemental census information, a comparison was made of the population characteristics of the targeted Perth Amboy area (census tract 45) and selected areas in Jersey City. This comparison was made to provide a profile of the Latino population in the study setting and to assist in evaluating the effectiveness of PACPY. The comparison was based on demographic characteristics, such as the percentage of the Latino population, age, family composition, and income. Two areas in Jersey City (census tracts 23, 25) were selected as the comparison community because the population characteristics were similar to Perth Amboy.

The second method used was a household survey conducted in 1990-1991. The main objective for conducting a household survey among Latinos in Perth Amboy (the intervention community) and in Jersey City (the comparison community) was to establish baseline information about key behavioral and attitudinal dimensions that the prevention interventions aimed to address. The survey was guided by the following questions:

What do Latinos think of their social environments?
How do they perceive their cities and city problems?
What are Latinos' attitudes toward the use and prevention of alcohol and other drug problems in their own communities?

HOUSEHOLD SAMPLE SELECTION

Because the project focused on a strictly defined area, a list of all streets and cross-streets in the targeted geographic areas was used for sampling purposes. The total number of households within each area was then counted. Perth Amboy had a total of 840 residential households, and 1,442 residential households were identified in the two census tracts in Jersey City. One hundred sample households were randomly selected in each area from among the identified households. All the households were screened to determine whether they met the key eligibility criteria, that is, a Latino household with household members between the ages of 10 and 18 years old. Respondents within each household were randomly selected on the basis of last birthday. Once the household was identified as Latino, one adult and one youth who had most recently had birthdays were asked to participate. One hundred adults 18 years of age or older and 50 children and adolescents, 10 to 18 years of age, were interviewed from each city. The final sample consisted of 200 adults and 93 youth. For the purposes of these analyses, the samples from both cities have been combined. No major differences of interest were found on major study variables between the Latino subgroups (i.e., Puerto Ricans and "other" Hispanics) or between the two community settings.

SURVEY INSTRUMENT DEVELOPMENT

The survey questionnaire was initially developed using core sets of Latino-appropriate questions asked in previous surveys, such as the HHANES. The instrument was modified for a 20-minute telephone interview. Data were obtained in four major areas:

1. Sociodemographic characteristics
2. Perception of the nature, origins, and extent of alcohol/drug use in general and in the community
3. Alcohol/drug use and related problems in the respondent's family
4. Current and potential involvement in community efforts to prevent and reduce alcohol/drug use

The adolescent questionnaire included an additional section on sexual behavior and tobacco use.

Results: A Profile of Perth Amboy

COMPARISON WITH
THE NONINTERVENTION COMMUNITY

Perth Amboy is a small, low-income, urban city situated in the middle of New Jersey. In 1986, it had a population of just over 40,000 people, 41% of whom were Latinos. Of the more than 16,000 Latino residents in Perth Amboy, more than half were of Puerto Rican origin (55%) and approximately 20% were Dominicans. The remainder were of Cuban or Central and South American origin. Perth Amboy is a microcosm of other poor urban Latino communities in the Northeast United States. In 1986, the city had the highest unemployment rate in the county (12.8% vs. 6.7% for the county and 5.3% for the state). About 21% of Latinos were receiving public assistance and Aid to Families with Dependent Children (AFDC), compared to 11.5% for all other ethnic groups. Compared to other cities in the county, Perth Amboy had, and continues to have, the highest rate of food stamp recipients (40.0 per 1,000 vs. 9.8 per 1,000) (U.S. Bureau of the Census, 1986).

Furthermore, the city had the lowest per capita income in the county ($6,067). More than 1 out of 5 households were, and continue to be, headed by female single parents with children. This represents 21.6% of all households. About 30% of Perth Amboy's Latinos lived below the poverty level in 1989, compared to only 15.5% of non-Hispanic Whites and 18.8% of African Americans. The city also had a higher rate of social problems than other cities in the county and most cities in the state. It had the highest suicide rate in the county (0.205 per 1,000 vs. 0.098 per 1,000). In the category of violent crime, New Jersey State Police reports for 1990 show that the city has a rate of 7.0 crimes per 1,000, compared to the county rate of 3.1 per 1,000.

In addition, the fertility rate of all young females, 15 to 19 years of age, was 75.36 per 1,000, four times the county rate of 19.64 per 1,000. For those 10 to 14 years of age, the fertility rate was 3.09 per 1,000, compared to the county rate of 0.48 per 1,000 (New Jersey Department of Health, 1988).

In Jersey City, the comparison community, the Latino population had similar fertility rates. The rate of births to all adolescents 15 to 19 years old was 84 per 1,000 in 1990, twice the state average (41 per 1,000). For girls 10 to 14 years old, the fertility rate was 2.14 per 1,000 (New Jersey Department of Health, 1992). In the same year,

36% of children were living with a single parent. The school problems in Jersey City schools are reflected in the fact that more than half of the ninth graders failed the 1991 High School Proficiency Test (Association for Children of New Jersey, 1992).

The comparison community in Jersey City is also similar to Perth Amboy in other important ways: ethnic group and adolescent age distribution, as well as portion of families with children under the age of 18. In addition, it has similarly high unemployment rates.

Results of the Community Survey

Survey data collected on adolescent and adult attitudes toward alcohol and other drug use and prevention strategies, as well as intergenerational comparisons, are presented. The data include the general demographics of the Latino respondents, their rating and perception of community problems, attitudes toward equity and empowerment, and attitudes toward use and prevention of alcohol and other drug problems. The youth's attitudes toward tobacco and birth control and their current sexual behavior are also reported.

DEMOGRAPHIC CHARACTERISTICS OF THE RESPONDENTS

Among the respondents surveyed, 58% of the adults and 62% of the youth identified themselves as Puerto Ricans; 18% of the adults and 15% of the youth identified themselves as Dominicans. The remainder were from different Latin American countries. Fewer adults (23%) than youth (62%) reported being born in the United States. About 38% of the adults and 15% of the youth were born in Puerto Rico, whereas 38% of adults and 23% of youth were born in other Latin American countries.

A similar pattern occurs with language usage. More adults (45%) reported that they used predominantly Spanish compared to 12% of the youth. English was less used by adults (13%) than by youth (30%). About 42% of adults and more than half of the youth were bilingual. Among the adults, more women (66%) than men (34%) were reached for the phone interview because of the higher participation rate of males in the workforce. Youth interviewed were more evenly distributed (see Table 7.1).

TABLE 7.1 Sociodemographic Characteristics by Percentages

Selected Characteristics	Adults *n = 200*	Youth *n = 93*
Ethnicity:		
Puerto Rican	58	62
Dominican	18	15
Other Latin American	24	23
Place of birth:		
Mainland United States	23	62
Puerto Rico	38	15
Other Latin American country	38	23
Language mostly used:		
English	13	30
Spanish	45	12
Bilingual	42	58
Gender:		
Male	34	47
Female	66	53
Age of adults:		
18-39	64	—
40-49	27	—
50+	9	—

As shown in Table 7.1, the age distribution of the sample is limited by the study design. Households selected were those with at least one youth between the ages of 10 and 18 years. Children and adolescents between the ages of 10 and 17 accounted for 27% of the sample. However, because Latinos are a younger population, almost two thirds were between 18 and 39 years old, 27% were between 40 and 49 years old, and only 9% were 50 years of age or older.

All children and adolescents were currently enrolled in school when interviewed. Among the youth, 47% were in middle school and the remainder were in high school. One youth was in the first year of college. The adults reflected the lower educational attainment of Latinos in the United States. Almost a fifth did not complete elementary school, and 20% had some high school. About a third obtained a high school diploma, and 22% continued on to college or technical or vocational school, but only 10% reported a 4-year college degree.

TABLE 7.1 *continued*

Selected Characteristics	Adults n = 200	Youth n = 93
Education:		
< 8 years of school	18	—
Some high school	20	—
High school diploma	30	—
Some college/technical school	22	—
College degree	10	—
Marital status:		
Married/living with someone	56	—
Separated, divorced, widowed	22	—
Single, never married	23	—
Employment:		
Employed	72	—
Not employed	26	—
Retired	2	—
Household income:		
< $10,000	24	—
$10,001-20,000	24	—
$20,001-40,000	43	—
$40,001+	9	—

When children and adolescents were asked "How far in school do you think you will go?" 17% replied that they will finish high school, and 15% reported that they will go to a technical, vocational, or junior college. About two thirds thought they would get a college degree or more. When they were asked "How much education would your parents like you to have?" 80% reported that their parents wanted them to go to college. About 70% of children and adolescents reported living with both parents or mother and stepfather, 26% with their mother only. About 4% reported living with other relatives. Among the adults, 56% reported being married or living with someone; 22% were separated, divorced, or widowed; and 23% were single. Among the adults, 72% reported they were employed, 26% were not in the labor force, and four persons were retired.

With regard to socioeconomic status, about a fourth of all individuals lived in a household with an income of less than $10,000, and another fourth indicated that their annual household income was between $10,000 and $20,000. About 40% reported incomes between $20,000 to $40,000, and only 9% reported incomes greater than $40,000.

PERCEPTIONS OF THE QUALITY OF THE ENVIRONMENT

Individuals in the two communities were asked to rate their city of residence on a 4-point scale: *excellent, good, only fair,* or a *poor* place to live. A small proportion of adults and adolescents (10%) rated their city as an excellent place to live. Another 10% rated their city as a poor place to live. About 45% of the adults rated their cities as only fair, compared to 28% of the adolescents. Half of the adolescents considered their city good, compared to 35% of the adult population interviewed. In general, however, adults and youth reported a similar rating of their city. As many Latinos have limited economic resources, they often choose to live in areas where cheaper housing is available. However, these urban settings may also have a higher rate of social problems.

PERCEPTIONS OF URBAN PROBLEMS

Both adults and adolescents were asked to rate a list of possible community problems on a 3-point scale (*very serious, somewhat serious,* or *not too serious*). Figure 7.1 depicts those problems rated as very serious.

For adults, teenage pregnancy (61%), drug abuse (57%), and unemployment (57%) were problems perceived as very serious. Among adolescents, drug abuse (60%), teenage pregnancy (57%), and juvenile delinquency (53%) were most likely to be rated as very serious problems. For 40% to 45% of both adults and adolescents, "too much drinking" and "poor school performance" were also seen as very serious problems. Half of the adolescents agreed that unemployment was a serious problem. Suicide and suicide attempts were perceived as a very serious community problem by a third of the adolescents, but by a smaller proportion of adults (18%). Overall, significant proportions of adult and youth perceived their community problems in a similar manner. No statistically significant differences between adult and youth perceptions were found, with the exception of juvenile delinquency ($p < .05$).

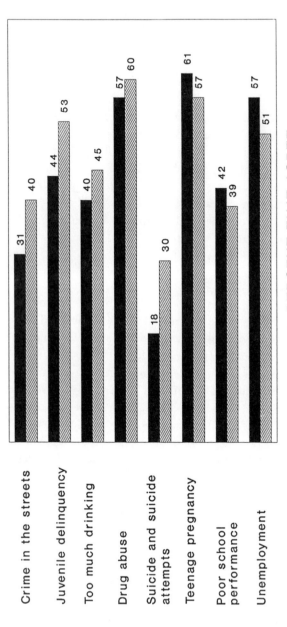

VERY SERIOUS

Crime in the streets — 31, 40

Juvenile delinquency — 44, 53

Too much drinking — 40, 45

Drug abuse — 57, 60

Suicide and suicide attempts — 18, 30

Teenage pregnancy — 61, 57

Poor school performance — 42, 39

Unemployment — 57, 51

PERCENT THAT AGREE

■ ADULT   ▨ ADOLESCENTS

Figure 7.1. Perception of Community Problems

145

RESPONDENTS' ATTITUDES
TOWARD EQUITY AND EMPOWERMENT

Finally, a set of four statements was used to measure the respondents' attitudes toward equity and empowerment and their awareness of possible sources for change in their communities (see Figure 7.2). Perception of inequality is similar among adults and youth. About 86% of the adults and 76% of the youth agreed that access to good education and jobs are not the same for Latinos and non-Hispanic Whites. About 75% of youth interviewed in both cities reported that the opportunities for education are unequal for Latinos, as compared to non-Hispanic Whites. More than half of the adults agreed that politicians are not interested in Latino issues and that services and programs are not available in Latino neighborhoods. Half of the adults considered it important for Latinos to take control of their own community if they want to reduce drug/alcohol abuse. About 40% of the youth agreed that most services and programs are allocated to non-Latino parts of the city and that Latinos should take control to resolve community problems. Only a fourth of youth agreed that politicians are not interested in Latino issues.

ATTITUDES TOWARD ALCOHOL
AND OTHER DRUG USE

The disparity between the values and behaviors learned at home and those modeled and socially sanctioned in the host community may lead to conflict between parents and children. Thus, the survey also explored the variations in the process of socialization and adaptation as reflected in the attitudes of adults and adolescents toward alcohol and other drug use and related problems.

As shown in Table 7.2, a higher proportion of adolescents (68%) than adults (54%) considered that the "example of alcohol abuse around them was the source of the problem"; 60% of adolescents agreed that the example of abuse came from parents, compared to 53% of the adults. A similar proportion of adults and youth (47% and 44%, respectively) agreed that advertising contributed to alcohol abuse. About 73% of adolescents said they believe that illicit drug use is caused by all the visible drug use around them, and 62% believed the example of parents is the cause of use, compared to 44% of the adult respondents. In response to the statement "People abuse alcohol/illegal drugs because they can't help themselves," 59% of adolescents agreed, compared to only 40% of the adults.

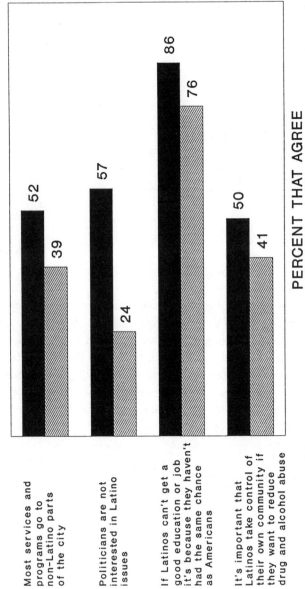

STATEMENTS

Most services and
programs go to
non-Latino parts
of the city

Politicians are not
interested in Latino
issues

If Latinos can't get a
good education or job
it's because they haven't
had the same chance
as Americans

It's important that
Latinos take control of
their own community if
they want to reduce
drug and alcohol abuse

52
39
57
24
86
76
50
41

PERCENT THAT AGREE

■ ADULT ▨ ADOLESCENT

Figure 7.2. Attitudes Toward Equity and Empowerment

TABLE 7.2 Attitudes Toward Alcohol and Drug Abuse by Percentages

Statement	Percent of Adults Who Agree	Percent of Youth Who Agree
1. People abuse alcohol because of the example of alcohol abuse they see around them	54 ($n = 196$)	68* ($n = 91$)
2. People abuse alcohol because they can't help themselves	41 ($n = 191$)	59* ($n = 92$)
3. People abuse alcohol because of the bad example of their parents	53 ($n = 198$)	60 ($n = 92$)
4. People abuse alcohol because of all the advertising for alcohol	47 ($n = 197$)	44 ($n = 93$)
5. People abuse illegal drugs because of the example of drug abuse they see around them	63 ($n = 197$)	73 ($n = 92$)
6. People abuse illegal drugs because they can't help themselves	40 ($n = 189$)	59* ($n = 92$)
7. People abuse illegal drugs because of the bad example of their parents	44 ($n = 197$)	62* ($n = 92$)

*$p < .05$, two-tailed.

When responses were analyzed to compare adult and youth attitudes toward alcohol and other drug use, significant differences were found in several areas. Adults' and youth's views on the "bad example of alcohol abuse around them" and the "bad example of parents regarding drug abuse" differed significantly ($p < .05$). For youth, people's inability to help themselves was perceived as a significantly stronger reason for alcohol or other drug use than for adults. In the prevention of alcohol use and problems, adults and youth reported similar attitudes. A strict enforcement of drinking age was supported by 99% of adults and 85% of adolescents. Police enforcement of no-drinking laws in public places, such as parks and beaches, was also supported by most adults (99%) and adolescents (90%). However, government prohibition of advertising alcoholic beverages was endorsed by 78% of adults, but only 51% of adolescents.

YOUTH'S ATTITUDES TOWARD
TOBACCO USE AND PREVENTIVE MEASURES

Youth respondents were asked a series of questions regarding tobacco use. Most of the youth surveyed (82%) agreed that tobacco is a drug

TABLE 7.3 Youth's Attitudes Toward Tobacco Use

Statement	Percent of Youth Who Agree (n = 93)
1. Tobacco is a drug	82
2. A real man smokes cigarettes	15
3. It's unpleasant to see a woman smoking cigarettes	67
4. Young people smoke cigarettes because the adults around them do	57
5. Young people smoke cigarettes because of all the advertising for cigarettes	38

(see Table 7.3). More than half reported that young people smoke because the adults around them do, whereas about a third agreed that advertisement for cigarettes promotes smoking among young people. It is interesting to note that relatively few youth (18%) indicated that smoking cigarettes is a "manly thing to do," and 67% considered it "unpleasant" to see a woman smoking cigarettes.

The youth surveyed had a low rate of smoking. A fourth reported they had smoked a few times or occasionally. Only two adolescents were frequent smokers (less than a pack a day). For all occasional and frequent smokers, the mean age when they started smoking was 14 years old. The youth's attitudes regarding the prevention of tobacco use reveal that 82% agreed that "no smoking" laws should be enforced more strictly. Three fourths agreed that the government should prohibit all cigarette advertisements for sporting events, and 61% agreed that government should not allow cigarette advertising at all. Approximately two thirds agreed that it is very easy to buy cigarettes.

These problems have prompted several corrective measures on the part of the PACPY. For example, the partnership has been pressing the appropriate authorities to enforce laws that prohibit the sale of cigarettes to minors, and it has been working with local businesses to encourage their compliance with the law.

SELF-REPORTED SEXUAL BEHAVIOR AND ATTITUDES TOWARD BIRTH CONTROL

One of the problems the communities were most concerned about is teenage pregnancy. This concern is based on the increase in the rate of teenage pregnancies in their communities over the last decade. Youth were asked about their current sexual behavior and about their attitudes toward birth control. As with many other studies of youth, this study also found a discrepancy between attitudes and sexual behavior. Almost all of the youth agreed that "it's smart to use birth control to prevent an unplanned pregnancy" (98%) and "to use condoms to protect against AIDS" (97%). For 82% of the adolescents "it's alright to use birth control," and only a fourth considered the use of birth control "a hassle." When they were asked if they had had intercourse, 26% (or 24 adolescents) responded positively. Almost half of these respondents reported that they did not use any contraceptive method at the time of first intercourse. One female respondent reported that the experience resulted in a pregnancy. Among those adolescents who reported that they did use contraception, the condom was the preferred method, followed by the pill. The mean age when respondents first had sexual intercourse was 15 years old.

Discussion of the Survey Results

The demographic distribution of the Latino population in the two cities surveyed is similar to other cities in the Northeast, where Puerto Ricans represent the largest proportion of Latinos (U.S. Bureau of the Census, 1993a). The socioeconomic profile of our sample is similar to the general demographic characteristics of Latinos in the United States. Latinos in the two cities surveyed tend to be young, have low educational attainment (38% do not have a high school diploma), and almost half report a family income of less than $20,000. Latinos are two and a half times more likely than the general population to live below the poverty level. In comparison, nationwide, 40% of Puerto Ricans, the poorest Latino subgroup, live below the poverty level. In our sample, most of the Latino families have limited economic opportunities, and parents themselves have low educational attainment. Nevertheless, the parents have high expectations for their child's education. Four fifths of the youth reported that their parents want them to go to college.

In both study sites, Latinos reported similar views regarding their city. More than half of the adults and 38% of youth gave their city a low rating. This can be explained by the diverse social problems faced in these communities. Drug abuse, teenage pregnancy, and unemployment were reported as the most serious concerns by approximately half of both the adult and youth respondents. However, fewer adults than youth respondents considered juvenile delinquency and suicide or suicide attempts as very serious. The greater concern of youth about these issues may be directly related to their more direct exposure to delinquent acts in the street and probably in school settings as well. In addition, they are more exposed to suicide ideation and attempts among their peers than are their parents or other adults. Special attention needs to be given to suicide prevention and delinquency in the schools and community, in light of the fact that suicide is a concern among the youth and that Puerto Ricans tend to have higher rates of suicide (Ungemack & Guarnaccia, 1993).

Results of the survey also indicated that Latino youth and adult attitudes toward equity and mechanisms for empowerment were similar. At a young age, Latinos are already aware of discrimination in jobs and education, as well as the marginalization of the Latino community in terms of services and programs. About 40% of the youth, as well as half of the adults, acknowledged the need to take control of their communities in order to bring about change. This demonstrates the importance of developing community-driven mechanisms whereby these issues can be discussed and addressed. To this extent, PACPY is an example that emphasizes processes that ensure active and ongoing participation of community members in the search for solutions to problems and that enhance community empowerment.

Attitudes toward alcohol, other drug use, and related problems reflect differences between adult and youth respondents. A larger proportion of youth believe that the use of alcohol and other drugs results from the example set by others around them, or the example of parents who themselves use drugs. This perception about alcohol and drug use is important. Recent studies have shown that drinking and other drug use by family members is a risk factor that considerably increases the likelihood of the adolescent engaging in such use themselves. (Gilbert & Alcocer, 1988; Vega, Zimmerman, Warheit, Apospori, & Gil, 1993).

Preventive measures for decreasing alcohol use and related problems were supported by an overwhelming majority of both adults and youth. Strict enforcement of the drinking age and no drinking in public places were strongly supported. Prohibition of advertising for alcoholic beverages was endorsed by three fourths of the adults and half of the adolescents. Thus, there is an apparent understanding of the effect of substantial amounts of advertising and availability of alcoholic beverages in their neighborhoods. These data suggest that the active participation of communities can be mobilized to counteract the advertising and marketing campaigns of the alcohol and tobacco industries that target Latinos.

Youth recognition of tobacco as a drug reflects the efforts in schools and other public health initiatives to warn children, and the public in general, of the effect of tobacco on health. Advertising for cigarettes and smoking was a concern of about 40% of the adolescent respondents. These data may reflect a trend whereby increasing portions of the Latino community are recognizing the detrimental role of advertising and cigarette availability as contributing to early initiation of tobacco use.

The statement "A real man smokes cigarettes" was endorsed by only 15% of the respondents. Thus, smoking is not considered a manly behavior. However, tobacco use among women was not considered acceptable by about two thirds of those surveyed. Although it might be expected that women are protected by cultural norms, this attitude has not deterred the increasing number of young Latina women who become smokers every year (Escobedo & Remington, 1989). Smoking among adolescent females appears to be the result of peer influences and more liberal norms outside of the home (Dusenbury et al., 1992). Also, adolescents are more likely to smoke if family members of the same sex smoke (MacGraw, Smith, Schensul, & Carrillo, 1991). With the increasing number of teenage pregnancies and teens who smoke, the risk of low-birthweight babies and other complications increases (Oster, Delea, & Colditz, 1988). Thus, both issues—adolescent pregnancy and tobacco use—require intervention.

Finally, the results of the survey bring attention to the importance of sex education and the availability of services for adolescents who initiate early sexual behavior. Nationally, there has been a steady increase in sexual activity among adolescents (Fielding & Williams, 1991). This is also true for Latino adolescents, who are less likely to practice contraception (Bachrach, 1984) and consequently more likely to become pregnant and keep their babies. Darabi and Ortiz (1987) found that rates of early childbearing in women less than 22 years old were higher among Mexican American (38.0%) and Puerto Rican women (30.1%) than among non-Hispanic White women. In our sample, half of the adolescents that had had intercourse did not use any form of protection. Thus, adolescents are exposed not only to the risk of pregnancy but also to sexually transmitted diseases, including AIDS. HIV/AIDS is increasing in the teenage community throughout the United States. Because Latino youth 13 years of age and older have a case rate of AIDS that is 2.7 times higher than non-Hispanic Whites, special attention should be given to this population (Diaz, Buehler, Castro, & Ward, 1993; Hein, 1993). Preventive measures that go beyond sex education and include the availability of contraception and health-related services are required (Fielding & Williams, 1991; Hein, 1993).

In conclusion, these data support the need for primary prevention and early intervention programs that target Latino children and adolescents. They also strongly underscore the principle that those who are at risk must be active participants in a process of change and community development so that empowerment may be achieved and that the necessary changes become institutionalized in the community. PACPY has incorporated these principles to guide its work with the community. Future public health endeavors are needed to create similar partnerships for prevention to assure that the perceptions and concerns of the community are the driving force of the intervention efforts. However, if risk reduction and disease prevention interventions are to succeed, they must take into consideration the multiple social, economic, cultural, and environmental factors that contribute to a community's well-being.

PART III

POLICY IMPLICATIONS

8

Family and Child Health

A Neglected Vision

RUTH E. ZAMBRANA

CLAUDIA DORRINGTON

DAVID HAYES-BAUTISTA

The purpose of this chapter is to present the current status of knowledge on the health and human service needs of Latino families and children and to identify current obstacles in developing culturally relevant Latino family and child services in the United States. Recent evidence clearly demonstrates the interdependent relationship between health and human services and the well-being of the population (Children's Defense Fund, 1991b; Danzinger & Stern, 1990; Schneiderman, 1990). The last 3 decades have yielded extensive information on the medical and nonmedical factors that influence the health status of low-income groups (Schorr & Schorr, 1988; U.S. Department of Health and Human Services, 1991). Factors such as stress or chronic life problems, availability of social support, and coping skills play a crucial role in overall health status and physical functioning. Furthermore, the broader but interrelated social welfare

AUTHORS' NOTE: The authors express their appreciation to Sally Alonzo Bell and Julie Solis for their contributions to this chapter.

issues, such as education, employment, and adequate nutrition, income, and housing, clearly influence the overall health status of the population.

In general, the health and human service needs of Latino families and children have been neglected in the United States. However an accurate assessment of these needs has proven to be a difficult task due to the historic lack of data on this group (Amaro, 1993; U.S. Public Health Service, 1992). The first comprehensive efforts to obtain health data on Latino populations were instituted in 1982-1984 through the Hispanic Health and Nutrition Survey (HHANES), the first national health survey to target this population, and more recently, in 1989, through revisions in the vital statistics birth records. It has long been observed that Latinos experience limited access to health services, have high levels of morbidity and mortality in selected clinical conditions, and make less use of public social services. However, a substantial number of articles have focused on cultural and organizational barriers rather than socioeconomic status in explaining determinants of disease patterns and use behaviors. There has been an implicit assumption that Latino health and help-seeking behaviors are a direct result of cultural factors, rather than consequences of the effects of social inequality.

Addressing the health and human service needs of the Latino population requires a broad comprehensive effort that includes confronting the causes of poverty and its consequences. Unemployment, poor housing conditions, residential segregation, poor quality of education, limited access to health and human services, and lack of health insurance represent a cluster of social and economic risk factors that are detrimental to the health and well-being of Latino families and children (Duany & Pittman, 1990). These structural and environmental factors jointly contribute to the unfavorable social, physical, and mental well-being of Latino children and families in the United States.

Health Within the Family Context: An Overview

Health represents a complex phenomenon that involves many dimensions of the individual, family system, community environment, and societal resources (Combs-Orme, 1990; Lillie-Blanton, Martinez,

Taylor, & Robinson, 1993; D. R. Williams, 1990). Moreover, the health and human service needs of Latino families and children are integrally related to family structure and available economic resources. Sardell (1990), in her cogent historical review of federal child health policy in the United States, demonstrates the "paradox of consensus" in the formulation of policy for women and children:

> Children live in families and communities. To become a society that produces healthy infants and children, we must deal with adult employment and family income, education, drug use, and housing issues. A universal prenatal and primary health care system providing transmedical services to pregnant women and children must be part of a comprehensive set of employment, wage, child care, and housing policies that support both the adults and children in families. (p. 302)

Thus, the health of women, men, and children is affected by their living conditions, the community resources available to them to enhance their physical and mental functioning, and their social environment. Documentation of the multidimensional factors that influence use of health services and health outcomes has led scholars to a new theoretical discourse, which in essence examines the interrelationships among individual attributes, family and behavioral risk factors, and institutional arrangements. Population characteristics alone are not focal explanations for low use of health and human services and poor health outcome among Latinos; rather, there is a focus on institutional arrangements and sociocultural barriers that occur at the level of the provider but are influenced by features of the larger society, such as discrimination and racism, poverty, and immigration law. For example, the high cost of medical care, difficulties of accessibility, language barriers, undocumented immigrant status, long waiting lines, lack of transportation, lack of evening and weekend services, lack of child care, and lack of knowledge of available resources assume a central role in understanding access to the use of appropriate health and human services among Latino families (De La Rosa, 1989; Giachello, 1994). Evidence suggests significant barriers associated with the allocation and distribution of economic resources and related health and human services for Latino families. These correlates of social inequality include poverty, lack of health insurance, segregated residential communities, and limited access to quality health and human service support services. All these significantly contribute to the persistent health and social disparities among Latinos.

HEALTH AND HUMAN SERVICE SUPPORT:
INCOME MAINTENANCE, EDUCATION, AND CHILD CARE

Data demonstrate that Latino families have limited economic resources available to them in comparison to non-Hispanic White
families. In 1991, over one quarter (26.5%) of Latino families and just
over 40% of all Latino children lived in poverty, compared to 7.1%
of non-Hispanic White families and 13.1% of non-Hispanic White
children. Intragroup differences show that Puerto Rican families and
children, followed by Mexican-origin families and children, are most
likely to be living in poverty. Although Latino children constitute
11.6% of all children, they constitute 21.5% of all children in poverty
(Garcia, 1993). Over the past decade, Latinos accounted for half of
the total growth in the number of poor children nationwide (Miranda,
1991). Furthermore, Latinos make up the largest proportion of children under the age of 3 who live in poverty, the fastest-growing
poverty group. In 1990, one third of Latino children under the age of
3 who lived with two parents and over two thirds (73%) who lived
with their mothers alone were poor (Carnegie Corporation, 1994).

Despite these high poverty rates, Latino families are also less likely
to receive assistance from publicly funded, means-tested, noncash
benefit programs, such as food stamps, subsidized housing, or Medicaid (U.S. Bureau of the Census, 1985), or from means-tested income
maintenance programs, such as Aid to Families with Dependent
Children (AFDC). In 1990, Latino families made up 16% of all AFDC
recipients, compared to 38% for non-Hispanic Whites (U.S. House of
Representatives, 1992). Available data from California suggest that
when we statistically control for income, Latino families are about half
as likely as non-Hispanic Whites or Asians and about one fifth as likely
as African Americans to receive AFDC (Hayes-Bautista, Hurtado,
Valdez, & Hernandez, 1992). Nationwide, the average AFDC monthly
grant for a family of three is $367, only 42.3% of the poverty level
(Children's Defense Fund, 1991b). Nonetheless, both cash and noncash government transfers remain of great importance to poor families. Government transfers are much more significant in lowering
income inequality than any benefits that might be gained through the
tax system (U.S. Bureau of the Census, 1993b).

Data on other human services related to income maintenance,
specifically with regard to Latinos, are not available. However, it can
be assumed that programs such as the various work incentive programs

for AFDC recipients have had mixed results for Latino families as they have for other poor families, depending on program design and regional differences. Designed to decrease unemployment and under-employment among poor families with the goal of lifting families out of poverty by providing job training, workfare programs have resulted in only modest increases in the number of people employed or in actual earnings, and they have had little effect on hourly wages (Grossman, Maynard, & Roberts, 1985; Hasenfeld, 1987).

Due to their low earning potential, work alone is frequently not enough to help many poor Latino families increase their economic resources. In other words, they participate in the secondary job market, which is generally characterized by low wages, poor working conditions, little opportunity for advancement, no retirement plans, and limited or no health care insurance. In 1989, over half of poor Latino families had a head of household who worked at least part of the year, and 1 in 5 had a household head who worked full-time all year. Latino families with children and with a head of household working full-time, year-round were three times more likely to be poor than similar non-Hispanic White families. Furthermore, immigration does not account for high rates of Latino poverty. Latino immigrants have lower rates of single parenthood and also have high rates of labor force participation. Latino families with a U.S.-born household head are still three times as likely to be poor as non-Hispanic White families (Miranda, 1991). Overall, Latino families lost economic ground between 1989 and 1992, experiencing a 9.9% drop in median family income compared to a 4.4% decline for non-Hispanic White families and a 7.5% decline for African American families (U.S. Bureau of the Census, 1993c).

Almost half (49.7 percent) of all poor Latino families are headed by women alone, compared to a quarter (24.6%) of non-Hispanic White families, even though Latinas are as likely to work full-time as non-Hispanic White women. Although many poor families receive subsidized child care, the federal government's child-care programs have tended to aid wealthier rather than poor families. As an example, in 1989, the largest federal program, the child and development care tax credit (CDCTC), awarded 77% of the $3.6 billion in credits to families with incomes over $30,000, and 43% to families earning over $50,000 (Marshall, 1991). According to the most recent available data, from 1986, families at the poverty level paid an average of 22% of their income for child care, compared with 4% paid by families with incomes of over $45,000. Poor women who have to pay for child care pay over 20% of their income for child care, compared to 7% paid by all working women (U.S. Department of Commerce, 1987). By the late 1980s only 30% of all federal child-care spending targeted low-income families, compared to 80% in 1972. Availability, cost, quality, and lack of information on accessible child care are all major problems for poor families (Marshall, 1991; Rogers, 1988).

Latino children make up 22% of children enrolled in Head Start, one of the more successful federally funded child-care programs designed to provide social as well as educational services for poor children between the ages of 3 and 5 (Costin, Bell, & Downs, 1991). However, the program reaches less than a quarter of all poor children in this age group, and most Head Start programs operate only half-day during the school year and thus do not accommodate working parents. Nonetheless, program evaluations clearly point to the benefits of quality preschool services, which can assist in promoting cognitive, social, and emotional development and preparing poor children to start school ready to learn. In addition, they are cost effective—for every dollar spent on preschool education, an estimated $4.75 is saved in social costs. Unfortunately, however, these benefits may not be lasting. Most gains have diminished by the third grade, suggesting not a failure on the part of Head Start, but rather a failure on the part of the school system (Marshall, 1991).

Certainly it would seem that the nation's schools are failing Latino children. In 1991, Latino youth had the highest school dropout rates in the country (35.3% compared to 8.9% among non-Hispanic Whites). Despite very modest gains since the early 1980s, compared to the population as a whole Latinos are still five times more likely to leave school before the sixth grade, "only about two thirds as likely to graduate from high school, and less than half as likely to obtain a bachelor's or other higher degree" (Darder, Ingle, & Cox, 1993, p. 2). Less educational attainment is clearly one of the factors influencing the occupational status of Latinos, and consequently the poverty rates of Latino families (Miranda, 1991). However, the problem is cyclical. Social inequalities hinder the educational achievement of many Latino children who are burdened by the stress of poverty and related conditions, such as poor health, poor housing, inadequate nutrition, and the environmental violence that often accompanies the poverty and lack of resources found in inner-city neighborhoods and schools.

Furthermore, many Latino children have parents who themselves have lower educational attainment, another factor, along with poverty, that influences academic success (Darder et al., 1993). A study by the Annie E. Casey Foundation (1994) determined that 1 in 10 Latino children currently lives in a "severely distressed neighborhood" compared to 1 in 63 non-Hispanic White children. By their definition, a "severely distressed neighborhood" has levels of poverty, unemployment, school dropouts, female-headed households, and welfare dependency that are higher than the national average by at least one standard deviation. The strain of these distressed conditions on Latino families and children is reflected in the increase in the number of Latino children who have entered the foster care system during the past decade.

Foster care is a primary social welfare service providing substitute care when parents are unable or unwilling to care for their children. Although over half of all the children in foster care are victims of abuse, the foster care placement frequently results from the combination of poverty, inadequate community resources and support networks to assist families in maintaining their equilibrium, and a disruption in a family's usual level of psychosocial functioning (Delgado, 1992). Data show that the number of Latino children in foster care rose between 1982 and 1990. In 1982, Latino children made up 6.7% of all the foster care children in 31 states, compared to 52.7% of non-Hispanic White children. By 1990, the percentage of Latino children had increased to 11.8%, compared to a decline in the number of non-Hispanic White children to 39.3%, representing a 172.2% increase between 1982 and 1990 (American Public Welfare Association, 1993). Overall, poor and minority children are overrepresented in the foster care system. For example, in 1990, 85% of the children in foster care in New York were African American and Latino. Furthermore, minority children are more likely than non-Hispanic White children to stay longer in care, either before returning to their families or before being placed for adoption. On average, Latino children spend 26 months in foster care, compared to 20 months for non-Hispanic White children (Delgado, 1992). However, of additional concern for Latinos is the apparent lack of Latino foster care home placements, resulting in many children being placed in homes where the child is at risk of losing his or her cultural identity and Spanish-language proficiency.

PSYCHOSOCIAL WELL-BEING:
MENTAL HEALTH SERVICES

There is a significant and well-established link between low socio-economic status, limited social support networks, traumatic life events, high stress, and psychological well-being. From a psychosocial perspective, many Latinos who are poor and experience high levels of work and environmental stress are vulnerable to mental health-related problems, such as anxiety and depression. In particular, recent Latino immigrants are vulnerable to feeling depressed or sad and anxious due to being uprooted from their countries or origin. They are more likely to be overwhelmed and unable to cope in a new environment in which they do not know the language, the predominant culture, the various systems, or how to manage the bureaucracy to access any available health and social service benefits. Data on adult Mexican immigrants have demonstrated higher levels of depression and psychosocial dysfunction, in comparison to U.S.-born Mexican Americans, independent of age, gender, marital status, or educational achievement (Warheit, Vega, Auth, & Meinhardt, 1985). As another more recent example demonstrates, relatively high levels of anxiety, depression, and post-traumatic stress disorder have been observed among Central American adults and children, particularly among those who arrived as refugees during the past decade and who may have lost family members, experienced violence themselves, or witnessed the murder or assault of friends or family, all events that impede their ability to function well (Aron, 1988; Arroyo & Eth, 1985; Cervantes, Salgado de Snyder, & Padilla, 1988; Rodríguez & Urrutia-Rojas, 1990).

Until recently, it has generally been held that Latinos underuse mental health services, perhaps preferring indigenous systems of care, such as *curanderismo* from the Mexican tradition and *espiritismo* from Puerto Rico. Latinos have a long history of developing various approaches to the treatment of people suffering from psychological problems, and as stated by Moore and Pachón (1985),

> Hispanics brought with them an indigenous system of health and mental health personnel. Further, some researchers argue that the Hispanic social structure provides its people with support and protection that seems to diminish the frequency of certain types of mental illness. (p. 158)

However, although natural social support networks (friends, family, and the church) are clearly important to Latino families, and although earlier studies suggest that some Latinos might prefer to seek assistance from indigenous practitioners, such as *curanderas,* geographical and "functional" barriers have been the major obstacles to mental health service use by Latinos in the United States (Chávez, 1986; Moore & Pachón, 1985).

Quality, affordable, mental health services are scarce, particularly in low-income communities, and receipt of services by Latinos has been one half or less than their representation in the population. Historically, Latinos who have had contact with the mental health system have been more likely to be misdiagnosed, admitted into psychiatric hospitals, or treated with medication and less likely to receive longer-term outpatient psychotherapy than non-Hispanic Whites. On the other hand, when outpatient services are made geographically and logistically accessible (e.g., flexible service hours), affordable, and culturally relevant (e.g., with bilingual and bicultural service providers), there appears to be no lack of use (Moore & Pachón, 1985; Morales & Salcido, 1992).

Overall, Latino families continue to face multiple barriers to obtaining quality mental health services, despite evidence of need. The problems of deficient funding and a shortage of accessible, quality services are exacerbated by a lack of Latino mental health professionals and cross-cultural training for other providers. Furthermore, a major barrier is insufficient knowledge on Latino mental health in general, with regard to assessment and diagnosis, psychopathology, reactions to stress, coping responses and related developmental issues, particularly among children and adolescents and across the diverse Latino populations (Vega, Warheit, & Meinhardt, 1985).

MATERNAL AND CHILD HEALTH

Overall, Latino women have higher fertility rates and tend to begin childbearing at younger ages than the general population. They are also less likely to use health services or to have public or private insurance. Among all racial and ethnic groups, Latinas are the least likely to use prenatal care. In 1987, the percentages of women receiving late (in the third trimester) or no prenatal care at all were 12.7% and 11.1% for Latinas and African American women, respectively, compared with 5% for non-Hispanic White women (U.S. Department of Health and Human Services, 1991). Among poor and racial and ethnic women, about 60% initiate care in the first trimester compared to 80% of the general population. Compared to women who receive timely prenatal care, women who do not receive prenatal care are three times more likely to deliver low-birthweight infants, and their infants are five times more likely to die in the first year of life (U.S. Department of Health and Human Services, 1991).

Patterns of use of prenatal care vary by Hispanic subgroup. Puerto Rican women are the most likely to receive late or no prenatal care (17%), followed by Central American (13.5%) and Mexican-origin (13%) women (U.S. Department of Health and Human Services, 1991). Several studies have demonstrated that Mexican-born women are the least likely of all groups in California to begin prenatal care during the first trimester. Among Mexican-origin women, Mexican-born women were less likely to initiate care in the first trimester than either African American or Mexican American women (Zambrana, Hernandez, Scrimshaw, & Dunkel-Schetter, 1991). Mexican immigrant women confront a number of barriers to prenatal care: low income; low education; limited financial access to prenatal care programs, including pregnancy-related social services; monolingual Spanish speaking; and the stressors of being immigrant, and undocumented.

However, although they are far less likely to begin prenatal care in the first trimester, Latina women have rates of low birthweight comparable to non-Hispanic White women. In 1987, the percentages of low birthweight among Mexican, Cuban, and Central and South American infants ranged from 5.7% to 5.9% compared to 5.6% for non-Hispanic Whites. The low birthweight rate among Puerto Rican infants was 9.3 per 1,000. Although they are at relatively low risk of low birthweight, Latino infants are at greater risk of being born prematurely. The preterm rates (infants born at less than 37 weeks of completed gestation) in 1987 were 9% for Cuban women, 12.6% for Puerto Rican women, and 11.% for Mexican-origin women, compared to 8.5% for non-Hispanic White women (U.S. Department of Health and Human Services, 1991).

Several studies have found that the generational status (or nativity) of the mother is an important predictor of low birthweight. U.S.-born (second-generation) Mexican-origin women were more likely than Mexican-born women to give birth to infants under 2,500 grams. This occurred despite the fact that, compared to Mexican-born women, U.S.-born women had higher education levels, better incomes, and higher health care use rates (Guendelman, Gould, Hudes, & Eskenazi, 1990). Cultural practices, such as abstention from substances, have been found to serve as protective factors and contribute to more favorable pregnancy outcome. Overall, Latinas are more likely to abstain from the use of drugs, alcohol, and cigarettes than women of other racial and ethnic groups (U.S. Department of Health and Human Services, 1991). However, second-generation Mexican-origin and Puerto Rican women are more likely than Mexican-born women to smoke or use alcohol and drugs (Guendelman et al., 1990). These differences in use of substances, combined with different family structure arrangements (that is, increases in women without partners) may explain the generational differences in low birthweight.

CHILD HEALTH

The overall health profile of Latino children reflects their tendency to be poorer and to live in "severely distressed" environmental conditions. Compared to other U.S. children, Latino children are less likely to have health insurance, to receive routine medical checkups, to have a source of health care, or to be immunized for infant and childhood diseases. They are also five times more likely to be involved in accidental injury and half as likely as non-Hispanic White children to have seen a dentist by age 11 (Children's Defense Fund, 1991b).

Less than half of poor Latino children are covered by public health insurance. In a national study of barriers to care for children, it was found that only 27.8% of Latino children were covered by Medicaid, about 40% reported some form of private insurance, and almost one third reported no insurance (Cornelius, 1993). An examination of data regarding older children from the 1984 National Health Interview Survey revealed that compared to non-Hispanic Whites, Latino adolescents are nearly three times as likely to be uninsured. That year, 30% of Latino adolescents and 44% of Latino young adults were completely uninsured (Lieu, Newacheck, & McManus, 1993).

Due to their low immunization rates, Latino children are at higher risk than non-Hispanic White children for such preventable illnesses as pertussis, tetanus, polio, diphtheria, measles, and rubella. The U.S. childhood vaccination programs (polio, DPT, measles) have not been made available to significant numbers of low-income racial and ethnic children in the last 10 years. The national rate in 1985 for adequate immunization of 2-year-olds was 44% compared to 25% for Latino 2-year-olds in California (Lazarus & Gonzalez, 1989). A possible consequence has been a measles epidemic; 25,000 cases have been identified since 1988, and more than 60 deaths were recorded in 1990 alone. The children most at risk of morbidity and possible mortality from these preventable diseases are low-income African American and Hispanic children under the age of 5 (National Vaccine Advisory Committee, 1991). In a study of hospital admission rates in Los Angeles County, low-income areas (which are heavily populated by Latinos and African Americans) were more likely than high-income areas to have hospital admission rates for conditions that could have been treated early in a primary-care setting. Latino and African American children living in poor areas were much more likely than non-Hispanic White children living in affluent areas to be hospitalized for pneumonia, bronchitis, asthma, gastroenteritis, and ear infections (Valdez & Dallek, 1991). Finally, higher rates of obesity have been reported among Latino school-age children in comparison with non-Latinos (U.S. Department of Health and Human Services, 1991).

PATTERNS OF USE OF HEALTH SERVICES

Overall, Latino families tend *not* to have a regular source of health care, are more likely to use emergency-room services for primary care, and are more likely to delay care for both themselves and their children (Valdez, Giachello, Rodríguez-Trias, Gomez, & De La Rocha, 1993). The primary barriers to use of health services for Latino families have been identified as lack of child care, lack of transportation, lack of knowledge of where to go for care, and lack of health insurance and/or ability to pay. Lack of health insurance is a burden disproportionately carried by Latino families (Trevino, Moyer, Valdez, & Stroup-Benham, 1991). This is no more clearly evident than in the significantly high number of Latinos without health insurance. Hispanics represented only 8.4% of Medicaid beneficiaries in 1986, and Medicaid covered only about 46% of the eligible poor (U.S. Department of Health and Human Services, 1991). Intergroup differences indicated that nationwide, 35% of Mexican Americans, 29% of Cuban Americans, and 22% of Puerto Ricans are uninsured (Trevino et al., 1991).

Literature on the health use patterns of Latinos suggests that youth and children underuse health services and, consequently, are at high risk of health problems. Compared to non-Hispanic White children and their parents, Mexican American children and their parents are less likely to use such services as routine medical checkups, family planning, prenatal care, and dental and eye examinations. An analysis of national data found that 25.2% of uninsured Hispanic children did not have a usual source of care, and only 10.6% of these uninsured children had made at least one routine visit to a physician in 1987 (Cornelius, 1993). Little is known about the health care patterns of older Latino children; however, school-age children have been found most at risk of medical underuse. Furthermore, underuse of preventive health care services by Hispanic women is reflected in the increase in rates of breast cancer and the high incidence and mortality rates of cervical cancer (Valdez, Delgado, Cervantes, & Bowler, 1993).

The data show that Latinos tend to underuse or delay care. However, when barriers to care are reduced, the limited knowledge available suggests that Latinos, like other groups, place a high value on health, seek health care services as needed, and comply with the medical regimen if it is explained, understood, and economically accessible. Culturally, Latino families value the importance of health care professionals and do not systematically use folk healers over medical providers. In fact, a recent analysis of the HHANES data showed that only 4% of adult Mexican Americans interviewed reported that they had consulted a curandero or folk healer within the previous 12 months (Higgenbotham, Trevino, & Ray, 1990). On the other hand, Latinos, like other families, do use informal sources of health care information. These sources tend to be extended family members, especially mothers and mothers-in-law, close female friends, and husbands. These intra- and intergenerational networks serve important functions in transmitting positive health beliefs and attitudes, as well as referrals to community providers.

Over the past decade, the health status of Latinos has deteriorated as poverty rates have increased and as human service programs have become more stringent in their eligibility criteria and/or funds for programs have been cut. Inadequate health insurance coverage for Latino families and children contributes to lack of appropriate use of preventive and primary care services, lack of a usual source of care, and increased risk for acute and chronic illnesses such as pneumonia, asthma, and diabetes. Early detection of treatable conditions, such as breast cancer and hypertension, is less likely. An analysis of the health status of low-income, Latino families shows that poverty, psychosocial stressors, behavioral risk or lifestyle behaviors, and environmental conditions contribute to poorer health status and less access to institutional resources (Lillie-Blanton et al., 1993). Socioeconomic indicators and institutional barriers, rather than cultural and ethnic-specific factors, explain the patterns of health use and risk in Latino populations.

HEALTH BEHAVIORS, CHRONIC DISEASE PATTERNS, AND MORTALITY RATES

Recent analyses of intragroup data show significant differences in morbidity and mortality rates (Desenclos & Hahn, 1992). The disproportionate share of illness and mortality burdens experienced by Puerto Rican and Mexican-origin groups reflects their low socioeconomic status in comparison to Cuban and other Hispanic groups. Health behaviors or behavioral risk factors have a significant relationship to chronic disease patterns and mortality. Latinos tend to engage in a range of moderate lifestyle behaviors, although there are differences by nativity, gender, and generational status. Overall, the data suggest that Latino immigrants, particularly Mexican immigrants, tend to exhibit more positive lifestyle behaviors than the native born. Such lifestyle behaviors may be major contributors to better infant health, longer life spans, and lower incidences of heart disease and certain forms of cancer (Hayes-Bautista, 1990; Scribner & Dwyer, 1989; Valdez, Delgado, et al., 1993).

Health behaviors such as diet, exercise, and use of alcohol, tobacco, and other drugs are linked to socioeconomic status and morbidity and mortality pattern. Current thinking views health behaviors and practices as individual choices, with limited recognition of the influence of stress, poverty, environmental conditions, and knowledge and beliefs regarding health practices. There has been a tendency to hold individuals responsible for behaviors that are greatly influenced by institutional and societal failures. For example, poverty is highly correlated with poor nutrition, unemployment, multiple jobs for low pay, or exposure to environmental dangers, which may in turn decrease preventive health behaviors such as exercise.

An accurate and comprehensive review of Latino patterns of substance use is limited by lack of data. However, substance use among Latinos represents a growing health care issue. Alcohol use represents a serious behavioral risk factor in Hispanic communities, especially among the Mexican American and Puerto Rican male population (Austin & Gilbert, 1989). Overall, Mexican American men abuse alcohol 5.5 times more frequently than other drugs, compared to non-Hispanic Whites. Furthermore, liver disease is the sixth leading cause of death among Latinos, and Latino elderly are twice as likely to die from cirrhosis of the liver as non-Hispanic Whites. Evidence suggests a higher prevalence of frequent and heavy drinking among U.S.-born Latino males and females than among immigrants (Valdez, Delgado, et al., 1993). Hispanic women generally appear to be less at risk for alcohol problems than women in general; however, the amount of drinking and incidence of heavy drinking are increasing among young and acculturated Mexican American women (Austin & Gilbert, 1989).

Smoking prevalence among Latino populations is higher than among the non-Hispanic White population, specifically among Latino adult and adolescent males, but it is lower than among the African American population. Overall it appears that Cuban men, ages 25-34, and Puerto Rican women, ages 25-54, have higher rates of smoking and higher consumption of cigarettes than other Hispanic subgroups (U.S. Department of Health and Human Services, 1991). On the other hand, many Hispanic females never smoke, and, if they do they begin smoking at a later age, they smoke fewer cigarettes and are more likely to quit. Tobacco use rates among Latinas have been far lower than those of non-Hispanic White and African American women, although with acculturation, researchers have noted an increasing number of young Hispanic female smokers. Paralleling the increase in tobacco use has been a marked increase in the rates of lung cancer and other pulmonary diseases, especially among Latino males (Maxwell & Jacobson, 1989; Valdez, Delgado, et al., 1993).

Regarding other drug use among Latinos, reliable data are even more limited and vary by subgroup and gender. Contrary to the stereotype, the prevalence of other drug use does not seem to vary substantially by race and ethnicity. Among Latinos, 17% of the men and 11.7% of the women reported use of illicit drugs in 1990. However, the type of drugs used and the method of use seems to vary. African Americans and Latinos are more likely to use cocaine and crack cocaine than non-Hispanic Whites. For both males and females, current and lifetime use of crack is higher among African Americans and Latinos. In addition, emergency-room data indicate that Latinos are more likely to report primary presenting problems with heroin, PCP, or cocaine than non-Hispanic Whites. Mexican Americans appear to have higher rates of marijuana and other drug use than other Latino groups. On the other hand, Mexican immigrants are less likely to have a diagnosis of drug abuse/dependence compared to non-Hispanic Whites (U.S. Department of Health and Human Services, 1991).

Related to the use of drugs is the prevalence of HIV/AIDS among the Latino population. Latinos accounted for 16% of all AIDS cases between 1982 and 1992. By 1989, 40% of Latino AIDS cases were related to the use of intravenous drugs and 7% to homosexual/bisexual male contact and intravenous drug use. Nationwide, Puerto Ricans had the highest incidence of AIDS related to intravenous drug use. As of 1992, Hispanic women represented 21% of all women diagnosed with AIDS, and Hispanic men accounted for 16% of all men so diagnosed. Among children, 25% of all children with AIDS are Latino. As of 1991, AIDS was the fifth leading cause of death among Latinos. The risk of contracting AIDS for Latinos is 2.8 times higher than for non-Hispanic Whites. The cumulative incidence of AIDS among Hispanic women is 8.1 times higher than for non-Hispanic women. The majority of cases among women and children are reportedly related to intravenous drug use by the women's partners (Office of Minority Health, 1990). Latinas as a group tend to be sexually conservative with respect to the number of past sexual partners and age at sexual initiation. Recent Latina immigrants tend to be the most sexually conservative, followed by bilingual Latinas, and then non-Hispanic White women. However, sexual practices are clearly related to the prevalence of AIDS and other sexually transmitted diseases. In one study, approximately half of the Latinas reported rarely or never using contraceptive birth control measures. The use of contraception and other protective sexual practices was highly related to educational level, age, and traditional values (Rapkin & Erickson, 1990).

Nutrition and diet are other important areas where limited information is available for Latino groups. However, the research suggests that obesity, which is related to high blood pressure, high cholesterol, and diabetes, among other health problems, is a relatively serious problem among certain Latino groups, especially among women. Data from the HHANES study found that between 30% and 40% of Puerto Rican, Cuban, and Mexican-origin women were overweight, compared to just under 25% of a comparable sample of non-Hispanic White women. Cuban Americans were found to have the highest percentage of overweight men, almost 30%, in comparison to 24% of non-Hispanic White men and 19% of Mexican Americans.

Data from the same study also showed relatively high rates of anemia among Latinos, 17% to 25%, irrespective of gender and age. In addition, there is some preliminary evidence that Latinos tend to do less overall physical exercise than other U.S. racial/ethnic groups and to consume more fast food and cola soft drinks than other groups, further contributing to their diet-related health problems. Furthermore, at the same time that death and disease related to alcohol, tobacco, and poor nutrition are increasing within the Latino communities, so are efforts by the producers of these commodities to target Latino consumers through major advertising campaigns (Maxwell & Jacobson, 1989; Valdez, Delgado, et al., 1993).

Overall, the leading causes of death for Latinos in order of frequency are heart disease (25%), cancer (17%), nonintentional injuries (9%), stroke (6%) and homicide (5%). Liver disease, pneumonia/influenza, diabetes, HIV infection, and perinatal conditions each account for 3% of mortality. However, the actual prevalence of diabetes among Latinos is much higher than the mortality rates might suggest, because most diabetics die from complications of the diabetes, primarily heart and kidney disease. Latino males are more likely than non-Hispanic White males to die as a result of homicide, unintentional injuries, cirrhosis, and infections. The low overall rate of mortality among Latinas, in comparison to non-Hispanic White females, is related to lower rates of suicide and unintentional injuries. However, although the incidence of breast cancer is significantly lower among Latinas, they are 2.4 times more likely to die from both cervical and breast cancer, due to limited knowledge of early symptoms of the disease and limited access to preventive and primary care. Furthermore, the burden of premature mortality varies widely by Latino subgroup. Mortality rates are highest for Puerto Ricans, followed by Mexican-origin persons and Cubans (Desenclos & Hahn, 1992).

The socioeconomic characteristics of the Latino population represent a set of shared risk attributes with other poor and racial/ethnic groups in the United States. The correlates of poverty, such as poor housing, lower educational attainment, inadequate nutrition, use of substances, and unsafe and poor quality environmental conditions, all contribute to the higher prevalence of both acute and chronic health conditions (Adler, Boyce, Chesney, Folkman, & Syme, 1993). Latinos of higher socioeconomic status, as defined by education and income, have health care patterns similar to the general population. The data suggest that the overall well-being and health status of Latinos are being adversely affected by their lack of access to quality health care services, as well as other supportive human service programs.

Obstacles in Promoting Latino Family Health

The dramatic increase and the diversity in Latino populations in the United States, coupled with their lack of access to health care and public social service resources, constitute a serious policy concern. Latino health and human service needs require serious consideration and attention from legal scholars, health and human service practitioners, and policymakers. The issues encompass both institutional changes and family-focused efforts. Although increased attention has been directed at public health policy and welfare reform in the 1990s, Latinos, as an emerging culturally distinct population, have received little or no attention. This results from the commonplace assumption that "all minorities suffer from the same problems and have the same needs" (Hayes-Bautista, 1990).

Recent scholarly developments and data on the unique health and human services needs of Latino families and children provide a relevant base from which to shape appropriate, effective, and responsive services for Latinos (Furino, 1992; U.S. Department of Health and Human Services, 1993). In effect, what is abundantly clear is that health promotion involves improving the standard of living and is the most important area of public health policy in this decade. Terris (1990) succinctly states the core of the solution:

> The concept of health promotion refers to the development of healthful living standards. These have a profound effect on positive health, which is not only a subjective state of well-being (including such elements as vitality, freedom from excess fatigue, and freedom from environmental discomforts such as excessive heat, cold, smog and noise), but also has a functional component, namely the ability of an individual to participate effectively in society; at work; at home, and in the community. (p. 285)

Improvements in the standard of living are crucial to Latino families and children, but equally important is access to primary and preventive services. All current data on use of public health and social service programs show that Latino families and children are not receiving needed services due to lack of awareness of services, lack of understanding of eligibility, and sociocultural and language barriers that impede access. Ginzberg (1991) states:

> Many Hispanics are poorly positioned to access the health care system by virtue of below average family income, above average employment

in establishments that do not regularly provide health insurance and a sizeable number who live in states with low Medicaid enrollments. (p. 238)

In addition, immigration status and the effects of differential eligibility within a single family are economically and psychologically damaging to Latinos. Immigration status is an obstacle to health care access, and clearly an obstacle to maximizing contributions to society. For example, differential definitions of *resident* for purposes of eligibility for county-funded services lead to inequitable access to health and family-support resources.

Another significant barrier is the severe underrepresentation of Latinos in the health and social service professions. Within the overall context of an oversupply of medical professional personnel, the system has failed to provide support, financial or affirmative, for health professionals who are bilingual and bicultural. Recent data from the Association of American Medical Colleges note that Latino enrollment in U.S. medical schools is a meager 1.7% for Mexican Americans, 2% for Puerto Ricans, and 1.7% for "other Hispanics" (Ginzberg, 1991). In our view, two potential pools of health personnel must be incorporated into the existing health care delivery system if we are to be responsive to the Latino community: the native-born Latino provider and the Foreign Medical Graduate (FMG). For native-born providers, the issues of affirmative action, recruitment, admissions, and retention to medical and related health professional schools remain salient. A vital program in the effort to increase the Latino physician supply is the National Health Service Corps, a mechanism to recruit and train Latino physicians in conjunction with the Hispanic Centers of Excellence in medical schools throughout the country. If training and educational resources were allocated for Latino health-service providers, this would represent an important commitment on the part of the United States to provide primary-care services in a culturally acceptable way to Latinos in the United States. The licensure of FMGs remains a legal limbo filled with unlicensed but trained personnel. This important and vital resource has remained unused within the Latino community.

The current health care and human service systems continue a long-standing tradition of unresponsiveness and ineffectiveness in addressing the needs and concerns of vulnerable and at-risk populations. A national health insurance program linked with a family income maintenance program and a child-care program can strengthen families, rather than serve to debilitate them. Furthermore, we need a focus on preventing problems, not on repairing the damage of neglect. These programs must be designed as an integrated system to provide comprehensive, family-focused, culturally and linguistically appropriate, community-based linked networks of health and human services, guided by the principles of prevention and primary-care interventions (Darder et al., 1993; Latino Coalition for a Healthy California, 1993).

This commitment requires reflection on our values as a nation. Current health and human service legislation must seek to redress the current inequities. Latinos bear a persistent and disproportionate burden of morbidity and mortality. In effect, Latinos, who have limited economic resources, confront extraordinary financial and sociocultural barriers to obtaining minimal health and human services. Current patterns set the foundation for a new generation of Latinos, who will continue to experience the adverse social, psychological, and medical effects of living in a society that denies them adequate access to health care and child and family welfare services. With certainty, it can be argued that Latino families and children have not elected to be economically and socially disadvantaged, but rather that the society in which they live has made that choice for them.

9

Social Science Theorizing
for Latino Families in
the Age of Diversity

MAXINE BACA ZINN

In the last two decades of the 20th century, the United States has
once again become a nation of immigrants. This population transition is taking place in a historical context that has included the
restructuring of the U.S. economy and the advent of a more conservative political climate. Immense changes in American life, together
with a great influx of people from around the world, have created a
nation of diversity.

The flux of these changes has a special bearing on families. In a
highly charged intellectual climate, social critics lamenting the state
of the family often assert that the emerging array of alternatives
weakens and undermines society (Briemelow, 1992; Popenoe, 1988;
Whitehead, 1992, 1993). Diverse family arrangements now place a
special spotlight on racial/ethnics[1] and non-European immigrants
(Fukuyama, 1993). As minorities become an ever larger share of the
U.S. population, the ability to understand the new social diversity will
become a central task within family studies.

Latinos are at the epicenter of several transformations that are
changing our conceptions of the family. This chapter addresses some
pressing theoretical issues for studying Latino families in light of the
demographic shift from an Anglo-European society to a multiracial,
multicultural society. Although research of the past two decades has

disputed many distortions of the past, the social and political changes now sweeping the country pose new intellectual challenges. Current social changes require renewed efforts to dislodge dominant thinking about Latino families.

This chapter identifies ongoing currents in social science thinking about Latino families. The following questions are posed:

1. What social science themes in family studies have shaped our visions?
2. To what extent has the revisioning of the Latino family during the past two decades touched the mainstream of family studies?
3. Why are certain troublesome themes about Latinos and other racial/ethnic families resurfacing today?
4. How can we avoid the pitfalls of earlier theories in understanding various Hispanic groups?
5. What further changes does the ongoing reconstruction of Latino families face?
6. How can we apply our new knowledge about Latinos and other racial/ethnics where it belongs—at the core of family theory?

Conventional Social Science Frameworks

The formal academic study of Latino families in the United States originated in the context of immigration and social problems. Much of our thinking about Latino families today is muddled by concepts and ideas that emerged during the late 19th and early 20th centuries. During this time, sociologists concluded that Mexican immigration, settlement, and poverty created problems in developing U.S. urban centers. The new field of "family study" emerged out of a deep fundamental belief in the need to document and ameliorate social problems (Thomas & Wilcox, 1987). The field of family studies has a tradition of being heavily normative, moralistic, and mingled with social policy and the social objectives of various action groups. Furthermore, it lacks a strong tradition of theory (Morgan, 1975).

The underlying assumptions in mainstream family scholarship produced a deeply flawed framework that misrepresented the family experiences of Latinos and other racial/ethnics by using a dominant family form as the normative experience for all. This framework was fused with and embedded in prevailing theories of race relations. Both fields were strongly influenced by the Chicago School of Sociology.

The dominant paradigms of assimilation and modernization guided and shaped research. Race relations' preoccupation with "traditional" and "modern" forms of social organization joined family sociology's preoccupation with the nuclear family, its wage-earner father and domestic-earner mother. This explained the different family arrangements of Latinos and other immigrants. Compared to mainstream families, they were analyzed as traditional *cultural forms.* Studies of Mexican immigrants highlighted certain *ethnic lifestyles* that were said to produce social disorganization. Structural conditions were rarely a concern. Instead, researchers examined (a) their foreign patterns and habits, (b) the moral quality of family relationships, and (c) the prospects for their Americanization (Bogardus, 1934).

As transplants from traditional societies, the immigrants and their children were thought to be at odds with social requirements in new industrial settings. Their family arrangements were treated as cultural exceptions to the rule of standard family development. Their slowness to acculturate and take on Western patterns of family development left them behind, as other families in American society modernized. They were peripheral to the standard family and viewed as problems because of their failure to adopt the family patterns of the mainstream (Baca Zinn, 1990). Social reforms of the times favored the "modern" family (nuclear in form with women in the home), as a way of combating social problems. (Even today, conservatives uphold this family ideal.)

In family studies, the twin pillars of modernization and assimilation influenced the main currents of thought and types of preoccupations through the 1950s, when functionalist theories came to prevail. Using a framework that took one type of family (by no means the only form, even then) and making it "the normal family" (Boss & Thorne, 1989), functionalism intensified the social science misinterpretation of Latino families. With its emphasis on fixed boundaries and a fixed division of labor, this normal family type presented a stark contrast with the familistic and traditional Mexican family of anthropological research (Heller, 1966; Madsen, 1964; Rubel, 1966).

Rethinking Latino Families

An extensive body of revisionist scholarship has reshaped our thinking about Latino families.[2] The new research developed with two major objectives. The first was reinterpreting Mexican-origin family life by uncovering new information about the history of these people and by analyzing their experiences with an "insider's" perspective. The second, an outgrowth of the first, has involved correcting social science generalizations about Latino families and ultimately about various aspects of family life in general.

Beginning with a critique of functionalist accounts of Mexican-heritage families as dysfunctional units that acted as barriers to individual and group mobility (Heller, 1966; Madsen, 1964; Rubel, 1966; Staples & Mirandé, 1980), scholars produced studies showing that alternative family patterns do not reflect deviance, deficiency, or disorganization. Instead of representing outmoded cultural forms handed down from generation to generation, Mexican family lifestyles often reflect adaptive responses to social and economic conditions. What were once labeled culturally deficient family patterns may now be viewed as family strategies that serve as solutions to constraints imposed by economic and social structures in the wider society.

Although the long-standing interest in cultural patterning in family life continues alongside a "social adaptation" approach, greater attention is now given to the social situations and contexts that affect Latino families (Vega, 1990). Structural approaches explore the close connections between the internal dynamics of family life and external conditions, such as changing labor markets and political systems. In the 1980s the frameworks shifted

> from a stereotypic model of family life, characterized by rigidity, authoritarianism, and a patriarchal structure, to a social adaptation perspective based on themes of family metamorphoses, resilience, flexibility, and cohesion in the face of changing social environments and economic circumstances. (Berardo, 1991, p. 6)

Connecting the New Body of Research on Latino Families With Other Revisionist Traditions

Latino family studies should be recognized as a vital thread in the overall family revisioning effort because the field has developed within and alongside other emergent social science discourses. Social history, feminism, and race and ethnic studies have offered unique challenges to past traditions of family thought. All together, these bodies of scholarship have produced new descriptions of family dynamics and identified new topics for investigation. Central to all of the scholarship is the strategy of "moving beneath and around the family as a unit of analysis" (Thorne, 1992, p. 12). Like other revisionist strands, this strategy has generated a proliferation of studies showing that Latino families are shaped by social and economic forces of particular times and particular places. As Zavella (1991) puts it, "household arrangements originate in the transition of larger social forces" (p. 318). This has produced a notable shift from earlier preoccupations with culture to the contemporary investigation of families and their encompassing social conditions.

The following themes capture some of the most important thinking in revisionist family scholarship and its infusion in Latino family studies.

1. *Conventional social science frameworks have falsely universalized the family.* What has long been upheld as normal was, in fact, only one of many family forms produced by uneven social and economic patterns of development occurring in society. Although long defined as the rule, the standard family was never the norm nor the dominant family type. It was, however, the measure against which other families were judged (Baca Zinn & Eitzen, 1993b).

2. *Families are socially constructed.* This means that they are not merely biological arrangements; nor are they the products of ethnic culture alone. Instead, families are shaped by specific historical, social, and material conditions. In challenging the assumption that minority family arrangements are merely the result of cultural or ethnic variations, researchers have discovered that many Latino family patterns are distinctive because their social settings produce and may even require diverse arrangements.

3. *Families are closely connected with other structures and institutions in society.* Rather than being separate spheres, they cannot be understood in isolation from outside structures. This has directed attention to basic social divisions and structures of power. Whereas the importance of economic factors in making a living and hence shaping family life has long been acknowledged in family research, other structural forces have been invisible. Along with social class,

gender and race are structured inequalities producing widely varying experiences of family life (Thorne, 1992).

4. *Gender is a basic organizing principle of society that shapes families in historically specific ways.* Making gender a basic category of analysis has profoundly altered family studies in general, and it has advanced research on Latino families as well. Latino family research has long been preoccupied with women's and men's differentiated family experiences. No assumption about Latino families is more deeply ingrained than that of male dominance. But cultural frameworks explained male dominance as traditional patriarchy; that is, an ethnic or machismo family dynamic. Although gender inequality remains an important theme, two developments have provided new explanations of male dominance. The first wave of studies conducted in the 1970s and 1980s challenged the distorted descriptions of macho-dominated Mexican-origin families (Baca Zinn, 1980; Ybarra, 1982). Often referred to as the "revisionist works" (Zavella, 1987), these studies found that Mexican American families exhibited many different patterns of marital decision making, including a patriarchal, role-segregated pattern and egalitarian patterns, with many combinations in between. In that early period, our engagement with questions about gender in Chicano families was very different from later approaches; nevertheless the questions we engaged were feminist.

The second wave of feminist research on Latino families was strongly influenced by the shift from the study of *sex roles* to the study of *gendered institutions* (Acker, 1992). This line of analysis has led Latina feminists, in dialogue with other branches of feminist thinking, to investigate how women's family lives are bound up with a broader system of gender inequality. Latinas' subordination, like that of other women, is rooted in the "pervasive social ordering of human activities, practices, and social structures in terms of differentiation between women and men" (Acker, 1992, p. 567). In conjunction with class and race inequalities, this ubiquitous gender order produces Latino family arrangements that constrain women in particular ways. Zavella's (1991) study of Chicano families is exemplary in its exploration of the close connections between women's family lives and economic conditions as they are bound up with a broader system of inequality. Others, too, have offered new insights about how specific structural inequalities make the family experiences of Latinas and Latinos different from other women and men. From motherhood (Segura & Pierce, 1993) to household decision making (Pesquera, 1993) to migration (Hondagueau-Sotelo, 1992), gender inequalities intersect with race, ethnicity, and social class to shape family life.

5. *Racial stratification is a powerful shaper of family life.* Like the class and gender hierarchies, racial stratification is a fundamental organizing principle of social relationships in U.S. society (Omi & Winant, 1986). Although social science has tended to treat race as fixed, we now have a better understanding of how racial categories change over time. New patterns of immigration are making the end of the 20th century a period in which our conceptions of racial categories are being dramatically transformed. Omi and Winant (1986) call this "racial formation," meaning that society assigns different worth and unequal treatment to groups on the basis of its definition of race. Racial formation touches people throughout society, not just those who are subordinated. This racial formation perspective offers important insights and challenging avenues for studying Latino families, because Latinos are not simply an ethnic group but an integral component within the U.S. racial hierarchy. Racial inequalities place families in different social locations, giving some greater access to resources and rewards and denying or limiting access to these same conditions for others.

I have pushed for a reconstruction of family theory through incorporating race as a dimension of social structure rather than merely an expression of cultural differences (Baca Zinn, 1990, 1994). Several formidable problems remain in applying this perspective to Latinos. In conventional thought and even in much social science, race is treated as if it were the property only of African Americans, or of African Americans and Whites. This biracial or dichotomous thinking (Collins, 1990) is one of the reasons for the long-standing invisibility of Latinos in social science. Bonilla (1990, p. 215) has called this "The American Dilemma of Latinos." In Gunnar Myrdal's classic on the sociology of race, *An American Dilemma*, Bonilla found practically no references to Latinos. The four decades following publication of that classic have consistently left Latinos out of the race relations analysis.

The perspective of Latinos as an ethnic group—simply another variant of standard ethnic immigrants—has long held sway in mainstream sociology. Despite the fact that "the single biggest change facing the United States is the increasing racial and ethnic diversity of its population" (Landry, 1991, p. 206), public discussions about "the new politics of race" (as well as the pervasive images in mainstream family theory) remain couched in images of Black and White.

To be sure, mainstream scholarship on race and ethnicity acknowledges that Latinos are structurally denied those opportunities that are available to White people. In other words, scholars know that Latinos fare poorly in the social order, that dramatic shifts in the population will render Latinos the largest minority in only half a decade, and that these trends portend new forms of social inequality and ethnic conflict.

Federal data sources classify Latinos as an ethnic category, not a race. However, classifying information by "race and Hispanic-origin" does not help us think about Latinos as being situated in a changing racial hierarchy. The U.S. Bureau of the Census has recently acknowledged the limitations of a White, non-White division and the need to move beyond this division. The current system of classifying information on Hispanics is in need of reassessment and refinement to more accurately reflect a diverse society (Lott, 1993). Current shifts in the composition of the U.S. population are producing a multiracial society that bears little resemblance to the way things once were. Race is not just about tensions, conflicts, and negotiations between Black and White; rather, racial politics entail further hierarchies of domination and subordination.

Applying the racial formation perspective to Latinos is complicated. Latinos are "racially heterogeneous populations made up of a variety of racial ancestries: Europeans, Africans, Amerindians, Asians, and various mixtures thereof" (Massey, 1993a, p. 8). Latinos do not possess a single unifying racial identity. Nevertheless, they are distinguished as a social category and dominated within a racial hierarchy. This last point is important because the crucial aspect of any racial category is that the distinguishing characteristics are *socially* defined.

The racial order works with and through the class system to determine opportunities for making a living, and hence for family well-being. Of course, we cannot speak of Latino families as a universal category. Not only do Latinos represent a diverse collection of national origin groups, they occupy many social statuses. Latinos are divided along the same lines that divide all families. Race, class, gender, nationality, and sexual orientation intersect with each other to produce a variety of Latino family experiences. Still, within these hierarchies, most Latinos are forced to acquire their life necessities in locations that are far removed from society's opportunity structures. One of the most important ways racial stratification penetrates and shapes households is in determining the kind of work people do and the wages they receive. Racialized economic contexts have created similar opportunities for people of color. Composite portraits of people of color show them to have family configurations that differ from those of White Americans. Although each group is distinguishable from the others, Latinos, African Americans, and Asians share some important commonalities (Glenn & Yap, 1993). These include an extended kinship structure and informal support networks spread across multiple households.

How Revisioning Traditions
Can Enlarge Family Studies

Using macrostructural inequalities to contextualize family life has given us new understandings of why Latino families exhibit distinctive configurations. We know that race, class, and gender inequalities create varied patterns in the way families and individuals are located and embedded in different social environments. Those environments structure social opportunities differently, and they position groups in systematic ways. Such findings and insights are not limited to Latino families. Instead the family experiences of Latinos and other racial/ethnics require a rethinking of family life in general.

Stratifying forces in U.S. society structure family life in fundamentally different ways. Today we have the analytic frameworks to reshape the basic assumptions and concepts of family studies by showing how all families are affected by interconnected systems of social inequality. The family that mainstream social science has upheld as standard is no less a product of social structure and culture; it emerged as a result of social and economic conditions that are no longer operative for most Americans and that never were operative for many poor Americans and racial/ethnics. From the original settlement of the American colonies through the mid-20th century, families of European descent often received economic and social supports to establish and maintain families (Dill, Baca Zinn, & Patton, 1993).

Rather than being an expression of group-specific differences alone, family diversity in the United States is an outgrowth of distinctive patterns in the way families and their members are embedded in environments with varying opportunities, resources, and rewards. (The following is adapted from Baca Zinn & Eitzen, 1993b.) These differences have enormous effects on the quality of marital relations, on the size of families, on lifestyles and life chances. Social locations, not cultural differences, are the key to understanding family differences. Favored positions in the racial and class hierarchies offer advantages and supports that are unavailable to those in less favorable social locations. Although the structures of race, class, and gender create disadvantages for some, they provide unacknowledged benefits for those who are at the top of their hierarchies—non-Hispanic Whites, members of the upper classes, and males. In addition, the availability of privilege for those at the top of their hierarchy is dependent on those at the bottom. This approach decenters and problematizes advantaged families rather than treating them as the norm.

Establishing a critical perspective in which systems of race, class, and gender differently shape families will make other contributions to family theory. For example, an important theme within several bodies of revisionist scholarship is that women and men create meaningful lives for themselves and their families. Despite severe structural constraints, they forge strategies that help them survive, resist, and cope. The study of Latinos offers fertile ground to explore not only *pathogenic* but *salutogenic* responses (Portes & Rumbaut, 1990, p. 144) of individuals and their families to limited opportunities. This is not meant to create mythical images of family life among subordinated peoples. Poor immigrant and racial minority families were and are found in contradictory settings of conflict as well as survival.

Excluding Latinos and other racial/ethnics from the mainstream of society has important consequences for family theory. Ultimately, such exclusion prevents a full understanding of the relationship between family and society. The failure to make racial/ethnic families a vital building block of family theory will cost the field the ability to provide a broad and comprehensive analysis of family life and social organization. It will render family theory incomplete and incorrect.

The Dangers of a Conventional Diversity Model

Although these revisions offer family studies several transformative directions, we should not anticipate an imminent mainstreaming of the new themes within family studies. Two developments could severely forestall the intellectual contributions produced by revisionist studies of Latino families. The first is the marginalization of racial/

ethnic families. The second is the increase of new immigration within a historical context that includes the restructuring of the U.S. economy and the advent of a more conservative political climate characterized by growing immigrant backlash. (See Vega, this volume.)

INTELLECTUAL MARGINALIZATION

Family scholars now routinely note the importance of diversity: of race, class, gender, and other differences in family study. Although the field of family studies is expanding to include a discussion of various kinds of difference, such differences do not inform the core of thinking about family dynamics in general. Like the earlier ghettoization of gender studies in the discipline of sociology (Stacey & Thorne, 1985), the study of family diversity remains contained within a "cultural diversity" category. Of course, most mainstream perspectives have dropped the cultural *deviant* perspective. However, they still treat family diversity as if it were the intrinsic property of groups that are "different" rather than as the product of forces that affect all families but in varying ways.

Instead of asking how cross-cutting systems of structural inequality shape families differently, most explanatory frameworks treat difference culturally, just as they did 75 years ago. Family studies research remains remarkably unstructural in theorizing family diversity. By stripping diversity from the social and political contexts shaping all families, cultural diversity has come to mean "others." Fundamentally, mainstream family thought has failed to transcend the cultural legacy of the past. Until it does, the intellectual revisioning of the past 2 decades will relegate Latinos and other racial/ethnic families to the rubric of special interest topics.

THE DEMOGRAPHIC TRANSFORMATION

An intellectual climate that marginalizes racial/ethnic families breeds a far more dangerous possibility. Current demographic upheavals pose the risk that mainstream family thinking will fall back on the false analytic strategies of earlier generations.

There are striking parallels between the current turn-of-the-century transitions and the changes that swept the world in the late 18th century, when conventional thinking about families took hold (Baca Zinn & Eitzen, 1993a). The social science produced then was rooted in structural transformations that are once again sweeping the world: massive immigration, political and economic systems in flux, political unrest, ethnic and racial solidarity and strife, and social movements to restore or transform (Baca Zinn & Eitzen, 1993a).

As population shifts produce a new demographic profile and U.S. institutions seem more and more unsettled, many family scholars regard family diversity with renewed anxiety (Popenoe, 1988; Whitehead, 1993). Conservative rhetoric is fueling a growing social and ideological cleavage between traditional family forms and the emerging alternatives (Gerson, 1991). This polarized climate threatens many of the advances produced by revisionist scholarship. Whereas the rhetoric of "family values" was at one time a conservative theme that blamed social decay on bad people doing bad things, that theme has now entered the political mainstream. Even President Clinton has recently echoed the conservative claim that the breakup of the two-parent family is the source of social disarray.

As racial and ethnic minorities become an ever larger share of the U.S. population, forging their family lives within widely varying settings of structured opportunity, the themes of family diversity and family values will surely escalate. We must rigorously oppose all thinking that measures family difference against a false universal standard. Immigration is undoubtedly creating alternative family patterns. However, we must not allow mainstream family thinking to dredge up cultural reductionist theories in which immigrant families are the scapegoat for society's problems. Even well-meaning pleas for "culturally sensitive" approaches to the study of minority and immigrant families can be problematic because they unwittingly keep the family ensnared in a normative model. The great challenge facing us now is to press for greater understanding of family diversity, not in group-specific terms, but as part of a socially constructed system. The demographic transformation now occurring in the United States poses new opportunities for us to move beyond the hollow theories of the past and toward a richer understanding of family life.

Notes

1. The term *racial/ethnic* refers to groups that are socially and legally subordinated and remain culturally distinct within U.S. society. It is meant to include: (a) the systematic discrimination of socially constructed racial groups, and (b) their distinctive cultural

arrangements. Historically, the categories of African American, Latino, Asian American, and Native American were constructed as both racially and culturally distinct. Each group has a common culture and shares a common heritage within a larger society that subordinates them. The racial characteristics of these groups have become meaningful within a society that continues to change (Baca Zinn & Dill, 1994).

2. This is not a comprehensive overview of revisionist works. Such reviews have appeared frequently in the past 2 decades of scholarship on Latinos. These works offer incisive criticisms of past distortions (see Hurtado, this volume). Suffice it to say that scholars stripped the early studies of their academic facades to reveal the false assumptions contained within them.

10

Contemporary Issues
in Latino Families

Future Directions for
Research, Policy, and Practice

DOUGLAS S. MASSEY

RUTH E. ZAMBRANA

SALLY ALONZO BELL

The study of Latino families not only has been limited but has suffered from the lack of a comprehensive framework to guide its knowledge building. This volume analyzes the depth and breadth of our understanding of Latino families and advocates new approaches to the study of Latino populations in the United States. Several interwoven themes have emerged that reflect a strong and distinct heterogeneity within Spanish-speaking groups in the United States.

A striking theme is the disproportionate socioeconomic burden that Latino groups experience. All the chapters indicate that low socioeconomic status is a key marker within Hispanic groups in the United States, influencing their cultural adaptations within the dominant cultural society. The unique cultural adaptations of Latinos, however, have not been adequately explored. Rather, culture has been confused with poverty and its correlates. Each of this volume's authors advocates and encourages a process of intellectual discourse that places culture in a framework of strength, so as to separate the role of culture from the determinants and consequences of poverty.

The substantive content of these chapters also reflects a remarkable absence of Hispanic groups from both empirical work and large-scale national, state, and local data sets. Furthermore, in examining the available literature, a significant portion of studies have included only Mexican-origin groups, and many have failed to take into account important variables, such as socioeconomic status, immigrant generation, and nativity.

The concept of acculturation or assimilation has been used extensively in most studies. This concept can be most imprecisely defined as a preference for culturally specific foods, language, social activities, and English language, as well as level of education, place of birth, and number of years in the United States. In essence, this concept has served as a proxy indicator for socioeconomic status, generational status, and place of birth. Because most studies have been conducted with low-income Latino populations, it is not surprising that most have concluded that low acculturation is highly related to lower levels of education, limited English-language proficiency, and more favorable lifestyle behaviors.

The lack of information on family structure, family functioning, and lifestyle factors has seriously hindered any viable efforts to develop programs and policies for the fastest-growing ethnic group in the United States (Hayes-Bautista, Hurtado, Valdez, & Hernández, 1992). Perhaps the complexity of the Latino groups and their inability to fit neatly into existing dominant-culture social science paradigms has hindered significant scientific advancement in this area.

A well-developed principle of the development of scientific knowledge is that it must be informed and comprehensive in order to guide its application in practice and policy. Yet this principle has not been followed in the study of Latino families. More frequently, approaches to Latino families have been either cultural or structural. The contemporary debate on whether or not Latinos fit the underclass model is a case in point.

Given the surging interest in urban poverty during the early 1980s, researchers interested in studying Latino family issues faced a difficult dilemma. On the one hand they could tap into the wellspring of funds available to study the *underclass,* a concept developed primarily with African Americans in mind. Adopting this strategy meant accepting that Latinos formed part of the underclass and working with theoretical models and analytic methods originally derived to study African American poverty (Massey, 1993b).

On the other hand, Latinos could separate themselves from the underclass debate and formulate their own agenda for research. This path was more difficult and carried greater risks. Rather than simply appropriating existing theories and methods, new and untried analytic tools would have to be developed. Rather than simply riding a cresting wave of research funding, these untested theories and methods would have to be used to make a case for funds at a time of increasing competition for resources.

Instead of facing this daunting prospect, researchers generally took the path of least resistance and worked within the underclass paradigm. Looking back from the viewpoint of the 1990s, however, the wisdom of this tag-along strategy seems questionable. Efforts to insert Latinos into studies of the underclass generally failed. Not only were they resisted by poverty researchers, they irritated some African American scholars, who saw Latinos trying to muscle their way into the poverty limelight. The strategy also exposed divisions within the Latino research community, with some scholars questioning whether Latinos actually constituted part of the underclass and others questioning whether such a class even existed (Massey, 1993b).

Outside of the Hispanic research community itself, Latino families have remained an afterthought in most theoretical developments on urban poverty, and they are still being analyzed using methods and models developed with African Americans in mind. The time has come to decouple Latinos from the larger underclass debate and to forge a new Hispanic research agenda governed by its own theoretical models and analytic methods.

The fact is that issues surrounding Hispanic families and poverty are fundamentally different in five essential ways from those facing African Americans. The differences are related to

the coherence of the group,
the meaning of race,
the level and extent of segregation,
the relative importance of immigration, and
the role played by language in determining well-being.

These differences render standard methods and theories inappropriate for studying Latino families in general and the role of poverty in Latino family functioning in particular. Exploring the distinctiveness of the Latino population as a racial and ethnic minority in the United States sets the stage for theoretical advancement in the study of families.

The Distinctiveness of the Latino Population

Unlike African Americans, the Latino population is composed of a diverse collection of national origins fragmented by class and generation (Bean & Tienda, 1987). The category *Latino* does not really exist apart from the classification created by federal statisticians to provide data on people of Mexican, Cuban, Puerto Rican, Dominican, Colombian, Salvadoran, and other extractions. Although "Hispanics" in theory include all those who can trace their origins to an area originally colonized by Spain, in practice this definition delineates few common traits and embraces tremendous national diversity.

With heterogeneity in national origins comes great variation in the timing of each group's arrival in the United States.

- Cubans arrived largely between 1960 and 1990.
- Mexicans have been migrating continuously since around 1890.
- Puerto Ricans obtained citizenship through colonial conquest in 1898.
- Southwestern Hispanics were forcibly annexed to the United States in 1848.
- Dominicans, Salvadorans, and Guatemalans have just begun migrating to the United States within the past few years.

As a result of these varied origins and immigration histories, Hispanics may be found in a variety of generational and legal statuses. They may be fifth-generation Americans descended from Spanish colonists or new immigrants just stepping off the jetway; they may be native-born children of immigrant parents or naturalized citizens; they may be legal immigrants driving across the Rio Grande on a bridge or undocumented migrants swimming underneath. Depending on when and how they got to the United States, Hispanics may know a long history of discrimination and oppression, or they may perceive the United States as a land of opportunity where origins do not matter.

When applied to Hispanics, therefore, underclass theories that assume the common historical experience of African Americans are bound to obscure more than they reveal. In fact, a different analytic model may be required to understand poverty and family issues in each Latino group. The attempts to force the diverse experiences of Mexicans, Puerto Ricans, Cubans, Salvadorans, and Dominicans into conceptual boxes created by theorists of the African American underclass are not likely to be productive.

A second distinctive feature of the Latino experience is race (Rodríguez, 1990). Unlike African Americans, Hispanics form a racially heterogeneous population with a variety of origins: European, African, Asian, Amerindian, and various mixtures thereof. As a result, race is a divisive factor among Latinos, rather a force for unity, as it is among African Americans. In the encounter between Latino and White culture, moreover, this natural racial diversity causes Hispanics to be divided from one another in another way: They are alienated from their own cultural system of racial classification.

Within Latin America, race has traditionally been viewed not as a dichotomy but as a continuum. Hispanic immigrants arrive in the United States exhibiting a wide range of racial traits, skin colors, and physical appearances that are perceived through conceptual categories sharply at odds with the strict racial dichotomy characteristic of European American culture. Although color prejudice exists in Latin America, it is more subtle and more intertwined with social class, and it does not follow a well-defined color line.

White prejudice and discrimination in the United States act upon this racial diversity to fragment the Latino population. Research clearly shows that U.S. markets reward Hispanics differentially on the basis of skin color. In the labor market, dark-skinned Hispanics earn lower wages than those with lighter skins; and in the housing market, those with dark skins are more segregated than their lighter-skinned fellows. The probability of housing discrimination also increases steadily as skin color darkens. Although White racism creates a coherent racial identity and a unifying ideology among African Americans, it tends to fragment the Hispanic population along racial lines.

A third feature that distinguishes Hispanics from African Americans is the degree of segregation they experience in society (Massey & Denton, 1993). Unlike African Americans, Hispanics do not universally experience residential segregation. As a result, they are much less vulnerable to downturns in the economy and are less likely to form underclass communities. Rather than the prevailing high segregation of African Americans, studies of Hispanic segregation reveal a high degree of variability across metropolitan areas that generally reflects four factors: generation, socioeconomic status, race, and national origin.

As socioeconomic levels rise and generations in the United States increase, the degree of Hispanic segregation progressively falls. At the same time, the level of segregation also varies by national origin because of differences in racial composition. A relatively large percentage of Puerto Ricans (47%) identify themselves as African American or racially mixed, people who are more likely to experience discrimination in the housing market. As a result, Puerto Ricans display a much higher degree of segregation than other Latino groups. Although Mexican Indians and mestizos also experience discrimination and segregation in U.S. housing markets, the levels are much less severe than those faced by African American or racially mixed Hispanics from the Caribbean. Among Latinos, therefore, only Puerto Ricans experience anything approaching the high levels of segregation characteristic of African Americans.

A fourth feature separating Latinos from African Americans is that Latinos are an immigrant population (Portes & Rumbaut, 1990). Indeed, immigration lies at the heart of Hispanic population dynamics, and it is impossible to make a firm statement about the social, economic, or demographic position of Latinos in the United States without taking this movement into account. The study of Hispanic poverty requires that explicit consideration be given to international migration as a social process that is potentially confounded with other processes related to poverty and family composition in the United States.

Migration, of course, is a highly selective process. The diverse historical processes that brought different national-origin groups into the United States result in initial populations with widely discrepant socioeconomic distributions and rates of poverty. In general, the greater the barriers to entry, the more selective the immigration process. The more physical, legal, and economic impediments that stand in the way of an immigrant's entry to the United States, the greater the selection on traits such as motivation, education, and wealth. Different migratory processes have thus created a set of Latino national-origin groups that differed substantially at their point of arrival.

Whereas socioeconomic and family outcomes among African Americans and non-Hispanic Whites can safely be assumed to stem from socioeconomic processes that occur entirely within the United States, Hispanic outcomes also reflect immigration. Given data showing low levels of schooling among Hispanics, for example, we have no way of knowing how much of the deficit reflects family strains and the failure of educational institutions in the United States, or how much stems from the arrival of non-English-speaking immigrants with limited economic means and low levels of education from abroad. Both processes are important and may require some action by the government; but they are entirely distinct, and the policies required to deal with them are likely to be quite different as well. The simple, ad hoc inclusion of Hispanics in studies of the underclass thus provides no guarantee that anything useful will result, unless confounding migratory processes are explicitly taken into account.

Theories must also be modified to recognize the unique interplay of immigration, poverty, and family structure among Hispanics, and statistical models must control for the selective effects of international migration. Analyses should be longitudinal and focus not only on histories of employment, earnings, cohabitation, marriage, and fertility, but also on international movement. Migration constitutes a principal means by which Hispanic families adjust to uncertainty in the labor market and flux in economic circumstances, and this fact needs to be incorporated directly into theoretical and empirical analyses. An adequate understanding of Hispanic poverty and family dynamics requires taking immigration into account at all phases of design and analysis.

One last distinctive feature of the Latino population is its attachment to the Spanish language (Veltman, 1988). According to recent data, a majority of Latinos are either bilingual or monolingual speakers of Spanish. Although research has detected no penalty to bilingualism in the labor market—and in many local labor markets (Miami, San Antonio, Los Angeles) bilingualism may even be rewarded—a lack of facility in English has inevitable socioeconomic consequences.

Among Hispanics, research clearly shows that a lack of English-language ability lowers earnings and reduces occupational status, mainly by blocking access to higher-level jobs. Once Hispanics speak English well and graduate from high school, their attainments equal those of Whites. Research must therefore recognize that language is a principal mediating factor conditioning how Latino families adapt and react to changing social and economic conditions in U.S. society.

The Elements of a Research Paradigm

The foregoing review suggests that although African Americans and Hispanics share high rates of poverty and family difficulties, these problems are likely to be generated through very different mechanisms and for very different reasons. Studies should therefore move beyond methods and models developed with African Americans in mind to embrace the distinctive features of the Latino population. Specifically, a comprehensive agenda for research must satisfy five specific criteria.

1. It must recognize the diversity of Latinos. Although family processes may be described by a single theoretical model that incorporates common underlying factors, these factors will carry different empirical weights in different groups, which will lead to subtle but important differences in model specification.
2. It must recognize race as a key factor that differentiates the experience of Latinos in the United States.
3. It must incorporate residential segregation as a key factor structuring the opportunities open to different groups in U.S. society.
4. It must incorporate immigration as a socioeconomic process that is confounded with other processes affecting family structure and poverty.
5. It must recognize the unique role that Spanish language plays in conditioning the social, economic, and political experience of Latinos in the United States.

New sources of data and more sophisticated methods of analysis are required. Data sets, theories, and methods developed to analyze the determinants of African American poverty cannot address the complex interplay of forces generating poverty among Hispanic groups, because the key role of international migration is not recognized. A principal challenge for Latino researchers, then, is to create binational data sets that link comparable samples in sending and receiving areas. This design has been incorporated into several small-scale studies of Dominicans and Mexicans with considerable success, but it has not been implemented on a large scale using nationally representative data sets.

Because Puerto Rico is covered by the U.S. Census, all analyses of Puerto Rican poverty should begin by pooling Public Use Microdata Samples for the United States and the island of Puerto Rico to construct files of island-born and mainland-born respondents that contain returned migrants from each location. With these data files, selective migration processes can be modeled and directly incorporated into analyses of socioeconomic outcomes.

Constructing binational data sets is not enough, however. The unique attributes of the Latino population and its influences on Latino family process and dynamics must be formulated to guide future data collection efforts and investigations.

Future Research Directions

A broad set of research areas requires exploration and analysis to generate the knowledge needed for formulating family-support policies that can strengthen Latino families in the United States. The last decade has witnessed a new tradition of scholarship, conducted predominantly by Latino scholars; this tradition has taken new theoretical and analytic directions to understand the dynamic interaction between the cultural and structural forces that affect the adaptation and function of Latino families in the United States.

Like other racial/ethnic families, Latino families in the last two decades have also experienced extraordinary changes in traditional family forms. Crucial to developing family support programs that are relevant and useful to strengthening these families are studies that examine the effects of women's changing roles, parent's expectations and concerns with children and adolescent lifestyles, the stressors of being a parent, and behavioral risk factors.

The types of parental stressors and their influence on both parents' and children's mental and physical well-being are critical to understanding the quality of life among Latino families. Latino families have been viewed as having high levels of social support. Yet the levels and types of social support have been measured outside the context of the chronic stressors of poor socioenvironmental conditions, poverty, institutional discrimination, and limited access to quality health and human services.

Given the constraints of poverty, how are family, friends, and organizational social support systems defined, and what forms are most helpful to Latino families? These are questions that deserve attention. In addition, the nature and types of stressors experienced by many low-income Latino families have been virtually ignored in past and current studies. Stressors representing psychosocial dimensions of family functioning and adaptation that merit conceptual attention in the study of Latino families include the following:

1. Multiple jobs
2. Discrimination
3. Children with learning disabilities and related school problems
4. Drug and alcohol problems of other family members
5. Violence in the community

On the other hand, a neglected area of study has been the growing Hispanic middle class and its adaptation in dominant society. The effects of upward mobility on both adults and their offspring have remained unexplored areas of inquiry. Intergenerational family relations, the role of extended families, and the role of the elderly within the different forms of family structure require study. Equally important, women's changing roles within families and in society require separate investigation. The ways in which Hispanic women have experienced societal and cultural changes, as well as the influence of these changes on performance of their multiple roles, on the quality of their lives, and on their health status, can provide significant insight and contribute toward filling large informational gaps.

Health status, behaviors, and lifestyle are other areas of inquiry that require a cultural and socioeconomic context. For example, current emphasis on exercise and the consumption of fruits and vegetables represents dominant-culture, middle-class environmental practices and assumes access to economic resources that are unavailable to low-income Latino families. The assessment of other, more appropriate, and culturally specific practices might provide significant information in understanding current health status and outcomes in this population. Finally, future studies of Latino families should adopt a comparative approach, considering families separately by socioeconomic status to assess more accurately how class differences influence the adaptation of Latino families within the dominant culture and society.

CONDUCT OF FUTURE STUDIES: METHODOLOGICAL CONCERNS

Recent emphasis on cross-cultural methodological strategies and sensitivity highlights the fact that most research on racial and ethnic groups, and specifically on Latinos, has not been grounded in a solid understanding of the contextual, structural, and cultural factors relevant to the group being studied. Central issues are related to the measurement of social inequality indicators, namely, the repeated confounding of race, ethnicity, culture, and socioeconomic status; the use of instruments that have limited applicability to the Latino experience; and the lack of collaboration and partnerships with community-based agencies, organizations, and providers.

Approaches to the study of Latino family processes require rethinking and greater integration into broader conceptual paradigms. Betancourt and López (1993) articulate with lucidity the extensive conceptual confusion that permeates the literature on definitions of culture and the related concepts of race and ethnicity in American psychology. The authors propose that the understanding of culture and the cultural sensitivity of applications can be advanced by including theory and by conceptualizing and measuring cultural and related variables.

Methodological approaches are usually derived from relevant conceptual paradigms. When theory reflects the reality of the populations under study, and when reality, in turn, contributes to the development of theory, cross-culturally relevant data can emerge to guide policy and practice. To this end, methodological procedures must be refined in collaboration with the local community to assure the inclusion of representative groups in the research endeavor (Hatch, Moss, Saran, Presley-Cantrell, & Mallory, 1993). Research cannot accurately reflect the realities of a community if it is not developed within the context of a particular geographic region. The anthropological tradition provides an important approach for understanding the lives of individuals within their communities.

Thus, the design of sound investigations requires multiple approaches, using both qualitative and quantitative methods. The dynamic processes that Latino families are undergoing, combined with the persistent immigration patterns, argue for the use of multiple and interdisciplinary methods. Future formulation and implementation of a family policy that is responsive to the needs of Latino children and families must be based on accurate knowledge of the specific concerns of that population.

Family Policy and Support Services

Family policy in the United States has narrowly focused on minimal economic subsistence. It has not been beneficial in addressing the multiple needs of families. In its broadest definition, family policy can be described as those acts intended to strengthen or change patterns of family life, as opposed to acts that help individuals and may have an indirect effect on the family network (Morris, 1985). The ambiguity of current U.S. family policy has contributed to a series of fragmented programs and services, such as Aid to Families with Dependent Children, health care services, job training, and work incentive programs, which have been more detrimental than beneficial to maintaining and strengthening families (Morris, 1985).

The health and human service delivery system, at both the national and regional level, is in a state of crisis, operating as a fragmented and costly problem-specific group of ad hoc programs that do not effectively serve the needs of the Latino population. The state of health and human service policy in this country is shown no more clearly than in the fact that the United States ranks 20th with respect to infant deaths in developed countries, falling behind even less industrialized countries such as Singapore and Hong Kong.

> The fact that the only two industrialized countries that do not have a medical care system are South Africa and the United States is not accidental; in neither country have working people been able to surmount the racism and segregation that prevent them from joining together for independent action. (National Committee to Prevent Infant Mortality, 1990, pp. 284-285)

CULTURALLY SENSITIVE PRACTICE

Recent data show that Latino families and children represent a group that is at risk and vulnerable. Latino families, according to the limited information available, have not benefited substantially from access to existing health and human services. The main indicators of barriers to use of existing institutional resources are the following:

- A high portion of Latino families residing in segregated, low-income housing areas
- Persistent and high levels of school failure
- Low completion rates for secondary and higher education
- Low rates of participation in income maintenance programs and job training programs
- Increasing rates of youth in juvenile correctional facilities, particularly in large urban areas
- Low rates of health insurance coverage, both public and private, coupled with adverse health status

Yet, as has been argued above, Latino concerns have consistently been ignored or defined within conceptual models, such as the underclass model, that are inappropriate for understanding the dynamics for this group. As a result, it is not surprising that most programs and service interventions continue to be labeled as lacking cultural sensitivity and cultural competency. The new emphasis on multiculturalism, equity, and diversity represents a unique opportunity to initiate a new set of processes to understand the intersections of culture, race, ethnicity, and socioeconomic status. However, there is no need to assume that we do not know what works. Knowledge of Latino families and experimental programs is sufficiently advanced to develop policy and program interventions that can contribute to the social well-being of Latino families and improve their economic well-being. Policy that seeks to strengthen Latino families rather than debilitate them must be guided by a long-term preventive orientation that places families at the center of the intervention and within the context of their neighborhoods and communities. Furthermore, children must be viewed and treated as part of families. For their optimal growth and development, children require strong, stable, and consistent supportive and nurturing relationships.

The practice or the design of culturally sensitive programs and interventions must strive to incorporate a series of attributes that have been found to be effective. These include programs that are flexible, comprehensive, and responsive to the needs of the population being served; active collaboration across professions and agencies; and staff availability and skills to build relationships that assure quality and continuity of services provided (Schorr & Schorr, 1988). Furthermore, the concept of cultural sensitivity and responsiveness by definition means the incorporation of personnel at all levels of the organizational structures who can design and implement programs in relation to the needs of the Latino target population. These attributes constitute the core of family support programs for Latino families.

Family support programs need to consistently implement comprehensive, interlinked human service systems to strengthen and enhance family functioning, with specific attention to responding to the economic, social, and educational needs of families and children. Among Latino families, the information available calls for programs that are targeted at and based in local communities. In the end, a critical mass of high-quality services must be delivered in a culturally sensitive and responsive way within the social and environmental context of local communities. It has been adequately demonstrated that regional areas exhibit differences with respect to Latino subgroups as well as the availability and accessibility of human services.

In breaking cycles of persistent disadvantage, a point of entry is early school learning such as public preschool programs, where both children and their families are informed and prepared for constructively engaging in educational efforts. Parents whose children are enrolled in preschool programs, for example, might benefit from a parallel program to provide preparation for high school courses and college, as well as courses on child development and parents' optimal role in fostering a child's intellectual and social development. A number of programs have been instituted in communities of color that have significant relevance to Latino children and families. These include partnerships with the business community, health care institutions, and government agencies to provide training and mentorships for adolescents and young adults.

Another set of programs has been implemented through the Healthy Start initiative. These family-focused interventions aim to identify families at risk when a child is born and to provide a comprehensive set of resources to improve the family's functioning. For Latino families, an early assessment of psychosocial, medical, educational, and environmental risk factors at birth of first child represents an effective and cost-saving model to improve family well-being. The Latino family has been disproportionately affected by economic downturns in the United States. Thus, Latinos persistently experience high levels of underemployment, inadequate housing arrangements, failing school systems, and violence in their community environments. These stressors, coupled with high fertility rates, immigrant status, and limited English-language proficiency, may have adverse effects on the welfare of Latino children. It has been argued that the costs of preventive efforts are, and must be, less costly than the costs of failure to the individuals involved, their families, and society.

Conclusions

We need innovative reformulations of our national goals and strategies that seek to replace existing fragmented and unresponsive policy with a comprehensive family support legislative effort that truly serves the needs of the majority of the population (i.e., the working class, the poor, and people of color), as opposed to the needs of a few. We need a linked national health insurance program, a family income-maintenance program, and a child-care program, to make families strong, not debilitate or destroy them. Furthermore, we need a focus on preventing problems, not on repairing the damage of neglect.

Thus, what is urgently needed is a national policy that uses its tools in the service of equitable policy for all. This commitment requires reflection on our values as a nation. The models that guide our policy are driven by ideas of American parity that do not seek to achieve a collective resolution of inequities in health care access among social classes, racial and ethnic groups, or generations. In the short run, the lack of an equitable policy will perhaps serve the interests of the dominant culture structure; in the long run, it can serve the interest of no one. Rather, the direction of a family support policy would benefit from developing a universal vision. In relation to health policy, Sultz (1991) states that:

> Neither a society nor a health care system can survive without virtue or, in broader terms, a cause that supersedes individual interests. A health care delivery system cannot progress without an articulated purpose, some common vision that can be expressed as policy. We must become unwilling to sacrifice the public interest for personal interests or political interests, and we must begin creating a network of services that will care humanely for the poor, the sick, the elderly and the most vulnerable. (p. 419)

There is a common societal interest in critically assessing our knowledge on family-support programs. Yet, in the contemporary debates on family policy, cultural responsiveness has not been a central dimension. The insistence of the American polity on espousing family-oriented values while neglecting to develop sound family-support programs presents serious barriers to the effective functioning of Latino families. The effects of this nonfamily policy, via the pathways of institutional discrimination and exclusion, are detrimental to positive family functioning and children's development. Observational and empirical data have shown that the current family support and child welfare services are not only inadequate but reflect racial and ethnic bias (Delgado, 1992). The projected demographic increases, coupled with the child and family needs of the Latino population over the next decade, form a strong scientific rationale for developing culturally relevant policy and programs. Policy formulation builds on knowledge and need. Family policy that responds to the needs of Latino families will serve to prevent increased economic costs to our existing human service systems and reaffirm and strengthen the role that Latino families have a right to assume in our society.

References

Abraham, K. G. (1986). Ego-identity differences among Anglo-American and Mexican-American adolescents. *Journal of Adolescence, 9*, 151-166.

Acker, J. (1992). Gendered institutions: From sex roles to gendered institutions. *Contemporary Sociology, 21*, 565-569.

Adler, N. E., Boyce, T., Chesney, M., Folkman, S., & Syme, L. (1993). Socioeconomic inequalities in health. *Journal of the American Medical Association, 289*(24), 3140-3145.

Aguayo, S., & Fagen, P. W. (1988). *Central Americans in Mexico and the United States.* Washington, DC: Hemispheric Migration Project, Center for Immigration Policy and Refugee Assistance, Georgetown University.

Aguirre-Molina, M., Ramirez, A., & Ramirez, M. (1993). Health promotion and disease prevention strategies. *Public Health Reports, 108*(5), 559-664.

Alarcón, N. (1981). Chicanas' feminist literature: A re-vision through Malintzin/or Malintzin: Putting flesh back on the object. In C. Moraga & G. Anzaldua (Eds.), *This bridge called my back: Writings by radical women of color* (pp. 182-190). Watertown, MA: Persephone.

Aleinikoff, T. A., & Martin, D. A. (1985). *Immigration process and policy.* New York: West.

Almaguer, T. (1991). Chicano men: A cartography of homosexual identity and behavior. *A Journal of Feminist Cultural Studies, 3*(2), 75-100.

Alvarez, R. (1987). *Families: Migration and adaptation in Baja and Alta California from 1800 to 1975.* Berkeley: University of California Press.

Alvirez, D., Bean, F. D., & Williams, D. (1981). The Mexican American family. In C. H. Mindel & R. W. Habenstein (Eds.), *Ethnic families in America: Patterns and variations* (pp. 271-292). New York: Elsevier.

Amaro, H. (1988). Women in the Mexican-American community: Religion, culture, and reproductive attitudes and experiences. *Journal of Community Psychology, 16*, 6-20.

Amaro, H. (1993, July 19-21). *Using national health data systems to inform Hispanic women's health.* Paper presented at the National Center for Health Statistics Public Health Conference on Records and Statistics, Washington, DC.

Amaro, H., Whitaker, R., Coffman, G., & Heeren, T. (1990). Acculturation and marijuana and cocaine use: Findings from the HHANES 1982-84. *American Journal of Public Health, 80*(Suppl.), 54-60.

American Civil Liberties Union. (1984a). *The fates of Salvadorans expelled from the United States* (American Civil Liberties Union Fund of the National Capitol Area, Political Asylum Project). Washington, DC: Author.

American Civil Liberties Union. (1984b). *Salvadorans in the United States: A case for extended voluntary departure* (Public Policy Report, National Immigration and Alien Rights Project, Report No. 1). Washington, DC: Author.

American Public Welfare Association. (1993). Characteristics of children in substitute and adoptive care. Washington, DC: Author.

Americas Watch Committee and American Civil Liberties Union. (1984). *Free fire: A report on human rights in El Salvador.* New York: Americas Watch Committee.

Amnesty International. (1988). *El Salvador: Death squads a government strategy.* New York: Author.

Andrade, S. (1982). Social science stereotypes of the Mexican American woman: Policy implications for research. *Hispanic Journal of Behavioral Sciences, 4*(2), 223-244.

Aneshensel, C. S., Fielder, E. P., & Becerra, R. M. (1989). Fertility and fertility-related behavior among Mexican-American and non-Hispanic White female adolescents. *Journal of Health and Social Behavior, 30*, 56-76.

Angel, R., & Tienda, M. (1982a). Determinants of extended household structure: Cultural pattern or economic need? *American Journal of Sociology, 6*, 1360-1383.

Angel, R., & Tienda, M. (1982b). Headship and household composition among Blacks, Hispanics and other Whites. *Social Forces, 61*, 508-531.

Arce, C. H. (1982). Language shift among Chicanos: Strategies for measuring and assessing direction and rate. *Social Science Journal, 19*(2), 121-132.

Arguelles, L., & Rich, R. B. (1984). Homosexuality, homophobia, and revolution: Notes toward an understanding of the Cuban lesbian and gay male experience, Part 1. *Signs: Journal of Women in Culture and Society, 9*, 683-699.

Aron, A. (Ed.). (1988). *Flight, exile and return: Mental health and the refugee.* San Francisco: Committee for Health Rights in Central America.

Arroyo, W., & Eth, S. (1985). Children traumatized by Central American warfare. In S. Eth & R. S. Pynoos (Eds.), *Post-traumatic stress disorder in children* (pp. 103-120). Washington, DC: American Psychiatric Press.

Association for Children of New Jersey. (1992). *Kids count New Jersey: State and county profiles of child well-being.* Newark, NJ: Author.

Austin, G. A., & Gilbert, M. J. (1989). Substance abuse among Latino youth. In *Prevention Research Update* (No. 3, Spring). Portland, OR: Western Center for Drug-Free Schools and Communities.

Baca Zinn, M. (1980). Employment and education of Mexican American women: The interplay of modernity and ethnicity in eight families. *Harvard Educational Review, 50*, 47-62.

Baca Zinn, M. (1982a). Chicano men and masculinity. *Journal of Ethnic Studies, 10*, 29-44.

Baca Zinn, M. (1982b). Mexican-American women in the social sciences. *Signs: Journal of Women in Culture and Society, 8*(2), 259-272.

Baca Zinn, M. (1982c). Qualitative methods in family research: A look inside Chicano families. *California Sociologist*, Summer, 58-79.

Baca Zinn, M. (1982-1983). Familism among Chicanos: A theoretical overview. *Humboldt Journal of Social Relations, 10*, 224-238.

Baca Zinn, M. (1983). Ongoing questions in the study of Chicano families. In A. Valdez, A. Camarillo, & T. Almaguer (Eds.), *The state of Chicano research on family, labor,* and migration. *Proceedings of the First Stanford Symposium on Chicano Research and Public Policy* (pp. 139-146). Stanford, CA: Stanford Center for Chicano Research.

Baca Zinn, M. (1989). Family, race, and poverty in the eighties. *Signs: Journal of Women in Culture and Society, 14*(4), 856-874.

Baca Zinn, M. (1990). Family, feminism, and race in America. *Gender and Society, 4*(1), 68-82.

Baca Zinn, M. (1994). Feminist rethinking from racial-ethnic families. In M. Baca Zinn & B. T. Dill (Eds.), *Women of color in U.S. society* (pp. 303-314). Philadelphia: Temple University Press.

Baca Zinn, M., & Dill, B. T. (1994). Difference and domination. In M. Baca Zinn & B. T. Dill (Eds.), *Women of color in U.S. society* (pp. 3-12). Philadelphia: Temple University Press.

Baca Zinn, M., & Eitzen, D. S. (1993a). The demographic transformation and the sociological enterprise. *The American Sociologist, 24*(2), 5-12.

Baca Zinn, M., & Eitzen, D. S. (1993b). *Diversity in families.* New York: Harper Collins College Publishers.

Bachman, J. G., Wallace, J. M., O'Malley, P. O., Johnston, L. D., Kurth, C. L., & Neighbors, H. W. (1991). Racial ethnic differences in smoking, drinking, and illicit drug use among American high school seniors, 1976-89. *American Journal of Public Health, 81*(3), 372-377.

Bachrach, C. A. (1984). Contraceptive practices among American women 1973-1982. *Family Planning Perspectives, 16*(6), 253-259.

Bane, M. J. (1986). Household composition and poverty. In S. Danziger & D. Weinburg (Eds.), *Fighting poverty: What works and what doesn't* (pp. 209-231). Cambridge, MA: Harvard University Press.

Baratz, S. S., & Baratz, J. C. (1970). Early childhood intervention: The social science base of institutional racism. *Harvard Educational Review, 48,* 161-170.

Barrett, M. E., Simpson, D. D., & Lehman, W. E. K. (1988). Behavioral changes of adolescents in drug abuse intervention programs. *Journal of Clinical Psychology, 44*(3), 461-473.

Bean, F. D., & Swicegood, G. (1982). Generation, female education, and Mexican American fertility. *Social Science Quarterly, 63*(1), 131-144.

Bean, F., & Tienda, M. (1987). *The Hispanic population of the United States.* New York: Russell Sage.

Becerra, R. M., & de Anda, D. (1984). Pregnancy and motherhood among Mexican American adolescents. *Health and Social Work, 9*(2), 106-123.

Bernard, B. (1989). An overview of community-based prevention. In K. H. Rey, C. L. Faegre, & P. Lowery (Eds.), *Prevention research findings: 1988. Proceedings of the First National Conference on Prevention Research Findings* (pp. 126-147). Rockville, MD: Office for Substance Abuse Prevention.

Berardo, F. M. (1991). Family research in the 1980s: Recent trends and future directions. In A. Booth (Ed.), *Contemporary families: Looking forward, looking back* (pp. 1-11). Minneapolis, MN: National Council on Family Relations.

Berryman, A. (1983). *Central American refugees: A survey of the current situation.* Philadelphia: American Friends Service Committee.

Betancourt, H., & López, S. R. (1993). The study of culture, ethnicity, and race in American psychology. *American Psychologist, 48*(6), 629-637.

Bettes, B. A., Dusenbury, L. K., Kerner, J., James-Ortiz, S., & Botvin, G. J. (1989). Ethnicity and psychosocial factors in alcohol and tobacco use in adolescence. *Child Development, 61*(2), 557-565.

Bird, H., & Canino, G. (1982). The Puerto Rican family: Cultural factors and family intervention strategies. *Journal of the American Academic of Psychoanalysis, 10*, 257-268.

Bogardus, A. (1934). *The Mexican in the United States.* Los Angeles: University of Southern California Press.

Bonilla, F. (1990). Poverty and inequality in the 1990s. In H. D. Romo (Ed.), *Latinos and Blacks in the cities* (pp. 213-219). Austin: University of Texas Press.

Boss, P., & Thorne, B. (1989). Family sociology and family therapy. In M. McGoldrick, C. M. Anderson, & F. Walsh (Eds.), *Women in families* (pp. 78-96). New York: W. W. Norton.

Bowman, T. (1992). Group leadership issues. In Minnesota Fathering Alliance (Ed.), *Working with fathers: Methods and perspectives* (pp. 101-111). Stillwater, MN: Nu Ink Unlimited.

Briemelow, P. (1992, June 22). Time to rethink immigration. *National Review,* pp. 30-46.

Bronstein, P. (1984). Differences in mothers' and fathers' behaviors toward children: A cross-cultural comparison. *Developmental Psychology, 20,* 995-1003.

Bronstein, P. (1988). Father-child interaction: Implications for gender role socialization. In P. Bronstein & C. P. Cowan (Eds.), *Fatherhood today: Men's changing role in the family* (pp. 107-124). New York: John Wiley.

Browning, H. L., & de la Garza, R. O. (1986). *Mexican immigrants and Mexican Americans.* Austin, TX: Center for Mexican American Studies.

Bruce-Novoa, J. (1986). Homosexuality and the Chicano novel. *Confluencia: Revista Hispana de Cultura y Literatura, 2*(1), 69-77.

Bureau of the Census. (1985). Receipt of selected noncash benefits: 1985. In *Current population reports: Consumer income* (Series P-60, No. 155). Washington, DC: Government Printing Office.

Bureau of the Census. (1986). *Characteristics of population: Census of population and housing.* Washington, DC: U.S. Department of Commerce.

Bureau of the Census. (1990a). *Statistical abstract of the United States* (108th ed.). Washington, DC: U.S. Department of Commerce.

Bureau of the Census. (1990b). *Statistical brief. Hispanics in the United States.* Washington DC: U.S. Department of Commerce.

Bureau of the Census. (1991). *1990 census profile: Race and Hispanic origin* (Number 2, June 1991). Washington, DC: Economics and Statistics Administration.

Bureau of the Census. (1992). *The foreign born population by place of birth for California.* Washington, DC: Office of Public Affairs, Census Publications.

Bureau of the Census. (1993a). Hispanic Americans today. In *Current population reports* (Series P23-183). Washington, DC: Government Printing Office.

Bureau of the Census. (1993b). Measuring the effects of benefits and taxes on income and poverty: 1992. In *Current population reports* (Series P60-186RD). Washington, DC: Government Printing Office.

Bureau of the Census. (1993c). Money income of households, families, and persons in the United States: 1992. In *Current population reports* (Series P60-184). Washington, DC: Government Printing Office.

Bureau of the Census. (1993d). *1990 census of populations: Persons of Hispanic origin in the United States* (1990 CP-3-3). Washington, DC: Government Printing Office.

Bureau of the Census. (1993e). *Statistical abstract of the United States: 1993* (113th ed.). Washington, DC: Government Printing Office.

Burgess, E. W. (1926). *The urban community.* Chicago: University of Chicago Press.

Buriel, R., & Cardoza, D. (1988). Sociocultural correlates of achievement among three generations of Mexican American high school seniors. *American Educational Research Journal, 25*(2), 177-192.

Burke, V., Gabe, T., Rimkunas, R., & Griffith, J. (1985). *Hispanic children in poverty.* Washington, DC: Congressional Research Service.

Caetano, R. (1983). Drinking patterns and alcohol problems among Hispanics in the U.S.: A review. *Drug and Alcohol Dependence, 12*(1), 37-59.

Calhoun, G., Connley, S., & Bolton, J. A. (1984). Comparison of delinquents and nondelinquents in ethnicity, ordinal position, and self-perception. *Journal of Clinical Psychology, 40*(1), 323-328.

Canino, G. J., Rubio-Stipec, M., Shrout, P., Bravo, M., Stolberg, R., & Bird, H. R. (1987). Sex differences and depression in Puerto Rico. *Psychology of Women Quarterly, 4*, 443-459.

Caraveo-Ramos, L. E., & Saldate, M., IV. (1987). Relationship of language, family occupational history, and level of generation to attainment of upper-class status among Mexican-American college students. *Journal of Instructional Psychology, 14*(1), 17-25.

Carnegie Corporation. (1994). *Starting points: Meeting the needs of our youngest children.* New York: Author.

Annie E. Casey Foundation. (1994). *Kids count data book: State profiles of child well-being.* Greenwich, CT: Author.

Cervantes, R. C., Salgado de Snyder, V. N., & Padilla, A. M. (1988). *Post-traumatic stress disorder among immigrants from Central America and Mexico* (Occasional Paper N. 24). Los Angeles: Spanish Speaking Mental Health Research Center, University of California, Los Angeles.

Chapa, J. (1988). The question of Mexican American assimilation: Socioeconomic parity or underclass formation? *Public Affairs Comment, 25*(1), 1-14.

Chávez, E. L., Edwards, R., & Oetting, E. R. (1989). Mexican American and White American school dropouts' drug use, health status, and involvement in violence. *Public Health Reports, 104*(6), 594-604.

Chávez, E. L., & Randall, C. S. (1991). An epidemiological comparison of Mexican American and White non-Hispanic 8th- and 12th-grade students' substance use. *American Journal of Public Health, 82*(3), 445-447.

Chávez, L. (1985). Households, migration, and labor market participation: The adaptation of Mexicans to life in the United States. *Urban Anthropology, 14*, 301-346.

Chávez, L. (1988). Settlers and sojourners: The case of Mexicans in the United States. *Human Organization, 47*, 95-108.

Chávez, N. (1986). Mental health service delivery to minority populations: Hispanics— A perspective. In M. R. Miranda & H. H. L. Kitano (Eds.), *Mental health research and practice in minority communities: Development of culturally sensitive training programs* (pp. 145-156). Rockville, MD: U.S. Department of Health and Human Services.

Children's Defense Fund. (1989). Testimony of the Children's Defense Fund before the Select Committee on Children, Youth and Families. Washington, DC: U.S. House of Representatives.

Children's Defense Fund. (1990). *Latinos youth at a crossroads.* Washington, DC: Author.

Children's Defense Fund. (1991a). *America's Latino children* (a fact sheet). Washington, DC: Author.

Children's Defense Fund. (1991b). *An opinion maker's guide to children in election year 1992.* Washington, DC: Author.

Clark, M. (1959). *Health in the Mexican-American culture.* Berkeley: University of California Press.

Collins, P. H. (1990). *Black feminist thought: Knowledge, consciousness, and the politics of empowerment.* Boston: Unwin Hyman.

Comas-Diaz, L. (1988). Mainland Puerto Rican women: A sociocultural approach. *Journal of Community Psychology, 16,* 21-31.

Comas-Diaz, L., & Duncan, J. W. (1985). The cultural context: A factor in assertiveness training with mainland Puerto Rican women. *Psychology of Women Quarterly, 9,* 463-475.

Combs-Orme, T. (1990). *Social work practice in maternal and child health.* New York: Springer.

Comite Pro-Justicia y Paz de Guatemala. (1987). *The human rights in Guatemala.* Mexico: World Council of Churches.

Cooney, R. (1979). Intercity variations in Puerto Rican female participation. *Journal of Human Resources, 14,* 222-235.

Cooney, R. S., Rogler, L. H., Hurrell, R. M., & Ortiz, V. (1982). Decision making in intergenerational Puerto Rican families. *Journal of Marriage and the Family, 44*(33), 621-631.

Corcoran, M., Duncan, G. J., Gurin, G., & Gurin, P. (1985). Myth and reality: The causes and persistence of poverty. *Journal of Policy Analysis and Management, 4*(4), 516-536.

Cordoba, C. (1986). *Migration and acculturation dynamics of undocumented Salvadorans in the San Francisco Bay area.* Doctoral dissertation, University of San Francisco.

Cordoba, C. (1992). Organizing in Central American immigrant communities in the United States. In F. G. Rivera & J. L. Erlich (Eds.), *Community organizing in a diverse society* (pp. 181-200). Boston: Allyn & Bacon.

Cornelius, L. (1993). Barriers to medical care for White, Black, and Hispanic children. *Journal of the National Medical Association, 85*(4), 281-288.

Costin, L. B., Bell, C. J., & Downs, S. W. (1991). *Child welfare: Policies and practice.* New York: Longman.

Crahan, M. E. (1988). Religion and the Central American crisis. In N. Hamilton, J. A. Friedman, L. Fuller, & M. Pastor, Jr. (Eds.), *Crisis in Central America: Regional dynamics and U.S. policy in the 1980s* (pp. 126-137). Boulder, CO: Westview.

Cuellar, I., Harris, L. C., & Jasso, R. (1980). An acculturation scale for Mexican-American normal and clinical populations. *Hispanic Journal of Behavioral Sciences, 2*(3), 199-217.

Danzinger, S., & Stern, J. (1990). *The causes and consequences of child poverty in the United States* (Innocenti Occasional Papers, 10). Florence, Italy: International Child Development Center.

Darabi, K., & Ortiz, V. (1987). Childbearing among young Latino women in the United States. *American Journal of Public Health, 77*(1), 25-28.

Darder, A., Ingle, Y. R., & Cox, B. G. (1993). *The policies and the promise: The public schooling of Latino children.* Claremont, CA: The Tomás Rivera Center.

Darity, W. A., & Meyers, S. L. (1984). Does welfare dependency cause female headship? The case of the Black family. *Journal of Marriage and the Family, 46*(4), 765-779.

Davis, R. M. (1987). Current trends in cigarette advertising and marketing. *New England Journal of Medicine, 316*(12), 725-732.

de Anda, D., Becerra, R. M, & Fielder, E. (1988). Sexuality, pregnancy, and motherhood among Mexican-American adolescents. *Journal of Adolescent Research, 3*(3-4), 403-411.

de la Garza, R. O., Bean, F. D., Bonjean, C. M., Romo, R., & Alvarez, R. (Eds.). (1985). *The Mexican American experience.* Austin: University of Texas Press.

De La Rosa, M. (1989). Health care needs of Hispanic Americans and the responsiveness of the health care system. *Health and Social Work, 14*(2), 104-113.

Delgado, R. (1992). Generalist child welfare and Hispanic families. In N. A. Cohen (Ed.), *Child welfare: A multicultural focus* (pp. 130-156). Boston: Allyn & Bacon.

Delgado-Gaitan, C. (1988). Sociocultural adjustment to school and academic achievement. *Journal of Early Adolescence, 8*(1), 63-82.

Department of Commerce, Bureau of the Census. (1987). *After-school care of school-age children.* Washington, DC: Government Printing Office.

Department of Education, Office of Educational Research and Improvement. (1988). *Dropout rates in the United States.* Washington, DC: Government Printing Office.

Department of Education, Office of Educational Research and Improvement. (1988). *High school and beyond survey.* Washington, DC: Government Printing Office.

Department of Health and Human Services. (1986). *The 1990 health objectives for the nation: Mid-course review.* Washington, DC: Office of Disease Prevention and Health Promotion.

Department of Health and Human Services, Office for Substance Abuse Prevention. (1990). *Alcohol and other drug use among Hispanic Youth* (OSAP Technical Report-4; DHHS Publication No. ADM 90-1726). Rockville, MD: Author.

Department of Health and Human Services. (1991). *Health status of minorities and low-income groups* (3rd ed.). Washington, DC: Author.

Department of Health and Human Services, Public Health Service. (1993). *Surgeon general's report: Blueprint for improving Hispanic and Latino health: Implementation strategies.* Washington, DC: Government Printing Office.

Desenclos, J.-C. A., & Hahn, R. A. (1992). Years of potential life lost before age 65, by race, Hispanic origin, and sex—United States, 1986-1988. *Morbidity and Mortality Weekly Report, 6*(42), 13-23.

Diaz, T., Buehler, J., Castro, K. G., & Ward, J. W. (1993). AIDS trends among Hispanics in the United States. *American Journal of Public Health, 83,* 504-509.

Dill, B. T., Baca Zinn, M., & Patton, S. (1993). Feminism, race, and the politics of family values. *Philosophy and Public Policy, 13*(3), 13-18.

Dorrington, C. (1992). Central American organizations in Los Angeles: The emergence of "social movement agencies." Doctoral dissertation, University of California, Los Angeles.

Dryfoos, J. (1990). *Adolescents-at-risk: Prevalence and prevention.* New York: Oxford University Press.

Duany, L., & Pittman, K. (1990). *Latino youths at a crossroads.* Washington, DC: Children's Defense Fund.

Duran, R. (1983). *Hispanics' education and background.* New York: College Entrance Examination Board.

Dusenbury, L., Kerner, J. F., Baker, E., Botvin, G., James-Ortiz, S., & Zauber, A. (1992). Predictions of smoking prevalence among New York Latino youth. *American Journal of Public Health, 82*(1), 55-58.

Ellwood, D. T. (1988). *Poor support.* New York: Basic Books.

Ellwood, D. T., & Summers, L. H. (1986). Household composition and poverty. In S. H. Danziger & D. H. Weinberg (Eds.), *Fighting poverty* (pp. 78-105). Cambridge, MA: Harvard University Press.

Erickson, P. I. (1990). Combating school-age pregnancy among Latinas in Los Angeles County. In E. R. Forsyth & J. Solis (Eds.), *Recommendations for improving the delivery of human services to Latina immigrants and their children in Los Angeles County* (pp. 25-36). Claremont, CA: The Tomás Rivera Center.

Escobedo, L. G., & Remington, P. L. (1989). Birth cohort analysis of prevalence of cigarette smoking among Hispanics in the United States. *Journal of the American Medical Association, 261*(1), 66-69.

Espada, F. (1978). *An attempt to assess the present state of drug abuse in five selected minority communities.* Washington, DC: The White House, Office of Drug Policy.

Espín, O. M. (1984). Cultural and historical influences on sexuality in Hispanic/Latin women: Implications for psychotherapy. In C. Vance (Ed.), *Pleasure and danger: Exploring female sexuality* (pp. 149-163). London: Routledge.

Farley, R., & Allen, W. (1988). *The color line and the quality of life in America.* New York: Russell Sage.

Felice, M. E., Shragg, G. P., James, M., & Hollingsworth, D. R. (1987). Psychosocial aspects of Mexican-American, White, and Black teenage pregnancy. *Journal of Adolescent Health Care, 8,* 330-335.

Fielding, J., & Williams, C. A. (1991). Adolescent pregnancy in the United States: A review and recommendations for clinicians and research needs. *American Journal of Preventive Medicine, 7,* 47-52.

Fukuyama, F. (1993, May). Immigrants and family values. *Commentary,* pp. 26-32.

Furino, A. (1992). *Health policy and the Hispanic.* Boulder, CO: Westview.

Garcia, J. M. (1993). *The Hispanic population in the United States: March 1992* (U.S. Bureau of the Census, Current Population Reports, P20-465RV). Washington, DC: Government Printing Office.

Gardner, R., Bobey, B., & Smith, P. (1985). Asian Americans: Growth, change, and diversity. *Population Bulletin, 40*(4).

Gerson, K. (1991). Coping with commitment: Dilemmas and conflicts of family life. In A. Wolfe (Ed.), *In America at century's end* (pp. 35-57). Berkeley: University of California Press.

Giachello, A. L. (1994). Hispanics' access to health care: Issues for the 1990s. In C. Molina & M. Aguirre-Molina (Eds.), *Latino health: America's growing challenge for the 21st century* (pp. 83-114). Washington, DC: American Public Health Association.

Gil, A. G., Vega, W. A., & Dimas, J. M. (1994). Acculturative stress and personal adjustment among Hispanic adolescent boys. *Journal of Community Psychology, 22,* 43-53.

Gil, A. G., Warheit, G. J., Vega, W. A., Zimmerman, R. S., Biafora, F., & Aporpori, E. (1994). *Family influences on drug and alcohol use in a multiethnic sample of adolescents.* Unpublished manuscript.

Gilbert, M. J., & Alcocer, A. M. (1988). Alcohol use and Hispanic youth: An overview. *Journal of Drug Issues, 18*(1), 33-48.

Ginzberg, E. L. (1991). Access to health care for Hispanics. *Journal of the American Medical Association, 265*(2), 238-242.

Glazer, N., & Moynihan, D. P. (1975). *Ethnicity: Theory and experience.* Cambridge, MA: Harvard University Press.

Glenn, E. N., & Yap, S. H. (1993). Chinese American families. In R. L. Taylor (Ed.), *Minority families in the United States: Comparative perspectives* (pp. 115-145). Englewood Cliffs, NJ: Prentice Hall.

Golding, J., & Burnam, A. (1990). Stress and social support as predictors of depressive symptoms in Mexican Americans and non-Hispanic Whites. *Journal of Clinical and Social Psychology, 9,* 268-286.

Gonzalez, A. (1982). Sex roles of the traditional Mexican family. *Journal of Cross-Cultural Psychology, 13,* 330-339.

Gonzalez, J. T. (1988). Dilemmas of the high-achieving Chicana: The double-bind factor in male/female relationships. *Sex Roles, 18*(7/8), 367-380.

Gordon, M. M. (1964). *Assimilation in American life: The role of race, religion, and national origins.* New York: Oxford University Press.

Gould, S. (1982). Correlates of career progression among Mexican American college graduates. *Journal of Vocational Behavior, 20,* 93-110.

Gratton, B. (1987). Familism among the Black and Mexican American elderly: Myth or reality? *Journal of Aging Studies, 1*(1), 19-32.

Grebler, L., Moore, J. W., & Guzman, R. C. (1970). *The Mexican American people.* New York: Free Press.

Griffith, J., & Villavicencio, S. (1985). Relationships among acculturation, sociodemographic characteristics, and social supports in Mexican American adults. *Hispanic Journal of Behavioral Sciences, 7,* 75-92.

Griswold del Castillo, R. (1984). *La familia.* Notre Dame, IN: University of Notre Dame Press.

Grossman, J. B., Maynard, R., & Roberts, J. (1985). *Reanalysis of the effects of selected employment training programs for welfare recipients.* Princeton, NJ: Mathematica Policy Research, Inc.

Guendelman, S., Gould, J. B., Hudes, M., & Eskenazi, B. (1990). Generational differences in perinatal health among the Mexican American population: Findings from HHANES 1982-84. *American Journal of Public Health, 80*(Suppl.), 61-65.

Gurak, D. (1978). Sources of ethnic fertility differences: An examination of five minority groups. *Social Science Quarterly, 59*(2), 295-310.

Hamilton, N., & Chinchilla, N. (1986). Central American women refugees in Los Angeles. *Urban Resources, 3*(2). (LA1-LA4, Local Interest Insert: Los Angeles)

Hamilton, N., & Chinchilla, N. (1991). Central American migration: A framework for analysis. *Latin American Research Review, 26*(1), 75-110.

Hartmann, H. I. (1987). Changes in women's economic and family roles in post World War II United States. In L. R. Beneria & C. R. Stimpson (Eds.), *Women, households and the economy* (pp. 33-64). New Brunswick, NJ: Rutgers.

Hasenfeld, Y. (1987). *Welfare and work: The institutionalization of moral ambiguity* (Working Paper). Los Angeles: Institute of Labor Relations, University of California, Los Angeles.

Hatch, J., Moss, N., Saran, A., Presley-Cantrell, L., & Mallory, C. (1993). Community research: Partnerships in Black communities. *American Journal of Preventive Medicine, 9*(6/Suppl.), 27-31.

Hawkes, G. R., Guagnano, G. A., Acredolo, C., & Helmick, S. A. (1984). Status inconsistency and job satisfaction: General population and Mexican-American subpopulation analyses. *Sociology and Social Research, 68*(3), 378-389.

Hawkes, G. R., & Taylor, M. (1975). Power structure in Mexican and Mexican American farm labor families. *Journal of Marriage and the Family, 37,* 807-811.

Hawkins, J. D., Lishner, D. M., Catalano, R. F., & Howard, M. (1986). Childhood predictors of adolescent substance abuse: Toward an empirically grounded theory. *Journal of Children in Contemporary Society, 18*(1/2), 11-48.

Hayes-Bautista, D. (1989). *Latino adolescents, families, work, and the economy: Building upon strength or creating a weakness?* A concept paper prepared for the Carnegie Commission on Adolescent Development.

Hayes-Bautista, D. (1990). *Latino health indicators and the underclass model: From paradox to new policy models.* Los Angeles: Chicano Studies Research Center, University of California, Los Angeles.

Hayes-Bautista, D., Hurtado, A., & Valdez, R. (1990). *Redefining California: Latino social engagement in a multicultural society.* Los Angeles: Chicano Studies Research Center, University of California, Los Angeles.

Hayes-Bautista, D., Hurtado, A., Valdez, R., & Hernández, A. C. R. (1992). *No longer a minority. Latinos and social policy in California*. Los Angeles: Chicano Studies Research Center, University of California, Los Angeles.

Hayes-Bautista, D. E., Schink, W. O., & Chapa, J. (1988). *The burden of support*. Stanford, CA: Stanford University Press.

Hazuda, H. P., Stern, M., & Haffner, S. (1988). Acculturation and assimilation among Mexican Americans: Scales and population based data. *Social Science Quarterly, 69*(3), 687-706.

Hein, K. (1993). Getting real about HIV in adolescents (Editorial). *American Journal of Public Health, 83,* 492-494.

Heller, C. (1966). Mexican-American youth: Forgotten youth at the crossroads. New York: Random House.

Higgenbotham, J. C., Trevino, F. M., & Ray, L. A. (1990). Utilization of curanderos by Mexican-Americans: Prevalence and predictors. Findings from the HHANES, 1982-84. *American Journal of Public Health, 80*(December Suppl.), 32-35.

Hill, M. (1983). Trends in the economic situation of U.S. families and children, 1970-1980. In R. R. Nelson & F. Skidmore (Eds.), *American families in the economy* (pp. 9-53). Washington, DC: National Academy Press.

Hill, M. S., & Ponza, M. (1983). Poverty and welfare dependence across generations. *Economic Outlook U.S.A.,* Summer, 61-64.

Holsinger, D. B., & Fernández, R. M. (1987). School to work transition profiles: Mexican American and non-Hispanic White high school graduates. *Sociology and Social Research, 71*(3), 211-215.

Holtzman, E. H., & Gilbert, L. A. (1987). Social support networks for parenting and psychological well-being among dual-earner Mexican-American families. *Journal of Community Psychology, 15,* 176-186.

Hondagueau-Sotelo, P. (1992). Overcoming patriarchal constraints: The reconstruction of gender relations among Mexican immigrant women and men. *Gender & Society, 6*(3), 393-415.

Hurtado, A., & Gurin, P. (1987). Ethnic identity and bilingualism attitudes. *Hispanic Journal of Behavioral Sciences, 9*(1), 1-18.

Hurtado, A., Gurin, P., & Peng, T. (1994). Social identities—A framework for studying the adaptations of immigrants and ethnics: Mexicans in the United States. *Social Problems, 41*(1), 129-151.

Hurtado, A., Hayes-Bautista, D., Valdez, R. B., & Hernández, A.C. (1992). *Redefining California: Latino social engagement in a multicultural society*. Los Angeles: Chicano Studies Research Center, University of California, Los Angeles.

Hurtado, A., Rodríguez, J., Gurin, P., & Beals, J. L. (1993). The impact of Mexican descendants' social identity on the ethnic socialization of children. In M. E. Bernal & G. Knight (Ed.), *Ethnic identity: Formation and transmission among Hispanics and other minorities* (pp. 131-162). Albany: SUNY Press.

Immigration and Naturalization Service. (1953-1954). *Annual report*. Washington, DC: U.S. Department of Labor.

Immigration and Naturalization Service. (1976-1990). *Statistical year book(s)*. Washington, DC: Department of Justice.

Immigration and Naturalization Service. (1991). *Statistical year book of the Immigration and Naturalization Service, 1990*. Washington, DC: Government Printing Office.

Jaramillo, P., & Zapata, J. (1987). Roles and alliances within Mexican-American and Anglo families. *Journal of Marriage and the Family, 49,* 727-735.

Jessor, R., & Jessor, S. L. (1977). *Problem behavior and psychological development*. New York: Academic Press.

Jiobu, R. (1988). *Ethnicity and assimilation*. Albany: SUNY Press.

Johnson, L., & Palm, G. (1992). What men want to know about parenting. In Minnesota Fathering Alliance (Ed.), *Working with fathers: Methods and perspectives* (pp. 129-155). Stillwater, MN: Nu Ink Unlimited.

Jorgensen, S. R., & Adams, R. P. (1988). Predicting Mexican-American planning intentions: An application and test of a social psychological model. *Journal of Marriage and the Family, 50,* 107-119.

Karno, M., Jenkins, J. H., De La Salva, A., Sontana, F., Telles, C., López, S., & Mintz, J. (1987). Expressed emotion and the schizophrenic outcome among Mexican American families. *Journal of Nervous and Mental Disease, 175,* 143-151.

Karsada, J. (1985). Urban change and minority opportunities. In P. Peterson (Ed.), *The new urban reality* (pp. 33-67). Washington, DC: The Brookings Institution.

Kay, M. A. (1980). Mexican American and Chicana childbirth. In M. Melville (Ed.), *Twice a minority* (pp. 52-65). St. Louis, MO: C. V. Mosby Co.

Keefe, S. (1984). Real and ideal extended families among Mexican Americans and Anglo Americans: On the meaning of close family ties. *Human Organization, 43,* 65-70.

Keefe, S. E., & Padilla, A. M. (1987). *Chicano ethnicity.* Albuquerque: University of New Mexico Press.

Kelly, P. F., & Garcia, A. (1989). Power surrendered, power restored: The politics of home and work among Hispanic women in Southern California and southern Florida. In L. Tilly & P. Gurin (Eds.), *Women and politics in America.* New York: Russell Sage.

Knight, G. P., & Kagan, S. (1977). Acculturation of prosocial and competitive behaviors among second- and third-generation Mexican American children. *Journal of Cross-Cultural Psychology, 8*(3), 273-284.

Knight, G. P., Kagan, S., Nelson, W., & Gumbiner, J. (1978). Acculturation of second- and third-generation Mexican American children. *Journal of Cross-Cultural Psychology, 9*(1), 87-97.

Kutsche, P. (1983). Household and family in Hispanic northern New Mexico. *Journal of Comparative Family Studies, 14,* 151-165.

Lamare, J. W. (1982). The political integration of Mexican American children: A generational analysis. *International Migration Review, 16*(1), 169-188.

Landry, B. (1991). The enduring dilemma of race in America. In A. Wolfe (Ed.), *America at century's end* (pp. 185-207). Berkeley: University of California Press.

Laosa, L. M. (1990). Population generalizability, cultural sensitivity, and ethical dilemmas. In C. B. Fischer & W. W. Tyron (Eds.), *Ethics in applied developmental psychology* (pp. 227-251). Norwood, NJ: Ablex.

Latino Coalition for a Healthy California. (1993). *The American Health Security Act: A Latino perspective.* San Francisco: The Latino Coalition for a Healthy California.

Lawyers Committee for International Human Rights. (1984). *El Salvador's other victims: The war on the displaced.* New York: Author.

Lazarus, W., & Gonzalez, M. (1989). *California: The state of our children 1989.* Oakland, CA: Children Now.

Leibowitz, A., Eisen, M., & Chow, W. K. (1986). An economic model of teenage pregnancy decision making. *Demography, 23,* 67-79.

Leslie, L. A., & Leitch, M. L. (1989). A demographic profile of recent Central American immigrants: Clinical and service implications. *Hispanic Journal of Behavioral Sciences, 11*(4), 315-329.

Levine, J. A., Murphy, D., & Wilson, S. (1993). *Getting men involved: Strategies and models that work.* New York: Scholastic.

Lewis, O. (1960). *Tepoztlan.* New York: Holt, Rinehart & Winston.

Lewis, O. (1961). *The children of Sanchez.* New York: Random House.

Lieu, T. A., Newacheck, P. W., & McManus, M. A. (1993). Race, ethnicity, and access to ambulatory care among U.S. adolescents. *American Journal of Public Health, 83,* 960-965.

Lillie-Blanton, M., Martinez, R. M., Taylor, A. K., & Robinson, B. G. (1993). Latina and African American women: Continuing disparities in health. *International Journal of Health Services, 23*(3), 555-584.

Lindsey, R. (1982, July 6). Secrets of the ghetto on Pico Boulevard. *Los Angeles Herald Examiner,* p. 7, C-1.

Linsky, A. S. (1985). *A report of the first two stages of research into regular substance-use and related psychosocial stressors among younger adolescent along the Tamaulipas-Texas border.* Paper presented at the Annual Meeting of the U.S./Mexico Border Health Association, San Antonio, Texas.

López Garza, M. (1988). Migration and labor force participation among undocumented female immigrants from Mexico and Central America. *In Defense of the Alien, 10,* 157-170.

Lott, J. T. (1993). Do United States racial/ethnic categories still fit? *Population Today, 21*(1), 6-9.

MacGraw, S. A., Smith, K. W., Schensul, J. J., & Carrillo, E. (1991). Sociocultural factors associated with smoking behavior by Puerto Rican adolescents in Boston. *Social Science and Medicine, 33,* 1355-1364.

MacManus, S. A., Bullock, C. S., III, & Grothe, B. P. (1986). A longitudinal examination of political participation rates of Mexican American females. *Social Science Quarterly, 67*(3), 604-612.

Maddahian, E., Newcomb, M., & Bentler, P. M. (1985). Single and multiple patterns of adolescent substance use: Longitudinal comparisons of four ethnic groups. *Journal of Drug Education, 4,* 311-325.

Maddahian, E., Newcomb, M., & Bentler, P. M. (1988a). Adolescent drug use and intervention to use drugs: Concurrent and longitudinal analyses of four ethnic groups. *Addictive Behaviors, 13,* 191-195.

Maddahian, E., Newcomb, M., & Bentler, P. M. (1988b). Risk factors for substance use: Ethnic differences among adolescents. *Journal of Substance Abuse, 1,* 11-23.

Madsen, W. (1964). *The Mexican-Americans of south Texas.* New York: Holt, Rinehart & Winston.

Manz, B. (1988a). *Refugees of a hidden war: The aftermath of counterinsurgency in Guatemala.* Albany: SUNY Press.

Manz, B. (1988b). Repatriation and reintegration: An arduous process in Guatemala. Washington, DC: Hemispheric Migration Project, Center for Immigration Policy and Refugee Assistance, Georgetown University,.

Markides, K., Boldt, J. S., & Ray, L. A. (1986). Sources of helping and intergenerational solidarity: A three-generation study of Mexican Americans. *Journal of Gerontology, 41,* 506-511.

Markides, K., Hoppe, S., Martin, H. W., & Timbers, D. M. (1983). Sample representativeness in a three-generation study of Mexican Americans. *Journal of Marriage and the Family, 45,* 911-916.

Markides, K., Krause, N., & Mendes de Leon, C. (1988). Acculturation and alcohol consumption among Mexican Americans: A three-generation study. *American Journal of Public Health, 9,* 1178-1181.

Marshall, R. (1991). *The state of families, 3: Losing direction: Families, human resource development and economic performance.* Milwaukee, WI: Family Service America.

Martinez, A. L. (1981). The impact of adolescent pregnancy on Hispanic adolescents and their families. In T. Ooms (Ed.), *Teenage pregnancy in a family context* (pp. 326-343). Philadelphia: Temple University Press.

Martinez, M. A. (1986). Family socialization among Mexican Americans. *Human Development, 29,* 264-279.

Massey, D. S. (1993a). Latino poverty research: An agenda for the 1990s. Social Science Research Council Newsletter, *Items, 47*(1), 7-11.

Massey, D. S. (1993b). Latinos, poverty, and the underclass: A new agenda for research. *Hispanic Journal of Behavioral Sciences, 15*(4), 449-475.

Massey, D., Alarcón, R., Durand, J., & Gonzalez, U. (1987). *Return to Aztlan.* Berkeley: University of California Press.

Massey, D. S., & Denton, N. A. (1993). *American apartheid: Segregation and the making of the underclass.* Cambridge, MA: Harvard University Press.

Maxwell, B., & Jacobson, M. (1989). *Marketing disease to Hispanics—The selling of alcohol, tobacco, and junk foods.* Washington, DC: The Center for Science in the Public Interest.

McBride, B. A. (1990). The effect of a parent education/play group on father involvement in child rearing. *Family Relations, 39,* 250-256.

Melville, M. B. (1991). Latino nonprofit organizations: Ethnic diversity, values, and leadership. In H. E. Gallegos & M. O'Neill (Eds.), *Hispanics and the nonprofit sector* (pp. 97-112). New York: The Foundation Center.

Miller, M. V. (1979). Variations in Mexican American family life: A review synthesis of empirical research. *Aztlan, 9,* 209-231.

Mindel, C. H. (1980). Extended familism among urban Mexican Americans, Anglos, and Blacks. *Hispanic Journal of Behavioral Sciences, 2,* 21-34.

Minnesota Fathering Alliance (Ed.). (1992). *Working with fathers: Methods and perspectives.* Stillwater, MN: Nu Ink Unlimited.

Miranda, L. C. (1991). *Latino child poverty in the United States.* Washington, DC: Children's Defense Fund.

Mirandé, A. (1977). The Chicano family: A reanalysis of conflicting views. *Journal of Marriage and the Family, 39*(4), 747-755.

Mirandé, A. (1988a). Chicano fathers: Traditional perceptions and current realities. In P. Bronstein & C. P. Cowan (Eds.), *Fatherhood today: Men's changing role in the family* (pp. 93-106). New York: John Wiley.

Mirandé, A. (1988b). Que gacho ser Macho: It's a drag to be a macho man. *Aztlan, 17*(2), 63-89.

Mirandé, A. (1991). Ethnicity and fatherhood. In F. W. Bozett & S. M. H. Hanson (Eds.), *Fatherhood and families in cultural context* (pp. 53-82). New York: Springer.

Mirandé, A., & Enriquez, E. (1979). *La Chicana. The Mexican-American woman.* Chicago: The University of Chicago Press.

Mitchell, J., & Dodder, R. A. (1980). An examination of types of delinquency through path analysis. *Journal of Youth and Adolescence, 9*(3), 239-248.

Montes Mozo, S., & Garcia Vasquez, J. J. (1988). *Salvadoran migration to the United States.* Washington, DC: Hemispheric Migration Project, Center for Immigration and Refugee Assistance, Georgetown University.

Montiel, M. (1970). The social science myth of the Mexican American family. *El Grito: A Journal of Contemporary Mexican-American Thought, 3*(Summer), 56-63.

Moore, J. (1989). Is there a Hispanic underclass? *Social Science Quarterly, 70*(2), 265-284.

Moore, J., & Pachón, H. (1985). *Hispanics in the United States.* Englewood Cliffs, NJ: Prentice Hall.

Mora, J., & Gilbert, J. (1991). Issues for Latinas: Mexican American women. In P. Roth (Ed.), *Alcohol and drugs are women's issues* (pp. 43-47). Metuchen, NJ: Women's Action Alliance and Scarecrow Press.

Morales, A. T., & Salcido, R. (1992). Social work practice with Mexican Americans. In A. T. Morales & B. W. Sheafor (Eds.), *Social work: A profession of many faces* (pp. 557-578). Boston: Allyn & Bacon.

Morgan, D. H. (1975). *Social theory and the family.* London, UK: Routledge & Kegan Paul.

Morgan, M. C., Wingard, D. L., & Felice, M. E. (1984). Subcultural differences in alcohol use among youth. *Journal of Adolescent Health Care, 5*(3), 191-195.

Morris, R. (1985). *Social policy of the American welfare state: An introduction to policy analysis* (2nd ed.). New York: Longman.

Moss, N. E. (1987). Effects of father-daughter contact on use of pregnancy services by Mexican, Mexican-American, and Anglo adolescents. *Journal of Adolescent Health Care, 8,* 419-424.

Muschkin, C., & Myers, G. C. (1989). Migration and household family structure: Puerto Ricans in the United States. *International Migration Review, 23,* 495-501.

Myrdal, Gunnar. (1975). *An American Dilemma.* New York: Pantheon.

Namerow, P. B., & Philliber, S. G. (1983). Attitudes towards sex education among Black, Hispanic, and inner-city residents. *International Quarterly of Public Health, 75*(1), 33-38.

National Committee to Prevent Infant Mortality. (1990). *Troubling trends: The health of America's next generation.* Washington, DC: Author.

National Vaccine Advisory Committee. (1991). The measles epidemic: The problems, barriers, and recommendations. *Journal of the American Medical Association, 266,* 1547-1552.

Nelson, C., Treichler, P., & Grossberg, L. (1992). Cultural studies: An introduction. In L. Grossberg, C. Nelson, & P. Treichler (Eds.), *Cultural studies* (pp. 1-17). New York: Routledge.

Newcomb, M., Maddahian, E., & Bentler, P. M. (1986). Risk factors for drug use among adolescents: Concurrent and longitudinal analysis. *American Journal of Public Health, 76,* 525-531.

New Jersey Department of Health. (1988). *Annual narrative-school year 1987-1988.* Perth Amboy: Author.

New Jersey Department of Health. (1992). *Preliminary birth and infant death statistics 1989 and 1990.* Trenton, NJ: Maternal and Child Health Services, Division of Family Health Services.

Nielson, F., & Fernández, R. (1981). *Hispanic students in American high schools: Background characteristics and achievement.* Washington, DC: National Center for Education Statistics.

Nieto, D. S. (1983). Hispanic fathers: The growing phenomenon of single fathers keeping their children. *National Hispanic Journal, 1,* 15-19.

Oakland, T., de Mesquita, P., & Buckley, K. (1988). Psychological, linguistic, and sociocultural correlates of reading among Mexican American elementary students. *School Psychology International, 9,* 219-228.

Oetting, E. R., & Beauvais, F. (1987). Peer cluster theory, socialization characteristics, and adolescent drug use: A path analysis. *Journal of Counseling Psychology, 34,* 205-213.

Office of Minority Health, Public Health Service, Department of Health and Human Services. (1990). AIDS/HIV infection and minorities. In *Closing the gap* (0-860-815). Washington, DC: Government Printing Office.

O'Guinn, T. C., Imperia, G., & MacAdams, E. (1987). Acculturation and perceived family decision-making input among Mexican American wives. *Journal of Cross-Cultural Psychology, 18*(1), 78-92.

Olsen, D. H., Russell, C. S., & Sprenkle, D. H. (1980). Circumplex model of marital and family systems: II. Empirical studies and clinical intervention. In J. P. Vincent (Ed.), *Advances in family intervention, assessment, and theory* (Vol. 1, pp. 128-176). Greenwich, CT: JAI Press.

Omi, M., & Winant, H. (1986). *Racial formation in the United States.* London, UK: Routledge & Kegan Paul.

Ortiz, V. (1986). Changes in the characteristics of Puerto Rican migrants from 1955 to 1980. *International Migration Review, 20*(3), 612-628.

Ortiz, V., & Cooney, R. (1984). Sex-role attitudes and labor force participation among Hispanic females and non-Hispanic White females. *Social Science Quarterly, 65*(2), 392-400.

Ortiz, V., & Cooney, R. S. (1985). Sex-role attitudes and labor force participation among young Hispanic females and non-Hispanic White females. In R. O. de la Garza, F. D. Bean, C. M. Bonjean, R. Romo, & R. Alvarez (Eds.), *The Mexican American experience* (pp. 174-182). Austin: University of Texas Press.

Oster, G., Delea, T. E., & Colditz, G. A. (1988). Maternal smoking during pregnancy and expenditures on neonatal health care. *American Journal of Preventive Medicine, 4,* 216-219.

Pachón, H., & Moore, J. (1981). Mexican Americans. *The Annals of the American Academy of Political and Social Science, 454,* 111-124.

Padilla, A. M. (1980). The role of cultural awareness and ethnic loyalty in acculturation. In A. M. Padilla (Ed.), *Acculturation: Theory, models, and some new findings* (pp. 47-48). Boulder, CO: Westview.

Padilla, A. M., Cervantes, R. C., Maldonado, M., & Garcia, R. E. (1987). *Coping responses to psychosocial stressors among Mexican and Central American immigrants* (Occasional Paper No. 23). Los Angeles: Spanish Speaking Mental Health Research Center, University of California, Los Angeles.

Padilla, A. M., & Lindholm, K. J. (1983). *Hispanic Americans: Future behavioral science research directions* (Occasional Paper No. 17). Los Angeles: Spanish Speaking Mental Health Research Center, University of California, Los Angeles.

Park, R. E. (1936). Succession: An ecological concept. *American Sociological Review, 1,* 171-179.

Parsons, T., & Bales, R. (1955). *Family: Socialization and interaction process.* Glencoe, IL: Free Press.

Passel, J., & Woodrow, K. (1984, May). *Geographic distribution of undocumented immigrants: Estimates of undocumented aliens counted in the 1980 census by state.* Paper presented at the Population Association of America meetings in Minneapolis.

Pearce, D. (1978). The feminization of poverty: Women, work, and welfare. *Urban and Social Change Review, 10,* 28-36.

Pelto, P., Roman, M., & Liriano, N. (1982). Family structures in an urban Puerto Rican community. *Urban Anthropology, 11,* 39-58.

Peñalosa, F. (1986). *Central Americans in Los Angeles: Background, language and education* (Occasional Paper No. 21). Los Angeles: Spanish Speaking Mental Health Research Center, University of California, Los Angeles.

Perez, L. (1986). Immigrant economic adjustment and family organization: The Cuban success story reexamined. *International Migration Review, 20*(1), 4-20.

Perry, C. L. (1986). Community-wide health promotion and drug abuse prevention. *Journal of School Health, 56*(9), 359-363.

Perry, C. L., & Jessor, R. (1985). The concept of health promotion and the prevention of adolescent drug abuse. *Health Education Quarterly, 12*(2), 169-184.

Pesquera, B. M. (1984). "Having a job gives you some sort of power": Reflections of a Chicana working woman. *Feminist Issues, 4*(2), 79-96.

Pesquera, B. M. (1993). In the beginning he wouldn't even lift a spoon: The division of household labor. In A. de la Torre & B. M. Pesquera (Eds.), *Building with our hands: New directions in Chicana studies* (pp. 181-195). Berkeley: University of California Press.

Pierce, J. (1984). The implications of functionalism for Chicano family research. *Berkeley Journal of Sociology, 29*, 93-117.

Pittman, K., & Adams, G. (1988). *Teenage pregnancy: An advocate's guide to the numbers.* Washington, DC: Children's Defense Fund.

Popenoe, D. (1988). *Disturbing the nest: Family change and decline in modern societies.* New York: Aldine de Gruyter.

Portes, A., & Bach, R. L. (1985). *Latin journey.* Berkeley: University of California Press.

Portes, A., & Rumbaut, R.G. (1990). *Immigrant America: A portrait.* Berkeley: University of California Press.

Powell, D. R. (1988a). Client characteristics and the design of community-based intervention programs. In A. R. Pence (Ed.), *Ecological research with children and families* (pp. 122-142). New York: Teachers College Press.

Powell, D. R. (1988b). Emerging directions in parent-child intervention. In D. R. Powell (Ed.), *Parent education as early childhood intervention* (pp. 1-22). Norwood, NJ: Ablex.

Powell, D. R. (1990). The responsiveness of early childhood initiatives to families: Strategies and limitations. *Marriage and Family Review, 15*, 149-170.

Powell, D. R. (in press). *Parent education and support programs: The state of the field.* Chicago: Family Resource Coalition.

Powell, D. R., Zambrana, R., & Silva-Palacios, V. (1990). Designing culturally responsive parent programs: A comparison of Mexican and Mexican-American mothers' program preferences. *Family Relations, 39*, 298-304.

Procidiano, M. E., & Rogler, L. H. (1989). Homogenous assortive mating among Puerto Rican families: Intergenerational processes and the migration experience. *Behavior Genetics, 19*(3), 343-354.

Ramirez, O., & Arce, C. (1981). The contemporary Chicano family: An empirically based review. In A. Barron, Jr. (Ed.), *Explorations in Chicano psychology* (pp. 3-28). New York: Praeger.

Rapkin, A. J., & Erickson, P. I. (1990). Acquired Immune Deficiency Syndrome: Ethnic differences in knowledge and risk factors among women in an urban family planning clinic. *AIDS* (August).

Reimers, C. (1984). The wage structure of Hispanic men: Implications for policy. *Social Science Quarterly, 65*(2), 401-416.

Rodríguez, C. E. (1990). Racial classification among Puerto Rican men and women in New York. *Hispanic Journal of Behavioral Sciences, 12*, 366-380.

Rodríguez, N. P. (1987). Undocumented Central Americans in Houston: Diverse populations. *International Migration Review, 21*(1), 4-26.

Rodríguez, N. P., & Urrutia-Rojas, X. (1990). *Undocumented and unaccompanied: A mental health study of unaccompanied, immigrant children from Central America* (Monograph 90-4). Houston, TX: Institute of Higher Education Law and Governance, University of Houston.

Rogers, H. R., Jr. (1988). Reducing poverty through family support. In H. R. Rogers, Jr. (Ed.), *Beyond welfare: New approaches to the problem of poverty in America* (pp. 39-65). Armonk, NY: M. E. Sharpe.

Rogler, L. H. (1991). Puerto Rican families in New York City: Intergenerational processes. *Marriage and Family Review, 16*(3-4), 331-349.

Rogler, L. H., & Cooney, R. S. (1984). *Puerto Rican families in New York City: Intergenerational processes.* Maplewood, NJ: Waterfront Press.

References 221

Rogler, L. H., & Cooney, R. S. (1991). Puerto Rican families in New York City: Intergenerational processes. *Marriage and Family Review, 16*(3/4), 331-349.

Rogler, L. H., Cooney, R. S., & Ortiz, V. (1980). Intergenerational change in ethnic identity in the Puerto Rican family. *International Migration Review, 14*(2), 193-214.

Rogler, L. H., Malgady, R. G., Costantino, G., & Blumenthal, R. (1987). What do culturally sensitive mental health services mean? The case of Hispanics. *American Psychologist, 42,* 565-570.

Romo, H. (1984). The Mexican origin population's differing perceptions of their children's schooling. *Social Science Quarterly, 65*(2), 635-650.

Rothman, J., Gant, L., & Hnat, S. A. (1985). Mexican American family culture. *Social Service Review, 59,* 197-215.

Rubel, A. (1966). *Across the tracks: Mexican Americans in a Texas city.* Austin: University of Texas Press.

Rueschenberg, E., & Buriel, R. (1989). Mexican American family functioning and acculturation: A family systems perspective. *Hispanic Journal of Behavioral Sciences, 11*(3), 232-244.

Ruggles, P., & Fix, M. (1985). *Impacts and potential impacts of Central American migrants on HHS and related programs of assistance.* Washington, DC: The Urban Institute.

Sabogal, F., Marín, G., & Otero-Sabogal, R. (1987). Hispanic familism and acculturation: What changes and what doesn't? *Hispanic Journal of Behavioral Sciences, 9*(4), 397-412.

Saenz, R., Goudy, W., & Lorenz, F. O. (1989). The effects of employment and marital relations on depression among Mexican American women. *Journal of Marriage and the Family, 51,* 239-251.

Salgado de Snyder, N., López, C. M., & Padilla, A. M. (1982). Ethnic identity and cultural awareness among the offspring of Mexican interethnic marriages. *Journal of Early Adolescence, 2*(3), 277-282.

Sanchez-Ayendez, M. (1988). The Puerto Rican American family. In C. H. Mindel, R. W. Habenstein, & R. Wright, Jr. (Eds.), *Ethnic families in America: Patterns and variations* (pp. 173-195). New York: Elsevier.

Sardell, A. (1990). Historical review of federal child health policy. *Journal of Health Politics, Policy and the Law, 15*(2), 217-304.

Schlossman, S. (1976). Before home start: Notes toward a history of parent education in America, 1897-1929. *Harvard Educational Review, 46,* 436-467.

Schneiderman, L. (1990). Human services in California: Problems and prospects. *California Policy Seminar Brief, 2*(6), 1-6.

Schorr, L., & Schorr, D. (1988). *Within our reach: Breaking the cycle of disadvantage.* New York: Doubleday.

Schumm, W. R., McCollum, E. E., Bugaighis, M. A., Jurich, A. P., Bollman, S. R., & Reitz, J. (1988). Differences between Anglo and Mexican American family members on satisfaction with family life. *Hispanic Journal of Behavioral Sciences, 10*(1), 39-53.

Scribner, R., & Dwyer, J. (1989). Acculturation and low birthweight among Latinos in Hispanic HANES. *American Journal of Public Health, 79*(9), 1263-1267.

Segura, D. (1984). Labor market stratification: The Chicana experience. *Berkeley Journal of Sociology, 29,* 57-91.

Segura, D. A., & Pierce, J. L. (1993). Chicana/o family structure and gender personality: Chodorow, familism, and psychoanalytic sociology revisited. *Signs: Journal of Women in Culture and Society, 19*(1), 62-91.

Shorris, E. (1992). *Latinos: A biography of the people.* New York: Norton.

Siantz, M. L. de L. (in press). A profile of the Hispanic child. In G. Brookins & M. Spencer (Eds.), *Ethnicity and diversity: Implications for research and policy.* Hillsdale, NJ: Lawrence Erlbaum.

Sigel, I. E. (1983). The ethics of intervention. In I. E. Sigel & L. Laosa (Eds.), *Changing families* (pp. 1-21). New York: Plenum.

Smith, D. E. (1987). Women's inequality and the family. In N. Gerstel & H. E. Gross (Eds.), *Families and work* (pp. 23-54). Philadelphia: Temple University Press.

Snipp, M., & Tienda, M. (1984). Mexican American occupational mobility. *Social Science Quarterly, 65*(2), 346-380.

Sorensen, A. M. (1988). The fertility and language characteristics of Mexican-American and non-Hispanic husbands and wives. *The Sociological Quarterly, 29*(1), 111-130.

Soto, E. (1983). Sex-role traditionalism and assertiveness in Puerto Rican women living in the United States. *Journal of Community Psychology, 11,* 346-354.

Soto, E., & Shaver, P. (1982). Sex-role traditionalism, assertiveness, and symptoms of Puerto Rican women living in the United States. *Hispanic Journal of Behavioral Sciences, 4*(1), 1-19.

Sotomayor, M. (1989). The Hispanic elderly and the intergenerational family. *Journal of Children in Contemporary Society, 20*(3-4), 55-65.

Stacey, J., & Thorne, B. (1985). The missing feminist revolution in sociology. *Social Problems, 32*(4), 301-315.

Stanley, W. D. (1987). Economic immigrants or refugees from violence? A time-series analysis of Salvadoran migration to the United States. *Latin American Research Review, 22*(1), 132-154.

Staples, R., & Mirandé, A. (1980). Racial and cultural variations among American families: A decennial review of the literature on minority families. *Journal of Marriage and the Family, 42*(4), 887-903.

Stroup-Benham, C. A., Trevino, F. M., & Trevino, D. B. (1990). Alcohol consumption patterns among Mexican American mothers and among children from single and dual-headed households: Findings from HHANES 1982-1984. *American Journal of Public Health, 80*(Suppl.), 36-41.

Sultz, H. (1991). Health policy: If you don't know where you are going, any road will take you. *American Journal of Public Health, 81*(4), 419-420.

Sweet, J., & Bumpass, L. (1987). *American families and households.* New York: Russell Sage.

Szapocznik, J., & Hernandez, R. (1988). The Cuban American family. In C. H. Mindel, R. W. Habenstein, & R. Wright, Jr. (Eds.), *Ethnic families in America* (pp. 160-172). New York: Elsevier.

Szapocznik, J., & Kurtines, W. (1988). Acculturation, bilingualism, and adjustment among Cuban Americans. In A. M. Padilla (Ed.), *Acculturation theory, models, and some new findings* (pp. 47-83). Boulder, CO: Westview.

Tannen, D. (1990). *You just don't understand: Women and men in conversation.* New York: Morrow.

Terris, M. (1990). Public health policy for the 1990s. *Annual Reviews of Public Health, 11,* 39-51.

Thomas, D. L., & Wilcox, J. E. (1987). The rise of family theory. In M. B. Sussman & S. Steinmetz (Eds.), *Handbook of marriage and the family* (pp. 81-102). New York: Plenum.

Thomas, W. I., & Znaniecki, F. (1918-1920). *The Polish peasant in Europe and America* (5 Vols.). Chicago: University of Chicago Press.

Thorne, B. (1992). Feminism and the family: Two decades of thought. In B. Thorne & M. Yalom (Eds.), *Rethinking the family: Some feminist questions* (pp. 3-30). Boston: Northeastern University Press.

Tienda, M. (1983). Market characteristics and Hispanic earnings: A comparison of natives and immigrants. *Social Problems, 31*(1), 59-72.

Tienda, M. (1989). Puerto Ricans and the underclass debate. *The Annals of the American Academy, 501,* 105-119.

Tienda, M., & Lii, D.-T. (1987). Minority concentration and earnings inequality: Blacks, Hispanics, and Asians compared. *American Journal of Sociology, 93*(1), 141-165.

Tomás Rivera Center. (1993). Resolving a crisis in education: Latino teachers for tomorrow's classrooms. Claremont, CA: Author.

Torres-Rivas, E. (1985). *Report on the conditions of Central American refugees and migrants.* Washington, DC: Hemispheric Migration Project, Center for Immigration Policy and Refugee Assistance, Georgetown University.

Trevino, F. M., Moyer, M. E., Valdez, R. B., & Stroup-Benham, C. (1991). Health insurance coverage and utilization of health services by Mexicans, mainland Puerto-Ricans, and Cuban-Americans. *Journal of the American Medical Association, 255*(2), 233-237.

Triandis, H. C., Marín, G., & Hui, H. C. (1984). Role perceptions of Hispanic young adults. *Journal of Cross-Cultural Psychology, 15*(3), 297-320.

Trolander, J. A. (1987). *Professionalism and social change: From the settlement house movement to neighborhood centers, 1886 to the present.* New York: Columbia University Press.

Ungemack, J. A., & Guarnaccia, P. J. (1993). *Suicidal ideation and suicide attempts among Hispanics in the U.S.* Unpublished manuscript, Institute for Health, Health Care Policy and Aging Research, Rutgers University, New Brunswick, NJ.

U.S. Committee for Refugees. (1989). *World refugee survey: 1988 in review.* Washington, DC: American Council for Nationalities Service.

U.S. House of Representatives. (1992). *Green book.* Washington, DC: Government Printing Office.

U.S. Public Health Service. (1992). *Improving minority health statistics.* Washington, DC: Government Printing Office.

Valdez, R. B., & Dallek, G. (1991). *Does the health care system serve Black and Latino communities in Los Angeles County? An analysis of hospital use in 1987.* Claremont, CA: The Tomás Rivera Center.

Valdez, R. B., Giachello, A., Rodríguez-Trias, H., Gomez, P., & De La Rocha, C. (1993). Improving access to health care in Latino communities. *Public Health Reports, 108*(5), 534-539.

Valdez, R. B., Delgado, D. J., Cervantes, R. C., & Bowler, S. (1993). *Cancer in U.S. Latino communities: An exploratory review.* Santa Monica, CA: RAND.

Valle, R., & Bensussen, G. (1985). Hispanic social networks, social support, and mental health. In W. A. Vega & M. R. Miranda (Eds.), *Stress and Hispanic mental health* (DHHS Pub. No. 85-1410, pp. 147-173). Rockville, MD: National Institute of Mental Health.

Vasquez, M., & Gonzalez, A. (1981). Sex roles among Chicanos: Stereotypes, challenges, and changes. In A. Baron, Jr. (Ed.), *Explorations in Chicano psychology* (pp. 50-70). New York: Praeger.

Vega, W. A. (1990). Hispanic families in the 1980s: A decade of research. *Journal of Marriage and the Family, 52,* 1015-1024.

Vega, W. A., & Amaro, H. (1994). Latino outlook: Good health, uncertain prognosis. *Annual Review of Public Health, 15,* 39-67.

Vega, W. A., Hough, R., & Romero, A. (1983). Family life patterns of Mexican Americans. In G. J. Powell (Ed.), *The psychosocial development of minority group children* (pp. 194-215). New York: Brunner/Mazel.

Vega, W. A., & Kolody, B. (1985). The meaning of social support and the mediation of stress across cultures. In W. A. Vega & M. R. Miranda (Eds.), *Stress and Hispanic mental health* (DHHS Pub. No. 85-1410, pp. 1-29). Rockville, MD: National Institute of Mental Health.

Vega, W. A., Kolody, B., & Valle, R. (1988). Marital strain, coping, and depression among Mexican American women. *Journal of Marriage and the Family, 50,* 391-403.

Vega, W. A., Kolody, B., Valle, R., & Weir, J. (1991). Social networks, social support, and their relationship to depression among immigrant Mexican women. *Human Organization, 50,* 154-162.

Vega, W. A., Patterson, T., Sallis, J., Nader, P., Atkins, C., & Abramson, I. (1986). Cohesion and adaptability in Mexican American and Anglo families. *Journal of Marriage and the Family, 48,* 857-867.

Vega, W. A., Warheit, G. J., & Meinhardt, K. (1985). Mental health issues in the Hispanic community: The prevalence of psychological distress. In W. A. Vega & M. R. Miranda (Eds.), *Stress & Hispanic mental health: Relating research to service delivery* (pp. 30-47). Rockville, MD: U.S. Department of Health and Human Services.

Vega, W. A., Zimmerman, R. S., Warheit, G. J., Apospori, E., & Gil, A. G. (1993). Risk factors for early adolescent drug use in four ethnic and racial groups. *American Journal of Public Health, 83,* 185-189.

Velez, C. N., & Ungemack, J. A. (1989). Drug use among Puerto Rican youth: An exploration of generational status differences. *Social Science and Medicine, 29*(6), 779-789.

Veltman, C. (1988). *The future of the Spanish language population of the United States.* New York: Hispanic Policy Development Project.

Verdugo, N., & Verdugo, R. (1984). Earnings differentials among Mexican American, Black, and White male workers. *Social Science Quarterly, 65*(2), 417-425.

Vidal, C. (1988). Good parenting among Hispanic Americans. *Child Welfare, 27*(5), 453-459.

Wallace, S. P. (1986). Central American and Mexican immigrant characteristics and economic incorporation in California. *International Migration Review, 20*(3), 657-671.

Warheit, G. J., Vega, W. A., Auth, J., & Meinhardt, K. (1985). Mexican American immigration and mental health: A comparative analysis of psychosocial stress and dysfunction. In W. A. Vega & M. R. Miranda (Eds.), *Stress & Hispanic mental health: Relating research to service delivery* (pp. 76-109). Rockville, MD: U.S. Department of Health and Human Services.

Watts, D. W., & Wright, L. S. (1990). The relationship of alcohol, tobacco, marijuana, and other illegal drug use to delinquency among Mexican-American, Black, and White adolescent males. *Adolescence, 25*(97), 171-181.

Weeks, J. R., & Cuellar, J. (1981). The role of family members in the helping networks of older people. *Gerontology, 21,* 388-394.

Welte, J. W., & Barnes, G. M. (1987). Alcohol use among adolescent minority groups. *Journal of Studies on Alcohol, 48*(4), 329-366.

Whitehead, B. D. (1992). *The expert study of marriage* (Publication No. WP14, pp. 11-12). New York: Institute of American Values.

Whitehead, B. D. (1993). Dan Quayle was right. *Atlantic, 271*(4), 47-84.

Whitworth, R. H. (1988). Comparison of Anglo and Mexican American male high school students classified as learning disabilities. *Hispanic Journal of Behavioral Sciences, 10*(2), 127-137.

Williams, D. R. (1990). Socioeconomic differentials in health. *Social Psychology Quarterly, 53*(2), 1-99.

Williams, N. (1990). *The Mexican American family: Tradition and change.* Dix Hills, NY: General Hall.

Windle, M. (1991). Alcohol use and abuse—Some findings from the National Adolescent Student Health Survey. *Alcohol Health and Research World, 15*(1), 5-10.

Wirth, L. (1928). *The ghetto.* Chicago: University of Chicago Press.

World Council of Churches. (1985, 1988, 1989). *The human rights situation in El Salvador.* San Salvador, El Salvador: The Archbishop Oscar Romero Christian Legal Aid Service Report(s).

Ybarra, L. (1982). When wives work: The impact on the Chicano family. *Journal of Marriage and the Family, 44,* 169-178.

Ybarra, L. (1983). Empirical and theoretical developments in the study of Chicano families. In A. Valdez, A. Camarillo, & T. Almaguer (Eds.), *The state of Chicano research on family, labor, and migration. Proceedings of the First Stanford Symposium on Chicano Research and Public Policy* (pp. 91-110). Stanford, CA: Stanford Center for Chicano Research.

Zambrana, R. E. (1990, October). *Collaborative relationships in program development: Working with Latino communities.* Paper presented at the fifth annual meeting of Grantmakers for Children and Youth, St. Paul, MN.

Zambrana, R. E. (1991). Cross-cultural methodological strategies in the study of low income racial ethnic populations. In M. L. Grady (Ed.), *Primary care research: Theory and methods* (pp. 221-227). Rockville, MD: U.S. Department of Health and Human Services.

Zambrana, R. E., & Frith, S. (1988). Mexican American professional women: Role satisfaction differences in single and multiple role lifestyles. *Journal of Social Behavior and Personality, 3*(4), 347-361.

Zambrana, R. E., Hernandez, M., Dunkel-Schetter, C., & Scrimshaw, S. (1991). Ethnic differences in the substance use patterns of low income pregnant women. *Journal of Family and Community Health, 13*(4), 1-11.

Zapata, J. T., & Jaramillo, P. T. (1981). Research on the Mexican American family. *Journal of Individual Psychology, 37,* 72-85.

Zavella, P. (1984). The impact of "Sun Belt industrialization" on Chicanas. *Frontiers, 8*(1), 21-27.

Zavella, P. (1985). "Abnormal intimacy": The varying work networks of Chicana cannery workers. *Feminist Studies, 11*(3), 541-557.

Zavella, P. (1987). *Women's work and Chicano families: Cannery workers of the Santa Clara Valley.* Ithaca, NY: Cornell University Press.

Zavella, P. (1991). Mujeres in factories: Race and class perspectives on women, work, and family. In M. de Leonardo (Ed.), *Gender at the crossroads of knowledge* (pp. 312-336). Berkeley: University of California Press.

Index

About the Authors

Marilyn Aguirre-Molina is Senior Program Officer of the Robert Wood Johnson Foundation in Princeton, New Jersey. She was previously Assistant Professor in the Department of Environment and Community Medicine of the UMDNJ-Robert Wood Johnson Medical School, Piscataway, New Jersey. She is also codirector of the Health Education Behavior Sciences Track of the Graduate Program in Public Health, jointly sponsored by the medical school and Rutgers University. She is Vice-Chair of the Executive Board of the American Public Health Association and the Founding Chair of the Board of Directors for the Latino Council on Alcohol and Tobacco. She is currently principal investigator of grants from the DHHS Public Health Services Office of Minority Health and Center for Substance Abuse Prevention and from several foundations, working with a minority coalition to develop a community organizing model to prevent health-related problems among youth.

Sally Alonzo Bell is Professor and Chair, Department of Sociology and Social Work, Azusa Pacific University, Azusa, California. Her research interests include Mexican American high school dropouts and their later welfare as adults. Her doctoral dissertation (UCLA, 1991) examined the determinants of educational attainment among low-income Mexican American and non-Hispanic White secondary students. Recently, she coauthored, with Ruth Zambrana and Claudia Dorrington, two articles examining the influence of family and institutional barriers on women of color in higher education.

Maxine Baca Zinn, Professor of Sociology, Michigan State University, is a Senior Research Associate at the Julian Samora Research Institute. She is coauthor, with Bonnie Thornton Dill, of *Women of Color in U.S. Society,* and coauthor, with D. Stanley Eitzen, of the following books: *Diversity in Families, In Conflict and Order: Understanding Society,* and *The Reshaping of America.*

Claudia Dorrington is Lecturer in the Department of Sociology and Social Work, Azusa Pacific University, Azusa, California. Her research focuses on the development of Latino community-based organizations and the delivery and accessibility of services to Latino families and their children, especially immigrants and refugees from Central America. She has written articles on Salvadoran refugees in the United States and Central American organizations in Los Angeles.

David Hayes-Bautista is Professor at the School of Medicine, University of California, Los Angeles, and Director of the Chicano Studies Research Center. His research interests are in Latino social policy as developed in his 1988 book *The Burden of Support: Young Latinos in an Aging Society.* He is the author of numerous papers and monographs which use demographic projections to identify key policy issues in the areas of employment, income, education, health, political participation, immigration, and societal cohesion. He is on the editorial board of Salud Pública de México and a member of the Carnegie Council on Adolescent Development and the National Advisory Council on Health Care Policy, Research and Education.

Aída Hurtado is Associate Professor of Psychology, University of California, Santa Cruz. Her research interests include the effects of subordination on social identity, with special interest in group memberships, such as ethnicity, race, class, and gender, that are used to legitimize unequal distribution of power. Her expertise is in survey methods with bilingual/bicultural populations, and she has published extensively on issues of language and social identity for the Mexican American population in the United States. She is coauthor, with David Hayes-Bautista, Robert B. Valdez, and Anthony C. Hernández, of *Redefining California: Latino Social Engagement in a Multicultural Society.*

Douglas S. Massey is Dorothy Swaine Thomas Professor of Sociology at the University of Pennsylvania. He is coauthor of the book *American Apartheid: Segregation and the Making of the Underclass,* which is the culmination of 15 years of research on the topic of residential segregation. His publications on U.S.-Mexico migration include the coauthored books *Return to Aztlan: The Social Process of International Migration from Western Mexico* and *Miracles on the Border,* which examines Mexican immigration from the viewpoint of the migrants themselves by examining their religious folk paintings. Prior to joining the faculty of the University of Pennsylvania in 1994, he served on the faculty of the University of Chicago, where he directed its Latin American Studies Center and Population Research Center.

Vilma Ortiz is Associate Professor of Sociology at the University of California, Los Angeles. Her research focuses on issues related to gender, immigration, and economic status among Latinos. She has published extensively on the social conditions of Latinos in the United States. With Edward Telles, she is currently studying mobility and ethnic identity among Mexican Americans in Los Angeles and San Antonio.

Pilar A. Parra, Sociologist, Division of Nutritional Sciences, Cornell University, is recipient of a Minority Investigator Award by the National Institute of Mental Health. She was previously a postdoctoral trainee of the Rutgers-Princeton Program in Mental Health Research. Her research focuses on issues related to the health status of minorities, particularly Latinos. Her present work is on maternal and child health and risk behaviors found in national and state survey data. She has written several articles based on qualitative data on families' coping strategies in caring for a chronically mentally ill family member.

Douglas R. Powell is Professor and Head of the Department of Child Development and Family Studies, Purdue University, West Lafayette, Indiana. He has conducted major studies of parent education and support programs, including research on a program development initiative in the Los Angeles area for low-income Latinos. He is editor of the *Early Childhood Research Quarterly* and author or editor of five volumes on early childhood and parenting issues. He is a founding member of the board of directors of the Family Resource Coalition and currently is cochair of the coalition's national project to define best practices in family support.

Julie Solis currently directs her own consultant services in Whittier, California. She has 17 years of experience in planning, developing, and implementing health and human service programs and research projects. Her major areas of interest are the provision of services to Latinos and other racial/ethnic communities, particularly with regard to child and youth issues, health promotion, and health care access.

William A. Vega is Professor of Public Health at the University of California at Berkeley. Latino health, mental health, social epidemiology, and sociocultural issues are his primary research interests. He has written numerous articles and chapters about immigrant mental health and social adjustment, with a special emphasis on adolescent development. His current research focuses on the role of acculturation in Latino family process, intergenerational differences, and subsequent influences on lifestyles of adolescents. He is currently conducting two large federally sponsored research studies: a longitudinal panel of Latino adolescents in Miami, Florida, which is concerned with acculturative stress and other risk patterns associated with early drug use; and a comparison of major psychiatric disorders and services use profiles among urban and rural Mexican Americans in California.

Ruth E. Zambrana is Enochs Professor and Director of the Center for Child Welfare at George Mason University, College of Nursing and Health Science, in Fairfax, Virginia. She was formerly at the UCLA School of Social Work for 10 years and served for 18 months as a visiting Senior Research Scientist on minority health at the Agency for Health Care Policy and Research, Center for Medical Effectiveness Research, Washington, DC. She has conducted research for the past 15 years on the health of low-income Latino/Hispanic women, children, and families, with a special focus on maternal and child health. She has published extensively on issues related to health, education, employment, and research methodology among low-income women of color.